Dog of the Decade

"Dogs in Our World" Series

Dog of the Decade: Breed Trends and What They Mean in America (Deborah Thompson, 2022)

Laboratory Dogs Rescued: From Test Subjects to Beloved Companions (Ellie Hansen, 2022)

Beware of Dog: How Media Portrays the Aggressive Canine (Melissa Crawley, 2021)

I'm Not Single, I Have a Dog: Dating Tales from the Bark Side (Susan Hartzler, 2021)

Dogs in Health Care: Pioneering Animal-Human Partnerships (Jill Lenk Schilp, 2019)

General Custer, Libbie Custer and Their Dogs: A Passion for Hounds, from the Civil War to Little Bighorn (Brian Patrick Duggan, 2019)

Dog's Best Friend: Will Judy, Founder of National Dog Week and Dog World Publisher (Lisa Begin-Kruysman, 2014)

Man Writes Dog: Canine Themes in Literature, Law and Folklore (William Farina, 2014)

Saluki: The Desert Hound and the English Travelers Who Brought It to the West (Brian Patrick Duggan, 2009)

Dog of the Decade
Breed Trends and What They Mean in America

Deborah Thompson

Dogs in Our World
Series Editor Brian Patrick Duggan

McFarland & Company, Inc., Publishers
Jefferson, North Carolina

Also by Brian Patrick Duggan
and from McFarland

*Saluki: The Desert Hound and the English
Travelers Who Brought It to the West* (2009)

Library of Congress Cataloguing-in-Publication Data

Names: Thompson, Deborah, 1963– author. |
Duggan, Brian Patrick, 1953– editor.
Title: Dog of the decade : breed trends and what they
mean in America / Deborah Thompson.
Description: Jefferson, North Carolina : McFarland & Company, Inc.,
Publishers, 2022 | Series: Dogs in our world | Includes
bibliographical references and index.
Identifiers: LCCN 2021047562 | ISBN 9781476684338 (paperback : acid free paper) ∞
ISBN 9781476645568 (ebook)
Subjects: LCSH: Dogs—Breeding—United States—
History. | BISAC: PETS / Dogs / Breeds
Classification: LCC SF427.2 .T46 2021 | DDC 636.7/0887—dc23/eng/20211006
LC record available at https://lccn.loc.gov/2021047562

British Library cataloguing data are available

ISBN (print) 978-1-4766-8433-8
ISBN (ebook) 978-1-4766-4556-8

© 2022 Deborah Thompson. All rights reserved

*No part of this book may be reproduced or transmitted in any form
or by any means, electronic or mechanical, including photocopying
or recording, or by any information storage and retrieval system,
without permission in writing from the publisher.*

Front cover image © 2022 LightField Studios/Shutterstock

Printed in the United States of America

*McFarland & Company, Inc., Publishers
Box 611, Jefferson, North Carolina 28640
www.mcfarlandpub.com*

To Rajiv Bhadra and Pretzel, first loves

Acknowledgments

Throughout the writing of this book, Kelley Simpson took epic dog walks with me while he listened to, and nudged, my evolving thoughts about cultural mythologies of dogs in the United States. Those dog walks and dog talks course through this book.

The members of my group, Slow Sand Writers Society, workshopped my proposal and offered me wisdom and support. Thank you to J.S. Burton, Sara Hoffman, Karla Oceanak, Leslie Patterson, Elisa Sherman, and Melinda Swenson.

Many colleagues at Colorado State University gave me their time and insight. Thank you in particular to Drs. C.W. Miller, Bernie Rollin, and Stephen Withrow for allowing me an interview.

The Department of English and the College of Liberal Arts at Colorado State University helped fund the use of images in this book. Thank you, as well, to Melissa Merritt for help with the selection.

McFarland was a joy to work with. Thanks especially to Brian Duggan for his very helpful suggestions on my first draft and to Layla Milholen for her amazing guidance.

Thank you to Pretzel, Chappy, Houdini, Olive, Tiger, and Penguin, for all the inspiration and helpful distractions.

Table of Contents

Acknowledgments vi
Introduction: Breedologies: How We Look with Dogs 1
Chapter One. Made in America: Cocker Spaniels in the 1950s 17
Chapter Two. Thousands of Howls: Beagles in the 1960s 38
Chapter Three. Rewilding: Dogs as Wolves in the 1970s 55
Chapter Four. Breeding Bullies: Pit Bulls in the 1980s 83
Chapter Five. A Dog for All Seasons: Labrador Retrievers in the 1990s 112
Chapter Six. Mutty Waters: Mixed Breeds in the 2000s 138
Chapter Seven. Made to Order: Designer Dogs in the 2010s 158
Afterword: How Will We Look with Dogs? 182
Chapter Notes 187
Bibliography 193
Index 199

Introduction
Breedologies: How We Look with Dogs

An episode on the television show *Frasier* ends with Eddie, the family dog, about to receive "The Unkindest Cut of All."[1] The credits roll over the Jack Russell Terrier being taken from the veterinary waiting room, where Frasier sits with his father and his brother, a fellow psychiatrist. At the sight of Eddie heading toward castration, all three men simultaneously cross their legs.

It's a cheap laugh, but it says a lot about the role of dogs in American culture. Frasier, Martin, and Niles are not alone in finding that the dog brings out latent insecurities (in this case, insecurities concerning their masculinity and potency); many people think and feel through their dogs. I joke that my own dogs have played the role of my id, and that it's convenient when one can take one's id out for walks on a sturdy leash. For the past twenty years, I've projected my emotions and thoughts onto one or another of my five dogs. Just the other day I was saying to Olive, my thirteen-plus-year-old Border Collie, "It's tough, isn't it, being an aging diva, past your prime, with all these young puppies coming along to take your place. Nobody gives you a second look when there are younger, cuter dogs around. Right, Olive?" I looked into her impenetrable eyes. Even at thirteen, Olive hasn't lost her Border Collie stare. I decided those eyes were telling me she agreed with me.

You'll find my dogs making frequent cameo appearances in this book, which you can take as evidence that I'm as prone to these anthropocentric projections as anyone I know. They help me know myself; when I talk to my dogs, I find out what I'm thinking. If you're reading this book, you, too, probably know somebody who projects onto her dogs, if you don't do so yourself. The example of Frasier, albeit a fictional character, suggests that even psychiatrists are not immune from psychological projections and introjections. We may know very well that our dogs can't understand us, but still we talk to them. We may know that dogs experience the world very differently than we do, but still we see ourselves in them.

We use dogs as icons to signal much more than repressed id-like material. Not only do we project repressed emotions onto them, we may also borrow the imagery from their worlds to define ourselves. Often we work out our anxieties or identity crises through our dogs, whether they concern gender and power (as in the case of *Frasier*), sexuality (as evidenced in the nervousness of their human counterparts when dogs hump each other in the dog park), racial and class tensions (as we see in debates about Pit Bulls), ageism (as I find in Olive), or inconvenient emotions such as grief or anger or fear. Not only do we identify with our dogs, but we also use our dogs to identify ourselves.

Such projections onto dogs happen on the cultural level, too. It's not just as individuals that we project onto individual dogs; whole cultures can sometimes choose a dog as their icon, their unofficial cultural mascot. Through our dogs, we figure out what we're thinking, where we're at, and who we are. Sometimes, we allow our dogs to represent by proxy things that we don't quite want to recognize in ourselves. American culture in particular, perhaps, has expressed its cultural unconscious through the iconography of dogs, from Jack London's Buck in *Call of the Wild* to Disney's Lady and Tramp to Charles Schulz's Snoopy to Stephen King's Cujo to John Grogan's Marley, and from our First Dogs in the White House to our homeless shelter dogs.

My working assumption for this book is that sometimes our projections aren't on just individual dogs, but on entire breeds or types, which we use to imaginatively create an embodiment of our contemporary era, with all its needs, fears, desires, longings, aspirations, repressions, and hopeless contradictions. Since these are always in flux, our breeds of choice shift over the decades. Some of our knottiest contradictions concern our identities as human beings and our relations with non-humans. Our changing breed popularities reflect changes in how we see humans and animals. Dogs in our imagination give shape to our cultural identities and their crises.

In his book *Wild Ones: A Sometimes Dismaying, Weirdly Reassuring Story About Looking at People Looking at Animals in America*, Jon Mooallem looks at some of the ways in which Americans project onto wild animals. "America has been working out its feelings about wild animals this way since before it was officially America, using them to contemplate its own character."[2] He says that

Breedologies: How We Look with Dogs

[f]rom the very beginning, America's wild animals have inhabited the terrain of our imagination just as much as they've inhabited the actual land. They are free-roaming Rorschachs, and we are free to spin whatever stories we want about them. The wild animals always have no comment.[3]

Our understanding of wildness and the wilderness is in flux (as I'll discuss further in Chapter Three). While Mooallem suggests we use the wild animals of our imagination to think through concepts such as wilderness and American character, I propose that we make special use of dogs, those creatures at the threshold of the animal and human worlds, of the outdoors and the indoors. We use these not-so-free-roaming Rorschachs to spin stories about both them and ourselves. They walk by our sides as we humans take our first step in working out our relationship with non-human beings.

Of course we—as a culture as well as individually—work out these issues at multiple sites in addition to dogs and canine iconography, and to wild animals. There's a long tradition of cultural criticism tracing the cultural "mythologies" of our things. The origin of this line of criticism is often attributed to French critic Roland Barthes' 1957 classic *Mythologies*, which looks not at the seemingly timeless myths of the ages or at tales of gods and monsters but at the everyday cultural mythologies that mediate the meaning of things. Barthes posed mythologies not as misconceptions or falsehoods but as formulations, encapsulations, or embodiments of a cultural context and a worldview. They are stories that can be "read" for subtextual significance.

Barthes' book observes the processes of "mystification" in his culture. Mystification, for him, happens when we make our particular way of life and our worldview seem natural and universal. Our ideological beliefs, when naturalized and universalized, become "mythologies." In contemporary culture, mystification happens in all kinds of everyday places: fashion, cars, celebrities, sports, dance styles, interior design, even coffee cups—just about anywhere throughout our mediated culture. The everyday is where our cultural mythologies thrive, often hidden in plain sight. Since we tend to perceive these mythologies as common-sense realities—hence the power of mystification—it takes critical work to decode or de-mystify them. Barthes looked, for example, at such sites as wrestling (in its mystification of good-vs.-evil) and *On the Waterfront* (which he saw as mystifying the very class structure that the film [also] seems to be condemning). To go from the sublime to the canine, I'm proposing that we also mystify our worldviews through our dogs—or, rather, through our representations of our dogs. I'm dubbing these "breedologies." As one critic of the social meanings of dog breeds puts it,

Through representations of dogs, humans now say things about race that would otherwise go unsaid. Through dogs, popular culture speaks about its assumptions and its anxieties having to do with difference. At the bottom of many of these anxieties are the questions: What makes us human? What or who is domesticated, and what or who is wild? Portrayals of dogs work these concerns out through the category of breed, tapping into assumptions about pedigree, heredity, and race.[4]

In this book I'll be looking at Disney dogs and presidential dogs, at cover-model dogs and poster dogs, at real dogs and fantasy dogs, at barking dogs and talking dogs and silent dogs, at purebred dogs, pseudo-breeds, and mutts.

Mythologies, according to Barthes, enable us to universalize our worldviews. To do so, these mythologies have to actively repress competing and contradictory worldviews. Subsequent cultural critics have shifted the focus to teasing out those other, more marginal worldviews. They're interested in the ways that the objects and images of a culture don't simply mystify it but also make legible its irresolutions, its cultural anxieties and repressed voices. Furthermore, while Barthes' primary focus was on worldviews concerning class relations, subsequent cultural theorists have spun out from Barthes' line of argument to look at worldviews concerning gender and family relations, racial and (post)colonial identities, norms of sexuality, our place as a country in international politics, our understanding of what's healthy and unhealthy—or of what's "raw" and "cooked" (in the formulation made famous by anthropologist Claude Levi-Strauss) or of what's "clean" and "unclean" (in Ann Douglas' studies). And that's not even including those not-yet-named or classified elements of culture and identity still to be recognized and explored. Eco-critics and Animal Studies critics, for example, are currently exploring how we understand what's "wild" and what's "natural"—concepts we tend to pose in opposition to the "tame" and the "unnatural." This structure of opposition—wild/tame, natural/unnatural, raw/cooked, unclean/clean—is one of the most common of structures that get embedded and reinforced in cultural mythologies. Opposites help us go on to determine, for example, our "proper" relation to nature and the wild. Doing so demands that we figure out which side of the equation our dogs go in.

Other cultural theorists have offered alternative models to explore a culture's use of everyday objects as metaphors that give structure and meaning to our worlds. I'll also invoke Raymond Williams' "structures of feeling" and George Lakoff's "framing," among other models. Each of these models enables different kinds of understanding, but each gets at the way a culture organizes itself around subconscious structures—frameworks, metaphors, and mythologies—to make sense of things.

American iconography doesn't just reveal back to us the structures that we've already formed, and that are stable. It also becomes a place where we break the structures and rebuild them. Dogs as represented in popular culture, for example, are not just passive sites to be read; they actively engage in cultural work. Different cultural icons show us different things, and the ones that reach real cultural prominence often fill a niche by expressing something that hasn't found fitting expression in any other way. Each icon offers its own formulation.

This book is an attempt to think through what dogs have meant to people in the United States, and how we have made meaning through dogs. I'll visit specific dog breeds and types that embody specific aspects of an era. While our crudest expression of this phenomenon is the use of dog breeds as sports mascots (The Bulldogs, The Huskies), we regularly create informal and ad hoc cultural mascots. Not only do we reimagine our changing American identity through dogs, but our understanding of dogs and of proper human-dog relations keeps changing—and we express this change, too, through the breeds and types of dogs we favor. Perhaps no one intuits and exploits these shifting identities better than the advertising industry, with the entertainment industry not far behind. The images they produce, including images of dogs, help make the changing needs of American culture visible, if we stop to look (and sniff) around.

This book is itself something of a mutt—or at least an intermingling of multiple bloodlines. Coming from an academic background in literary criticism and Cultural Studies, I try to think critically about dogs in America and what they mean. Cultural Studies has accrued many different and useful approaches for combing into the deep undercoat of ideology, which does the real work of protecting and insulating, beneath a sometimes deceptive fluffy topcoat of adorableness. Such attempts to expose underlying ideologies otherwise rendered invisible by external representations have been applied to many aspects of popular culture, both in the United States and beyond. Popular culture studies have looked at such disparate "texts" as romance novels, punk fashion, and Black hairstyles—to offer just a few disparate examples. Often what seems to be a meaningless triviality is deeply shaped by—and shapes—the dominant worldviews of the era. Sometimes these underlying worldviews even clash with the conscious beliefs of the readers or wearers of these popular culture artifacts. Borrowing from the discipline of Cultural Studies to expose underlying ideology in this way can help us to understand why dominant ideologies are so enduring, even when we want to reject them. At the same time, the artifacts of popular culture also offer a chance to recognize emerging ideologies as they vie with dominant ones.

In this book, I treat an aspect of popular culture that's deeply meaningful in the United States but that hasn't received much cultural study: the iconography of dogs. I'm especially interested in why particular dogs and types of dogs thrive within a cultural moment. Looking at dogs in popular culture and in the popular imagination, it turns out, can reveal an awful lot not only about the human ideologies concerning race, gender, sexuality, and class—the usual suspects of Cultural Studies and obsessions of United States culture—but also about matters beyond "the big four" that we can't label quite so handily. Dogs in American popular culture also explore and/or enforce our ideologies about human-nonhuman relations, about "nature," about "personhood" and "self-hood," about ownership and consumption, and about national identity. With fashion and design, the reason a certain style "feels right" in a given moment is that it fits with the existing ideology of the moment—but also deviates from it just enough to be interesting and new. So, too, I'm arguing, with dogs.

My intended audience for this book, though, is not only an academic one; it's written just as much for my fellow "dog people," who don't necessarily speak the language of critical theory. So I've tried to write as accessibly as possible, to minimize jargon, and to prioritize accessibility over critical precision. Managing this mixed lineage in my writing has proven to be a difficult task; as I'll discuss in Chapter Seven in regard to designer dogs, the mixing of two bloodlines can result in an array of offspring, some of which may preserve the best of both bloodlines in equal measure, but others of which will frustrate the intended results. Jargon encapsulates concepts and debates that have been developed over years and can't be easily summarized to non-specialists. At times I find myself forced to use bits of jargon when no other term will suffice. As much as possible, though, I try to prioritize my non-critic dog people over academic insiders.

To further mutty the mix, even as I want to make this book both academically serious and widely accessible, I also want it to be playful. I don't want it to feel like a "study" in the stern sense that term conjures up, but something more like a foray, a trying-on of ideas, a musing (and sometimes amusing) journey through the past seven decades. But perhaps "journey" is the wrong metaphor too, since the foray is not driving toward a conclusive endpoint. Perhaps this book is best characterized as an intellectual dog walk, stopping to investigate interesting spots along the way.

Into this already mutty mix I also add personal narrative, especially in chapter codas. While my early career and training was in literary criticism and Cultural Studies, my second career has been in creative nonfiction, the artful shaping of true facts. For the most part, in this book, I include personal anecdotes to illustrate my critical musings. (I've written more full-on creative nonfiction about my dogs in my book *Pretzel, Houdini, and Olive: The Dogs of My Life*.) I offer myself and my mixed-species family as a fairly representative—though perhaps comically exaggerated—form of mainstream American dog relations. I have no formal training in veterinary medicine, animal behaviorism, or even dog training. I can only offer observations from my hundreds of hours logged at the dog park and from my thousands of hours cohabiting with my five variously neurotic rescue dogs in my oversized doghouse of a home.

So it should be abundantly clear by now that I'm not taking a scientific or empirical approach to dogs. Such an approach necessitates setting aside what dogs mean to people in order to get at the truth of what dogs really are. Instead, I take the scientific approach's set-asides as my object of study. I'm interested in what dogs mean to people, however rightly or wrongly—in how we make sense of and through dogs. Put another way, I'm not trying to argue for what dogs "really are" behind all the myths. I love books that do this, and have learned from many. (Especially useful to me have been Gregory Berns' *What It's Like to Be a Dog*, John Bradshaw's *Dog Sense*, and Alexandra Horowitz's *Inside of a Dog*.) I even refer to some of these more objective studies in this book. While there's a real use for such work, this book aims to try on the kinds of ideas that can't be objectively proven or disproven. It's not about confronting "false" mythologies and correcting them with the truth about dogs, or trying to prescribe how we really *should* relate to dogs (if a "proper" or "healthy" relationship to dogs can even be found). I'm less interested in looking behind a myth than I am in looking at the myth itself, and even—to shift the metaphor—to approach American dog mythology like my dog Tiger does a new toy, disemboweling the device inside that makes it squeak.

It should also be clear by now that I won't be taking a rigorous historical approach to American culture's representation of dogs, at least not in a scholarly way. That's important work to do, too, but that's not what this book does. (For that work, see such gems as Mark Derr's *A Dog's History of America* and Katherine C. Grier's *Pets in America*. Or, for a British context, see Harriet Ritvo's *The Animal Estate*.) I make no attempt at comprehensiveness, but rather look at specific aspects at play in specific eras. Nor am I even looking at dogs per se, but our representations of them—at dogs in the American imagination. I want this book to be a playful, speculative, even recklessly subjective attempt to "read" aspects of American culture through its canine self-representations. The appearances of my own five dogs—my five little Rorschachs—will demonstrate my decidedly subjective approach. You'll meet Pretzel the Spaniel–Border Collie mix, Chappy the Cocker-Pomeranian-Poodle pretty boy, Houdini the Cocker, Olive the Border Collie mix with a Sheltie shriek, and Tiger, my Husky-Terrier monster. Reading my dogs helps me see what I can't quite recognize in myself and in my culture.

Such subjectivity flaunts itself in my organizing this book around one exemplary breed or type per decade, starting in the 1950s (which, arguably, marks the beginning of the mass-production of dogs in the United States, though our interesting and contradictory relationships with dogs began decades—and centuries—earlier). I use the schema of a breed-of-the-decade to get both at our changing uses of dogs as cultural icons and our changing understanding of ourselves as humans. The changing meanings we give to different dog breeds (or pseudo-breeds) over the decades offer a special dog-door entrance into an understanding of facets of American culture, showing us things about ourselves we might not see from other focal points. Why do some breeds seem to capture our attention in some eras, then fall by the wayside in others? Why do we see such fluctuations in AKC breed popularities? Why, for example, have Labrador Retrievers risen from relative obscurity (as when they were first recognized by the AKC in 1917) to the number one dog in America for over two decades? These fluctuations have multiple causes, of course, but one of them is the cultural climate—the needs of certain elements of American culture at the time.

This layout—assigning a dog breed or pseudo-breed per decade for seven decades—could be seen as a gimmick—or what literary folks more politely call a "conceit." I'm the first to admit that there are problems with this conceit. One is the very notion of a breed as a stable, distinct entity, a problem I'll discuss further in Chapter Six. Another problem with this conceit is its reliance on the idea of decades themselves, as self-contained units of time, an idea that's ultimately indefensible, as anyone who's written anything based on a decade definition can attest to. But like breeds, decades serve as enabling fictions, starting points allowing more nuanced explorations.

An even bigger problem with this project is the idea of "American culture" itself. Up to this point I've been speaking of "American Culture" as if there is one—that is, as if there's one, singular, and it's stable and knowable. Which of course it isn't. The American zeitgeist, if "it" exists, is never unitary or monolithic, but messily multiple, more *pluribus* than *unum*. Raymond Williams speaks of dominant, emergent, and residual strands of ideology or worldview, coexisting (and often intermingling) at any given time.[5] And there are always subcultural, or co-cultural, ideologies running alongside—and at times ruffling up—the dominant ideologies. Sometimes, dominance creates resistance, and the resistant ideologies adopt the language of the dominant ones. Other times, these subordinate ideologies can diverge so significantly from the dominant ideologies that they go their own ways. Even so, the composition of coexisting ideologies shifts over time. Even if we can't believe in a singular "American identity," though, we can still note significant shifts in our varied attempts at self-identification, shifts that we mark through our cultural icons. I'm risking the oversimplifying of differences within an era in order to track the shifts from one era to another. Fictions such as breeds, decades, and identities make comprehensible our otherwise ungraspable realities. Even so, I put my focus on only selective and specific dog-moments that embody particular aspects—quirks, anxieties, debates, and obsessions—of their decade.

What follows, then, are my altogether subjective picks of the decade-defining breeds of the past seventy or so years. These are the dog types whose representations in film, advertisements, literature, legislation, and other media most embody meaningful features of their cultural moment.

I'm sure my choices will offend breed loyalists, both those whose breed of choice is left out and those whose breed I may seem to malign or misrepresent (though neither is my intention). Some readers may not be able to forgive me for not assigning a single Terrier breed an American decade (unless you count the Pit Bull Terrier). As the owner of a Terrier-ish mutt, I can hardly forgive myself. Also omitted are German Shepherds, Poodles, Collies, Boxers, Great Danes, Chihuahuas, Greyhounds, Pugs, and other equally worthy contenders for the status of representative American dogs, and all of these breeds have loyal human groupies. I simply tried to choose the breeds that seemed to me the very most defining of a decade's issues, knowing that no one breed could ever be sufficient, and that no breed should be left behind. Every decade is as messy and multifarious as the dog park my dogs and I visit every day.

Chapter One ("Made in America: Cocker Spaniels in the 1950s") tracks the Cocker Spaniel, that sentimental protagonist of American culture in the 1940s and especially 1950s, appearing as Butch on wartime covers of *The Saturday Evening Post*, Lady in the Disney film, and Spot in the "Dick and Jane" readers. *Lady and the Tramp* bears special attention as a cold-war era film, posing the innocent Cocker as the epitome of the American middle-class home front, in contrast to those devious and inscrutable Siamese cats.

Cockers so epitomized wholesomeness that in Nixon's "Checkers" speech, in which he deflected criticism with the imagery of his adorable Cocker Spaniel, the breed worked better than any other breed could have. By the end of the 1950s, however, Cockers were already being bred—as well as in-bred and over-bred—in puppy mills, resulting in a number of physical and behavioral problems, and tainting the Cocker's wholesome reputation. In my discussion of the rise of puppy mills, I admit to my own purchase of a pet store Cocker Spaniel and its rather disastrous results.

What the Cocker was to the 1950s, I suggest in Chapter Two ("Thousands of Howls: Beagles in the 1960s"), the Beagle was to the 1960s. Through the Beagle, more than any other breed, we represented and reimagined ourselves, and at the same time, the Beagle represented our changing ethos of human-dog relations.

Chapter Two begins with "The Great Ear Lift" controversy, the national kerfuffle over President Lyndon Johnson's lifting his Beagle by the ears to make him howl. At the same time as concern poured out for this dog, however, the use of Beagles for laboratory testing rose astronomically. (In this chapter I give special attention to one particular Beagle colony, the "Charlie lab" in the Foothills Campus of Colorado State University, where two thousand Beagles were radiated to study the late-term effects of radiation.) This would not be the first or last time that Americans showed simultaneous hyper-concern for one individual creature and flagrant disregard for a species. Even with the enactment of the Animal Welfare Act in 1966, which eased some of the worst suffering of laboratory dogs, Beagles (the favored breed for lab research) continued to suffer behind the scenes even as a fictional Beagle, Snoopy, the most visible dog of his era, garnered write-in votes in the 1968 presidential election.

Chapter Three ("Rewilding: Dogs as Wolves in the 1970s") considers wolves—and those dog breeds seemingly most wolf-like, such as Huskies—as the zeitgeist "dogs" of the 1970s. A wolf, of course, is not a dog, but the 1970s was a decade of new respect for both the wolf and the wolf-in-the-dog. In this decade, we significantly revised our view of dogs and their relations to wolves. This revision was part of a larger-scale change in attitudes towards the natural environment and its conservation. Some of the beliefs about dog-wolf relations that emerged in the 1970s have since been disproven, but their cultural influence remains powerful.

As a child in the 1970s, I first encountered this new respect for wolves in Jean Craighead George's Newberry Award–winning children's book *Julie of the Wolves*, published in 1972. Like many suburban American children of the time, I read this book and subsequently "played Eskimo"; my friends and I, our imaginations sparked, acted out scenarios from the book, in which we were Arctic Native Americans bonding with wolves. Our "playing Indian" (as Native American critic Philip Deloria calls it) was problematic in many of the ways the book itself (written by a non–Native woman) is, but it also reflected our nation's casting about for a revisionary approach to the wilderness—even as we were simultaneously (paraphrasing Joni Mitchell's words of the time) paving it and putting up parking lots.

By the 1970s, actual wolves were nearly extinct in the lower forty-eight states after the resoundingly successful eradication efforts of earlier decades. The 1973 Endangered Species Act reversed this approach, declaring gray wolves an endangered species in need of protection. While their population has since increased, the fate of gray wolves (and other wolf subspecies) remains uncertain to this day.

The year of 1973 was also the year that the Iditarod, Alaska's annual sled dog race, began. In the face of increasing anxieties about America's national power and natural resources, this northern sled race offered an alternative image through which Americans could understand their cultural identity. Commemorating and re-enacting the 1925 Serum Run, in which an antitoxin for a diphtheria outbreak in Nome was delivered by sled when weather conditions made airplane flight impossible, the race was also resurrected in the 1970s "to save sled dog and Alaskan Huskies, which were being phased out of existence due to the introduction of snowmobiles in Alaska."[6] Many of these dogs, including the lead dog, Balto, were "Indian Ehiskimo" or "Husky" dogs; the Eskimo heritage of the dogs was also being revalued (albeit problematically so) by (mostly white) Americans. A somewhat mystified image of both Native Americans and their dogs offered American culture at large a new model through which to imagine a different relationship to nature and the wilderness.

This re-envisioning is reflected in the changing theories of dog origins. In the 1970s, dogs were seen as close descendants of wolves, and the wolf in the dog was increasingly celebrated. Current scientific evidence (including mitochondrial DNA) puts today's dog and wolf farther apart than was believed in the 1970s. Changing understandings of dog descent sometimes reflect the cultural needs of the era creating them as much as they do the scientific evidence; like nature and nurture, they enable each other. Once again we see the dog, at the threshold between "the wilderness" and "human civilization," as a primary place where we work out our attitudes toward nature. At least in our imaginations, we tried to put the wolf back in the dog and the wilderness back in the American landscape.

In Chapter Four ("Breeding Bullies: Pit Bulls in the 1980s") I consider the Pit Bull as the iconic dog of the 1980s. This breed has, rightly or wrongly, become synonymous with toughness and viciousness. During the Reagan era of the 1980s, as American culture reimagined its national identity once again as one of toughness and dominance, the image of the tough Pit Bull began to assert itself.

But what exactly is a Pit Bull? The very definition of the (non-)breed spurs debate, and this debate is itself a microcosm of cultural identity debates. In fact, though it's commonly referred to as a breed, experts consider it a type, and prefer the term "Pit Bull type dog." Complicating matters further, the Pit Bull type dog (hereafter referred to, however problematically, as the Pit Bull) is notoriously difficult to identify visually, and can be indistinguishable from lab and Boxer mixes. In truth, the classification of "Pit Bull" often has more to do with the race and class of its owners than with genetic lineage.

The owners Pit Bulls have tended most to be associated with since the 1980s have been Black and Latino men. While there's some demographic truth to this association, it's in the realm of American cultural mythology that the equation between pits and men of color has its greatest strength, bestializing men of color and racializing Pit Bulls in the process. Almost every characterization of Pit Bulls (or justification for the prejudice against them) echoes earlier characterizations of black men and justifications of racism. Some people go so far as to say that prejudice against Pit Bulls is really a displaced and disguised prejudice against their owners, who are disproportionately Black and Latino men in the urban north and rural south.

Any discussion of Pit Bulls in the United States, then, is also inflected with race and class issues, even when all the participants involved are white and middle class. Racist discourse may inevitably infect and inflect the ways Americans conceptualize breeds. At the same time, though, prejudice against Pit Bulls is not reducible to racism. The dogs are not people, breeds don't equate to races, and breedism is not simply racism for dogs. Characterizing men of color as metaphorical Pit Bulls seems to me uncomfortable and harmful; however, ignoring this metaphor, so active in American culture, doesn't make it disappear.

Currently, the shelters are flooded disproportionately with Pit Bull type dogs, and will often label ambiguous pit mixes as Lab or Boxer mixes to avoid stigma and breed-specific laws. In the case of the Pit Bull, not only does the breed bear the metaphorical weight of culture's racial conflicts, but it also, sometimes, suffers very real consequences. Shelters also disproportionately collect black dogs, harder to place than their lighter-furred counterparts. The homeless of the dog population mirror, demographically, the homeless of the human population.

In 1997, when Bill Clinton brought a three-month-old chocolate lab to the White House and named him Buddy, the then-president chose the perfect puppy for his era. The Labrador Retriever reached the top of the AKC rankings for dog popularity in the United States in the 1990s and has remained there ever since. At the same time, Buddy confirmed the retriever's status as the iconic dog of the 1990s, as I'll present in Chapter Five ("A Dog for All Seasons: Labrador Retrievers in the 1990s"). The Lab is now as iconic of the late twentieth century as the Cocker was of the mid-century.

Buddy was named after a great-uncle who had recently died, and the very fact that a dog received the same name as a human, and that this was seen as an honor, speaks volumes about changes in the status of dogs in America. A breed once valued as a hunting dog and used for sport now played the role of buddy, friend, companion, even family member. Though dogs had long been referred to as family members by some Americans before the 1990s, this status was still looked on askance by the majority until well into the twentieth century. The 1990s may be seen as the decade when pets became accepted as family. In fact, our biggest pet store chain, PetSmart, which went public on the NASDAQ in 1993, bore the motto "Where Pets Are Family."

At the same time, though, "family" was a radically contested term in the 1990s, and one played out through our dogs even as those dogs themselves became family members. This contest over the meaning of family is one version of the decade's "culture wars." These clashing ideologies showed up in our different understandings of dogs as family members, as well as in approaches to dog training. Within this divisive era, the Labrador Retriever was the ideal dog for embodying both conservative and progressive concepts of family. Athlete and "big lug," servant and partner, hunter and heart-warmer—the Lab was one of those rare creatures able temporarily to reconcile Americans' irreconcilable differences.

One could argue that the decade of the nineties ended decisively on September 11, 2001, with the fall of the Twin Towers. In the wake of that disaster, Search and Rescue dogs were brought in—most famously Labs and Goldens (among other breeds). These rescue dogs received an extraordinary amount of media attention, partly because we were desperate for positive stories of heroism, but also because they gave us an image of a particular kind of heroism—and of resilience—that was hard to find in the human realm. In this key post–World War II event defining our nation, these search and rescue dogs became the nation's therapy dogs.

As president-elect Barack Obama indicated in his post-election press conference in 2008, the first presidential campaign promise he would keep was the one to his daughters to get a dog. When asked by an interviewer what breed of puppy the Obama family would get, the President-Elect couldn't say with certainty, because the plan was to get a rescue dog from a shelter, and "most of them are mutts, like me."[7] In Chapter Six ("Mutty Waters: Mixed Breeds in the 2000s"), I take the mutt to be the representative dog of the 2000s.

At the risk of over-analyzing what was almost surely an ad lib comment, I spend some time on that "mutts, like me" simile. The status of the mutt, a non-pedigreed mixed-breed dog, had clearly risen if it was being considered for the First Dog. The Obamas ended up with a (hypoallergenic) Portuguese Water Dog because of Malia's allergies. Had they adopted a rescue mutt, they might, by example, have challenged assumptions about the iconic American dog, as they have about the race of the iconic American family.

Even without the help of a mutt in the White House, the 2000s saw a backlash against puppy mills. Shelter dogs and mutts became cool. Back in the 1950s, the mutt Tramp might have been a protagonist in *Lady and the Tramp*, but in that film he was promoted to the clearly more desirable level/class of the purebred (as if given honorary purebred status). Now, the muttiness of the mutt was becoming classy. Or, put another way, the mutt has gone middle class.

In fact the very notion of "breed" (like "race") was losing its hold. The notion is ultimately a construction. Breeds themselves are unnatural, in the sense that they are almost all human creations, the product of artificially manipulating the gene pool to select for traits that might not have survived natural selection. In essence, breeds are the product of dog eugenics. Furthermore, many breeds were the result of mixing other already established purebreds together.

Obama's "mutts, like me" comment brings up an even more troubling "lived fiction": the concept of race. By the 2000s, the demographics were radically shifting. What's more, seemingly stable racial classifications were yet again stirred up, as seen in changes in the racial classification options on census forms. In academia, race was increasingly discredited as a scientific fact, and was instead seen as an ideological system. Cornel West, a proponent of this concept, titled his critical book on race in America *Race Matters*, suggesting that no matter how fictive, race is lived in material ways, and with very real consequences (as we saw in Chapter Four).

Even more troubling in Obama's comment is the aligning of breeds and races, however fictive these categories might both be. Any comparison of humans to (non-human) animals is treading dangerous ground. Still, Obama's ad-libbed comment was also spot on. Like it or not, our rhetorics of breed and of race inform each other. I considered titling this book *Breed Matters* in the shadow of Cornel West's *Race Matters*, in recognition of these troubling and uncanny parallels, and of their centrality to American culture.

Currently, the 2010s seem to be the era of designer dogs, as I argue in Chapter Seven ("Made to Order: designer dogs in the 2010s"). Puggles. Labradoodles. Goldendoodles. These are the dogs-of-the-decade for an era in which individuality—both of humans and of dogs—is completely integrated into the economy, which itself began to shift from mass-production to micro-consumption. In addition, it makes sense to me to see this proliferation of designer dogs in an era of GMOs, an era that actively undermines former nature-nurture and natural-artificial dualisms. Designer dogs are different from mutts. Mutts are accidental mixes. Designer dogs were specifically bred for the best traits of each breed—e.g., the hypoallergenic hair of the Poodle, the docility of the Beagle (but without the baying). These dogs were designed by humans—in essence, genetically modified. While with designer dogs, we don't actually go into cells and modify genes directly, the aim and results fit the GMO zeitgeist. Indeed, attempts at dog cloning and other genetic manipulations are already underway.

There's a real market for these designed Cockaliers, Maltipoos, Chiweenies, Chorkies, and Dorkies—and I want to put the emphasis on *market*. Unlike mutts, designer dogs are expensive and are part of a whole consumer economy. Indeed, the economy around dogs has vastly expanded, with pet stores offering far more than the food and leashes of yore. Dogs have now become thoroughly folded into consumer economy, both as products (objects of consumption) and as consumers-by-proxy. We might, of course, say the same of humans.

Americans are as crazy about our dogs as ever, if not more so, and we'll continue to see ourselves in our dogs, to mold our dogs to our needs, to represent ourselves through iconic dogs. As we use dogs to understand ourselves, and to work out our issues through our dogs, their representations will continue to be as contradictory as American culture. As we move into an era of genetic manipulation and hybridization, interspecies relations and ethics will become more puzzling and more urgent than ever, even as the very notion of species integrity becomes as muddled and unsustainable as the notion of breed. No doubt dogs will once again help us find our way through this identity thicket.

Looking at dogs, we look at ourselves. Dogs confront us with some hard truths. And some soft truths. Some curious truths, and some downright uncomfortable truths. Looking at Eddie in the veterinary office, the Cranes reflexively cross their legs. There's plenty in this book to make us all want to cross our legs, however we identify.

Chapter One

Made in America

Cocker Spaniels in the 1950s

In its heyday in the 1950s, the American Cocker Spaniel was synonymous with smiles. The spritely Cocker captured the "happy days" spirit that American culture strove to project back to itself. There's something inherently campy about a Cocker Spaniel, with its floppy ears, cartoonishly round eyes, and long eyelashes. The figure of the Cocker presents itself ready-made for representation in the form of sentimentalized drawings, cartoons, and knick-knacks. If you spend any time browsing in flea markets and vintage shops, as I like to do, you'll see oodles of kitschy Cocker Spaniel figurines from the 1950s. I recently splurged on a Cocker Spaniel toothpick holder in bold mid-century turquoise.

It's as if the breed were designed to attract customers to pause at a storefront window.

In the previous decades, many of our most iconic dogs had been more serious and serviceable. Susan Orlean's book *Rin Tin Tin: The Life and the Legend* compellingly explores the roles and representations of dogs in the era of the two world wars, an era in which German Shepherds like Rin Tin Tin were a particularly iconic breed. Among other contenders for the role of the era's iconic breed, we might include

Cocker kitsch: a vintage Cocker Spaniel toothpick holder (photograph by the author).

the Scottish Terrier—with FDR's Fala as the most famous—and the Collie, so capably represented by Lassie. (Lassie the character was herself capably represented by several different actual dogs, some of them lads.)

By the 1950s, however, farming and ranching work was decreasing as we saw the beginnings of factory farms. No longer needed as agricultural laborers, dogs became increasingly valued for their companionship rather than for their utility. The decades before the 1950s already saw the rise of dogs primarily as family pets. They were not yet routinely thought of as family members, but were increasingly coming indoors to eat and sleep, making our human identities and self-images even more bound up with dogs. Herding breeds, like Lassie, bred to work outdoors all day long, were less appropriate as household pets than some other breeds. Then, too, by the end of the 1950s, as German Shepherds evoked images of those police dogs photographed attacking nonviolent civil rights protesters, the breed lost some of its associations with rescue and safety. As post-war families began to baby-boom, and the middle class surged, new breeds and new brands entered the mainstream marketplace. Kim Kavin notes in her book *The Dog Merchants: Inside the Big Business of Breeders, Pet Stores, and Rescuers* that the Westminster Kennel Club Dog Show was first televised in 1948, and purebred (or knock-off purebred) dogs began appearing in newspaper classifieds. "The purebred dogs, as much as the suburban houses," writes Kavin, "became a middle-class lifestyle status symbol."[1] Breed began to function as brand.

The American Cocker Spaniel

Dogs can perhaps best be understood as prolonged wolf puppies, or pedomorphic wolves. A man-modified if not man-made species (or subspecies), dogs have no natural habitat outside the human realm. Hypotheses about the evolution of dogs abound (as I discuss in later chapters), but the most common one during the Cocker's heyday in the 1950s, and one still considered viable today, is that humans probably began breeding dogs from wolves around 12,000 years ago by selectively supporting the least aggressive and most friendly—that is, the most puppy-like—of wolf cubs, creating in the dog a permanently infantilized wolf, forever fawning, face-licking, and, in many cases, floppy-eared. Wolf pups, too, are born with floppy ears, but those ears stand erect within weeks of birth.

Cockers, in particular, maintain the look of infant wolf pups throughout their lives. In my experience, they maintain the infantile personality, too, even into old age. A 1958 description of the American Cocker Spaniel, in *The National Geographic Book of Dogs*, states,

> The affectionate, flop-eared Cocker ingratiates himself with every member of the household. Active by nature, he particularly loves to romp with children. The playful little dog does not accede to full spaniel dignity until relatively late in life.[2]

Indeed, Cockers are eternally the dogs of childhood, the dogs of nostalgia. They connote the good old days (that probably never were).

Cocker Spaniels were bred centuries ago by hunters to flush woodcocks out of the forest undergrowth. Those dogs with traits that made them pursue potential food without pause and follow every slight movement with exuberant curiosity—that is, with puppy-like traits—were allowed to reproduce. Cockers were not bred for patience or guidance or loyalty or retrieving ability; their purpose was to stir things up. As that same 1958 *Book of Dogs* says, "The Cocker's comportment in the field is all exuberance, and he shows his delight in his work by the incessant, enthusiastic wagging of his tail."[3] It's no wonder, then, that many Cockers have the curiosity—and attention span—of a human two-year-old. Still, they made better pet dogs than some of the higher-energy herding and working breeds, especially as dogs became increasingly confined to backyards.

The American Cocker Spaniel is itself a breed made in America, a product of adapting and redefining the droopier English Cocker Spaniel to American cultural needs. Both were originally bred for hunting, with ears designed to raise up scents from the underbrush as the dogs ran. The American Cocker Spaniel split off from the English version of the breed as America was coming into its own. In 1936, the American and English were shown in the kennel club rings as separate breeds for the first time. In the coming decades, America established itself as the upwardly mobile world power, full of energy and optimism and dogged mirth. Not all United States citizens benefited equally, but young white men, at any rate, could have the cockiness to believe that in the sweep of history, America was now the protagonist.

In the decades leading up to the 1950s, as the American Cocker Spaniel emerged as a breed, it also emerged as a cultural icon.

"Butch"

The American Cocker Spaniel offered something different from policing German Shepherds and vigilant Collies: not a dog as protector, but a dog who needed protection. Already in the 1940s, while the war thundered abroad and the United States represented its *military* identity through war dogs, especially those Shepherds, the *home front* was being represented by more domestic dogs such as Cocker Spaniels. On the covers of the *Saturday Evening Post*, a playful black and white Cocker endeared himself to readers with antics such as raiding pantyhose or stealing socks or snatching newspapers (sometimes bearing headlines from the war front). This little fellow was ironically named "Butch," although he was more femme than butch, more a charming inhabitant of the domestic realm and the home front than a warrior or frontier trailblazer.

Drawn by illustrator Albert Staehle, who purchased his own Cocker at a local pet store, Butch represented the young, innocent, wholesome nation back home. Butch debuted on the cover of the February 19, 1944, *Saturday Evening Post*, caught in the act of chewing wartime ration stamps. Oops! The issue, Sharon Damkaer notes in her piece on Staehle in the *American Art Archives*, "sold out quickly and mail poured in to defend the mischievous puppy; some folks even sent rationing stamps to replace those Butch had appeared to destroy."[4]

Butch went on to misbehave or to be misbehaved upon by humans (for example, by finding himself knitted into a sweater) on another twenty-four covers of the *Saturday Evening Post* in the 1940s-50s. These include such classics as "Butch Weighs In" (1945), "Butch Breaks the Lamp" (1946), "Butch and the Sunday Paper" (1947), "Butch Chews the Mail" (1948), and "Butch Gets a Bath" (1956).[5] Other illustrations show him getting into trouble with open paint cans, mousetraps, and stolen baseballs. He was the poster child-dog for putting on a happy face. Staehle drew Butch with an enlarged head and eyes, which puppied up the dog even further. Butch's crimes, such as they were, were really just cute misdemeanors, after all. Although his childlike naughtiness and high spirits may have destroyed a few wardrobe accessories and household goods, Butch's eyes were so pure and innocent and happy, so opposite to the evil Nazis and the Axis forces, that he elicited instant forgiveness. As the good-hearted, defenseless underdog, this Cocker was the face of the home front that America drew for itself, covering over other possible mythologies or narratives we could have told ourselves about ourselves.

After the war, when the United States sought to redefine itself as a nation yet again, it drew on this image of eager innocence, an image that may already have been obsolete. Butch continued to scamper across magazine pages in the 1950s, including thirty covers for the *American Weekly*, as well as on advertisements and merchandise.[6] One illustration for *American Weekly* even depicts Butch watching a dog show on television.[7] He was literally the poster boy for dogs, appearing on the official poster for National Dog Week in 1950. He also featured on a 1956 recruitment poster for the United States Navy and was sworn in as the official U.S. Navy mascot.[8] The optimistic Cocker did not so much represent who we were as how we chose to imagine ourselves.

Run, Spot, Run!

The American Cocker Spaniel emerged as a breed around the same time as highways emerged for the ever-increasing masses of cars. Expanded roads allowed for white flight from cities and middle-class sprawl into the developing suburbs. As single-family homes and lawns replaced farms and forests, the dog's role as pet replaced its role as hunter and herder. The Cocker Spaniel was the quintessential suburban dog. Like the lawns of American suburbs, Cockers gave us a simulation of nature, but without nature's annoying wildness. Dogs became a privileged representative of nature, while natural landscapes were razed to create the suburban lawns on which canine pets cavorted.

"Run, Spot, Run," children across the country recited as the mottled Cocker Spaniel scampered across the pages of the Scott-Foresman *Fun with Our Friends* readers of the 1930s to the 1960s (better known as the "Dick and Jane" books). Indeed, "Run, Spot, Run!" has become part of our pop cultural lexicon, though over the years it's gone rancid with cynicism. In the early readers of the 1930s—the era of FDR and his Scottie, Fala—the little dog appeared as a black-and-white Terrier, but starting in the 1940s the dog metamorphosed into a Cocker. Spot, the epitome of guileless mischief, evoked an idyll of innocence and childhood. Readers watched Spot bark at cows and chase chickens on the grandparents' farm. When not running, Spot was constantly at play, hiding in a picnic basket, yanking on the end of a blanket, digging in the sandbox and tossing sand onto Sally, or leaving a paw print in the drying concrete. Always he supplemented and accentuated the human life around him. Tolerating being dressed up in fancy hats as he followed the children on their mundane adventures, he asked only for attention. His needs were as simple as elementary grammar. Often grouped with dolls, Spot is essentially the children's child, and pet-keeping is seen in these readers as a juvenile activity. The pet is clearly for the children, not their adult parents.

Spot represented the dog as an integral part of childhood. Pet-keeping can even be seen as a childhood rite of passage in America. Katherine C. Grier, in her book *Pets in America: A History*, tracks a "domestic ethic of kindness" that emerged alongside modern pet-keeping.[9] This "domestic ethic of kindness" arose in the nineteenth century and is still very much with us. We see a child's relationship to a pet as training in family values of love, loyalty, and stewardship. A child's cruelty to animals, by contrast, is seen as a primary sign of anti-social behavior. Spot's prominent but subservient role among Dick, Jane, Sally, and the other children models this connection between playful dogs and healthy childhood. The Cocker Spaniel makes a choice symbol for a phase of wholesome innocence in American childhood, one in which we learn how to "play well with others" and through which we must pass before moving on to less innocent phases.

Although black-and-white in color, Spot may have been the whitest dog in America. His human owners, Sally, Dick, and Jane, bear all the signs of a purebred WASP ethnicity, especially the girls, with their cherubic blond curls. They even had—literally—a white picket fence around their highly cultivated green lawn. Not until the 1960s did they see a glimpse of any non-white humans. By the time the African American family of brother Mike and twin sisters Pam and Penny moved into the neighborhood, the series was in its waning years, overtaken by such contending books for beginning readers as the Dr. Seuss books that I grew up on, books sprawling with far more diverse and imaginative species, with their star bellies and green diets.

Had the series survived into later decades, it may have had to adjust its depiction of Spot's mobility. In the series, there's nary a leash in sight (unless he's harnessed like a sled dog to pull the roller skate-shodden Dick); Spot romps freely around the family grounds, though rarely leaves his natural habitat, the lawn. Beyond the yard, though, the nation saw an inflation of leash laws around the 1950s, which arose partly out of a fear of rabies among free-roaming dogs, partly as a protection against dog theft, and partly (among many other reasons), because the increasing automobile traffic through the suburbs resulted in a disturbing incidence of car-on-dog accidents. Increasingly, family dogs would be confined to the family property, their ownership increasingly privatized as their freedom narrowed. We would soon not see Spot run as much as he would have liked.

Like a Lady

Perhaps no dog is more iconic of the 1950s than Lady, the American Cocker Spaniel of the 1955 Disney classic *Lady and the Tramp*. This film ostensibly tells the story of class conflict in the romance between the pedigreed Lady and her homeless and streetwise mongrel beau, Tramp.

The film was Disney's 15th feature-length animated film and its first in CinemaScope's widescreen format, which allowed characters to more naturalistically move across a set backdrop.[10] The dogs, too, are depicted more naturalistically than past cartoon dogs, and Disney illustrators took pains to study and model their images on actual dogs.

The film is set in an anachronistic amalgam of time and place, calling up a nostalgic pre-war era, when Walt Disney himself was a child. Although the story technically takes place in New England in 1909 (as reflected in the film's late-Victorian footwear, floor-length skirts, and horse-and-buggy transportation), the backdrop feels very mid-twentieth-century America in its manicured, fenced lawns, the accents of its protagonists, and above all the cold war ideology invisibly suffusing it. This mixture of times and places gives the film a universalizing effect, as if normalizing middle-class, mid-century values onto anytime and anyplace. This film is not exactly an allegory, but it does have allegorical elements operating beneath its plot. Like the animal characters in Aesop's fables, the animated dogs in this film embody human characteristics. These characteristics, however, aren't so much universal human traits (although they seem to pose as such) as they are those consistent with a mid-century, middle-class, implicitly white culture. A classic romance of the boy-meets-girl, boy-loses-girl, boy-gets-girl formula, *Lady and the Tramp* also reveals major ideological forces dogfighting with each other in the 1950s. The film appears more innocent than it is.

The story, which goes from Christmas to Christmas, begins with a husband gifting his wife a hatbox, whose contents begin to squirm and yip and poke at the lid. Inside the hatbox we find not the expected headwear but an entirely different commodity: a floppy-eared puppy. I remember a similar scene in my own childhood in the early 1970s, when a friend of mine opened her wrapped-and-bow-tied birthday package to find a kitten. That practice, I suspect, is rarely performed in the twenty-first century, when we treat new pets more like adoptees than gifts. The dog in the Christmas-wrapped hatbox suggests that in the 1950s, while a puppy may not have denoted a *thing*, exactly, its position in the household overlapped with that of other household goods and accessories.

Like so many heroines of fairy tales and Disney films, Lady appears without a mother. Feminist critics have long noted the uncanny absence—even erasure—of mothers in these kinds of stories. Fairy tales abound with widowed fathers (and more than a smattering of unmotherly stepmothers). In the case of Lady, however, the lack of mothers for fairy tale heroines overlaps with the invisibility of parents for store-bought dogs. Both maternal absences reinforce each other and feed into the notion that dogs come to us without a history or a past, and no labor or loss went into their creation.

Lady's ambiguous status in the household soon becomes clear. At first, the husband and wife—who, from Lady's perspective, are named Jim Dear and Darling—resolve to keep Lady out of the bedroom and have her sleep in a basket downstairs. However, her lonesome puppy-howls soon sway them into making space for her at the foot of their bed. Many actual dogs of the era made this trip from the downstairs doghouse or dog bed to the human bed upstairs. Lady rests on the edge, or foot, of the family bed but not yet its center. Somewhat like a doll, she is a kind of surrogate child, or practice-child, who will eventually be replaced by the clearly preferable, more valuable human version.

Although her coat is golden in color, Lady is, like Spot, unquestionably white in race. Her own accent of Standard American English echoes that of her owners, Jim Dear and Darling, whose white skin further confirms an unmarked whiteness to the entire household. Lady's canine neighbors, Trusty and Scotty, too, are coded white. We first meet them when Lady proudly shows them her new collar, which bears a medal license. It proclaims her a legitimate citizen.

Trusty is an aging, Southern-drawled Bloodhound, described in the original (1955) movie trailer as "the Bloodhound of the Old South, but now given to dreams of faded glory." Like his granddaddy, "Old Reliable," he once "tracked criminals." We might understand "criminals" as a euphemism for escaped slaves; Bloodhounds were reputed to be the dog of choice in the nineteenth century for tracking enslaved people seeking freedom. Staged versions of *Uncle Tom's Cabin* employed Bloodhounds to particular dramatic effect. Bloodhounds were seen in late nineteenth- and early twentieth-century America as among the most vicious dogs and as the particular enemies of African Americans. By the 1950s, though, many Americans preferred to shed this vicious history. They welcomed displacing a history represented by the Bloodhound with a future embodied by the Cocker Spaniel, who now takes over as protagonist. Trusty the Bloodhound is allowed to retire quietly and with dignity and even a last gasp of heroism. The sweet old Trusty, however, like the American South, bears a dark history, which this film successfully represses. Indeed, there are no people of color in this film, but the implicitly not-white dogs under incarceration, who Lady will briefly share a cell with, sing the blues.

Alongside Trusty trots Scotty, Lady's other neighbor, an aging Scottish Terrier. In 1955, viewers might well have remembered FDR's beloved wartime dog Fala, perhaps the most famous presidential dog in his time. Scotty's heavy Scottish brogue marks him as an immigrant of the Old World, but a blue-blooded, documented immigrant with the all-important license worn around his neck. Next to Scotty's Old World past, Lady represents the new, up-and-coming, post-war United States.

Into this suburban scene wanders Tramp, who lives "on the other side of the track" from this circle of respectable canine citizens. Tramp fashions himself as a kind of Disney-fied Beatnik or James-Dean-like rebel, who rejects the conformity and confinement of the "leash-and-collar set." He is nobody's property, and has no regard for

Lady and the Tramp, **poster, top left to right: Lady, Tramp; bottom left to right: Bull, Boris, Pedro, Si and Am, Trusty on poster art, 1955 (photograph by LMPC via Getty Images).**

private property; instead, he believes in The Commons. In other words, he's a bad capitalist, perhaps an inchoate communist. He's also an undocumented outsider. He hangs out with people who were once considered "ethnic" or "not white, not quite." Much has been written about Italian Americans, Jewish Americans, and Irish Americans as immigrants who "became white" only in the nineteenth and twentieth centuries. (See, for example, Noel Ignatiev's *How the Irish Became White*.) These are Tramp's people. He roams from household to household, one for every night of the week, dining on different ethnic cuisine leftovers. Most famously, he woos Lady at Tony's Italian restaurant, resulting in a spaghetti noodle-induced kiss.

Farther beyond the normative "home" of the suburbs are the canine illegal aliens, especially the ones who end up in the pound. Most of these dogs—including Boris, the Russian Borzoi, and Pedro, the Mexican Chihuahua—are undocumented immigrants, and not from what our current president might call "nice countries" like Norway. (The original movie trailer says that Pedro's "visa and luck wore out at the same time.") Or they're street-smart lowlifes, like Peg (voiced by Peggy Lee), the butt-twitching, tail-swishing showgirl past her prime, who celebrates Tramp's trampiness, and can't be put in a monogamous, heteronormative box. These are the ones who must be excluded from the suburbs and on whose exclusion the suburbs' suburbanness depends.

Even farther from American norm—so far that they're represented by another species—are the Siamese cats. It's these invaders that displace Lady from her own home and render her unable to perform her civic duty. In contrast to the American protagonists, and their close canine allies, a pair of Siamese cats, with caricatured Indo-Chinese accents, introduces a menace into the idyllic Western household. Smuggled into the household in Aunt Sarah's basket, these cats, the villains of the film, set in motion a plot that has mostly been missing until now. As they reconnoiter their new "domicile" ("If we like we stay for maybe quite a while"), they sing the infamous "We Are Siamese." The two cats are identical not only in appearance but also in their movements. Both are voiced by Peggy Lee, further adding to their sameness, and evoking the McCarthy-era stereotype of communists as being so anti-individualistic as to be identical. The Siamese cats invade the American household with a red menace and try to displace the (American) family dog. Although nominally Siamese (or Thai), these cats are a mish-mash of Orientalist tropes, with communist China as their greater target. Their buck teeth, their hisses, and their sly treachery call up "yellowface" traditions, in which white people represented Asians in stereotypical ways that had little resemblance to actual Asians. (Today this song is considered downright racist and only appears in the 2019 live-action remake of *Lady and the Tramp* in a radically revised form.) As they sing, they cause havoc on the domestic front, leaving Lady to take the blame, before slinking and slithering upstairs to steal milk from the baby.

When Aunt Sarah sees the war-torn living room, she punishes Lady by taking her to a pet shop to get a muzzle. Lady panics at the muzzle and runs out of the store and into more trouble, only to be saved by Tramp. He then romances her, takes her for a walk on the wild side, and tries to woo her into his "footloose and collar-free" life. But Lady declines, citing her duty to look after the baby. Before she can return home, though, she is temporarily put into the pound. There she learns of the (seemingly only) alternative to her suburban "leash-and-collar" life of living in confinement on private property. She could be like the mournfully howling inmates, or, worse, like Nutsy, who we see only in shadow taking his last walk "thru d' one-way door."[11] Fortunately, Lady's documentation makes her life worth more than the lives of her fellow inmates.

Rescuing Lady from the pound, Aunt Sarah restrains the Cocker to the outdoor doghouse. When Lady is tied up in the backyard and a rat invades the household, threatening the baby—the baby!—she calls on Tramp to police the domestic borders and save the day. Tramp can choose Lady and risk confinement, or he can choose his independence.

Tramp chooses Lady, and nearly gets confined to the pound, but is ultimately only confined to the suburbs. Enchanted by Lady, he willingly accepts a life of documentation and surveillance. Tramp's patriotic heroism in protecting the home front is rewarded along the lines of so many 1950s films: he gets the girl (or girl dog). In doing so, the gray Tramp, too, ultimately "becomes white." He may be wayward, but he's not foreign. He's ultimately assimilable, in terms of class and ethnicity, into the white, suburban, middle-class lifestyle. What's more, he becomes a real man (or dog) when he fathers a litter of pups at the end of the film. These Disney dogs show us that true happiness resides in a reproductive heterosexual relationship nestled in a middle-class hearth and home. The happily-ever-after ending teaches us that love transcends class—or, in essence, levels us all to the middle class. Because they're dogs, presumably creatures of nature, the film's values seem all the more natural to its audiences. In other words, *Lady and the Tramp*, as an ideological mediator, *naturalizes* the nuclear family, as well as naturalizing what Tramp calls "the leash-and-collar set" as the American way of (animal) life.

Throughout this book, I'll be exploring ways in which dogs in popular culture (such as Lady, Tramp, and friends) serve as a place to talk about race without talking about race. Same thing goes for gender, class, sexuality, ethnicity, immigration status, age, and all kinds of other social identities. Through dogs we offer ideas, whether progressive or reactionary, that might otherwise risk censure.

At the same time as they symbolize racial, ethnic, and national identities, however, dogs in this film are not merely symbols of human beings. These dogs are also dogs. If the film is subtextually about the national drama of cold war anxieties, it's also, and overtly, about the changing place of dogs in the middle-class American household. Tramp's journey from a free-ranging hobo to a collared and house-bound family pet encapsulates a larger mass movement of dogs into the household. Their territories correspondingly narrowed to their lawns. Although we rarely see any leashes attached to the collars of the "leash-and-collar set" (as we soon will in, for example, Disney's 1961 animated film *101 Dalmations*), these dogs don't wander beyond their neighborhoods, and barely beyond their lawns. This problematic partitioning and narrowing of a dog's space becomes, in the film, a mark of prestige and progress. Though arguably a most unnatural infringement on a dog's freedom of movement, this leashing and collaring of dogs is naturalized by the film.

Checkers

The meaning of Cockers in pop culture as the epitome of suburban middle-class American values provided the ideal backdrop for Richard Nixon's famous campaign speech of 1952, when the politician was a Vice Presidential candidate. Accused of accepting illegal campaign contributions, Nixon claimed that the only "bribe" he accepted came from a man in Texas who'd heard Nixon's wife, Pat, mention on the radio that her daughters wanted a dog. The Nixons got word that a package arrived for them at Union Station in Baltimore.

> You know what it was? It was a little Cocker Spaniel dog in a crate that he'd sent all the way from Texas, black and white, spotted. And our little girl Tricia, the six year old, named it Checkers. And you know, the kids, like all kids, love the dog, and I just want to say this, right now, that regardless of what [Nixon's detractors] say about it, we're gonna keep it.[12]

Response to Nixon's speech was overwhelmingly positive, and Nixon got to stay on the ticket as Eisenhower's running mate. In part people responded to the American Cocker Spaniel and the daddy who let his daughters keep her as the family dog. To Nixon's frustration, the speech became known as the "Checkers Speech"; even though the Cocker took up only one paragraph of a forty-paragraph speech, she became the icon.

While the outpouring of support for Nixon was great, the outpouring of support for Checkers was proportionately greater, as people sent her a year's supply of dog food, collars, leashes, and toys.

Instantly parodied as the nadir of sentimental manipulation, the "Checkers Speech" nevertheless worked—in large part because Checkers was a Cocker Spaniel, visual proof of guileless innocence. A Doberman wouldn't have worked as well, or a German Shepherd, or even a Border Collie. Using any dog as a stand-in for American culture may be manipulative and saccharine, but using a Cocker multiplies the "aw" factor. You can't think of a Cocker without smiling.

Like in the soon-to-appear film *Lady and the Tramp*, the American Cocker Spaniel made the perfect foil to the threat of communism. Soon after his protective stance toward his family dog Checkers, Nixon says in his Checkers speech that he thinks his "country is in danger ... look at the record. Seven years of the Truman Acheson Administration, and what's happened? Six hundred million people lost to the Communists." In Nixon's imagery, he and Dwight Eisenhower were the men to defend the American Cocker Spaniel way of life against the dangerous spread of Communism.

In retrospect, of course, America's halcyon Cocker era was always more checkered than many of its members may have wanted to believe.

It's no accident that these most iconic of Cockers of the 1950s were graphic, not actual. In part this is because Cockers are notoriously difficult to train—or, to put it less politely, many remain stubborn and dumb despite being extremely food-motivated (which should help with training). The stars of live TV shows and movies about dogs would be smarter breeds: Collies, Shepherds, and Terriers. But Cockers peaked in the 1950s during the rage for animation. The technology of animated film had reached a level of sophistication that, at the time, was bedazzling. Animation fit the zeitgeist. Americans liked to relate to animals as humans. We grew to love those animals that most seemed to resemble us, offering cute imitations of human life. We learned to think of animals—and of nature in general—as plastic, malleable, and bendable to our ends. What got left behind, for a time, was the animality of animals, the wildness of nature. But as Sigmund Freud, newly revived to popularity in 1950s America, famously said, the repressed always returns.

From Lady to Laika

As the fictional Lady and Tramp, along with thousands of real dogs in the United States, were settling into their suburban homes to grow comfortably into middle age, an actual Soviet dog was leaving the shelter of her planetary home to go into orbit. On November 3, 1957, the Soviets launched Laika, a Husky-Terrier mix, into space in *Sputnik II*. This launch followed quickly on the heels of the October 4 launch of *Sputnik I*, the first human-made satellite to orbit the earth. Momentous as it was, *Sputnik I* flew uninhabited. Could life withstand the effects of microgravity and the heightened irradiation believed to exist beyond the earth's protective atmosphere? That's what Sputnik II would investigate. Doctors surgically embedded medical devices in Laika's body to track heart function, blood pressure, and breathing rate. The little dog was fitted up in an excrement-collecting contraption and then strapped into her seat at the rocket window, from which she could look down on earth—or at least that's what many of us choose to envision.

In the United States humiliation over the Soviet Union's once again having beaten us into space converted into concerns over Laika's survival. Americans did not know that Laika was never expected to return alive, or that, at any rate, she only had enough food and oxygen for seven days. Historian Alice George reports in a *Smithsonian* article that in

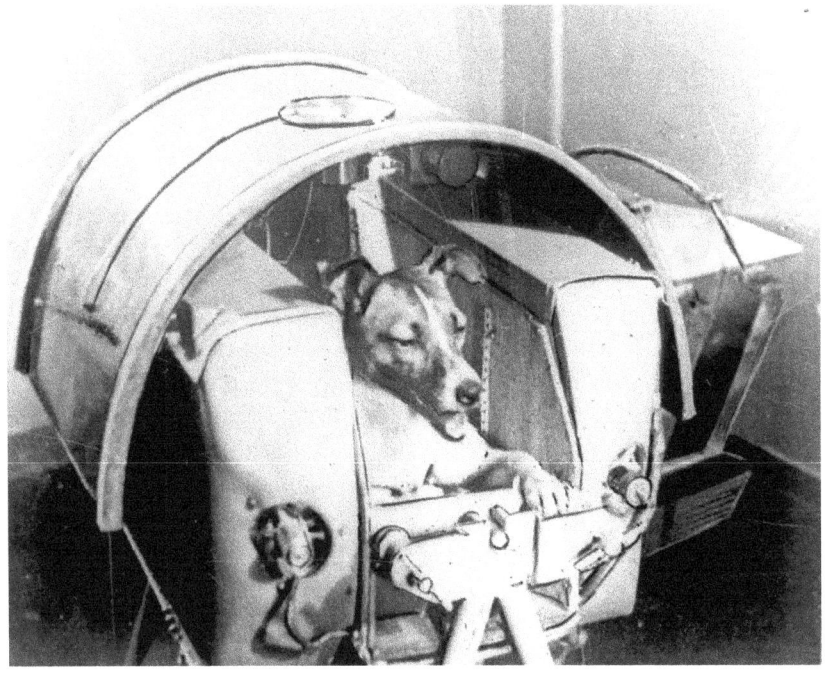

Laika ensconced in her *Sputnik II* cabin, 1957 (photograph by Keystone-France/Gamma-Keystone via Getty Images).

Great Britain, both the Royal Society for the Prevention of Cruelty to Animals (RSPCA) and the British Society for Happy Dogs opposed the launch. In the United States, a "pack of dog lovers attached protest signs to their pets and marched outside the United Nations in New York."[13] Americans across the country hoped and prayed for the dog's safe return to earth.

Laika became an important *ad hoc* symbol for Americans; we did not want to imagine ourselves a nation that sent dogs off to die in space. We saw ourselves as kind and gentle in our post-war power, in contrast to the Soviet Union and other communist countries. And so we condemned Laika's launch, and condemned it even more fervently when she did not make it. Amidst the tensions of the Cold War and the arms race, the treatment of Laika became symbolic evidence against our Soviet enemy. They may have beaten us into space, but they did so by exerting horrifying cruelty on a helpless little dog. (Never mind that we launched chimpanzees and many other research animals into space; at least we didn't hurt dogs.) As Kurt Caswell says in his book *Laika's Window: The Legacy of a Soviet Space Dog*, the little dog became "a symbol of Soviet godlessness, a cruel sacrifice to the technological advance of a state fallen from God's grace."[14]

Soviet broadcasts did not report Laika's death. In actuality, Laika demonstrably survived the first two orbits around the earth, albeit with a tripled heart rate and quadrupled breath rate. She probably survived a third orbit, but likely not a fourth. Decades later, we've learned that Laika probably died within hours, not days, as the Soviets had reported, and that she probably died a painful death from overheating, rather than the gentler death from oxygen deprivation that they'd expected. Had we known this at the time, the American outrage would undoubtedly have been even greater. To be honest, as a current owner of a Husky-Terrier mix, I'm still having a hard time with Laika's fate, even all these decades later.

One thing that was clear following the *Sputnik II* "sacrifice" of Laika was that dogs had entered United States politics as crucial symbols.

Pet Shops and Puppy Mills

In 1952, Pattie Page recorded "The Doggie in the Window," heralding in the era of the pet store. These shops began to pop up along with the emerging American strip malls. The song asks how much "the doggie in the window" costs; puppies were becoming commodities, for which one could window-shop on a stroll. The dark underside of pet stores, which could be as shameful as the puppies in their windows were innocent and guileless, was also emerging in the 1950s.

Pet stores were a creation of the late-nineteenth and twentieth centuries. At first, they were for the birds; the nineteenth century hosted an extended fad of bird ownership that spanned the classes, as Katherine C. Grier discusses in *Pets in America: A History*. Keeping birds in cages in the home was seen as a way of appreciating these birds, as well as being stylish and pleasurable. With this fad of bird-keeping emerged shops to supply these pets along with cages and other avian-keeping paraphernalia. The seeds of the modern pet industry were planted, and pets joined the American commercial network. It wasn't just pet stores, however, that made pets into commodities. Grier notes that from the 1920s through the 1960s, everyday venues such as five-and-ten shops also sold canaries, parakeets, aquarium fish, and other small pets.[15]

The bird-keeping fad began to wane in the twentieth century just as pet dogs were becoming popular among urban and suburban people. Canines began to fill the birds' niche in pet stores. In earlier eras, dogs, if they were purchased at all, would have been bought directly from breeders, who usually worked closely with their stock. With the emergence of pet stores, the dog became further removed, for its owners, from the realm of nature to become a domestic product.

These pet stores needed to keep their inventory stocked. The rise in demand for purchasable puppies coincided with changes in agricultural practices. Multiple factors intersected to create "factory farms," or large-scale farms prioritizing efficiency and profit over animal welfare and sustainability. Early in the twentieth century, the industrialization and drive for efficiency that made factories like Henry Ford's so profitable now moved into agriculture. Agricultural colleges grew, along with new majors like agricultural business and agricultural economics. Researchers in these fields envisioned new ways to bring the factory model into farming. Economies of scale made large, industrialized farms out-compete with individual family farms. At the same time, post–World War I, the loss of labor due to the war and the Spanish flu caused many family farms to go under and to be repossessed by banks, which merged them into larger industrial farms. This was now possible because newly developed antibiotics allowed masses of animals to be crowded into small spaces without causing epidemics. The antibiotics also made livestock get larger and develop more quickly, creating faster turn-over.[16]

The movement toward factory farms and large-scale agribusiness after World War II increasingly displaced smaller farms, particularly in areas of the Midwest such as Pennsylvania, Ohio, Iowa, Arkansas,

Oklahoma, Kansas and Missouri. The struggling owners of these family farms sometimes turned to dog breeding for money. The industrialization of agriculture, with its large-scale electric machinery, hit Amish family farms in the mid-west particularly hard, which is why we see the Amish over-represented in dog (and exotic animal) trade. The dogs in these repurposed farms could be held in abandoned chicken coups and other structures in run-down farming facilities. In this way, puppies became a new form of livestock, mass-produced in "puppy farms."

Ironically, these new large-scale dog breeders shared a business model with the factory farms that displaced them, in that they put efficiency and profit over the welfare of animals. They also used the animal's body itself as a kind of factory. In factory farms (now also referred to as CAFOs, or Concentrated Animal Feeding Operations), animals became mechanisms for converting plants into meat. In puppy farms, bitches became little factories producing saleable puppies. Treating dogs as livestock, puppy farms objectified and commodified animals according to the same logic as factory farms. And so people began to call such re-purposed farms "puppy mills."

The decline of small farms also coincided with a new interest in purebred dogs among the middle class. Dog fancy, which had long been developing in Europe, and particularly England, for almost a century, had crossed the Atlantic in the early twentieth century. By mid-century, a growing middle class could now afford these interesting new dogs, as well as suburban houses with yards. The Westminster Kennel Club Dog Show began airing on television in 1948, which further spread interest in purebreds.[17] Kim Kavin, in her study of "dog merchants," suggests that "purebred dogs, as much as the suburban houses, became a middle-class lifestyle status symbol."[18] By mid-century, then, multiple factors had coalesced to produce the phenomenon of puppy mills.

The term "puppy mill" is contested, both in meaning and origin. The *Oxford English Dictionary* offers as its example for the use of the term "puppy mill" a quotation from 1980, when the *Christian Science Monitor* noted, "Some shops get animals from reputable local breeders, but others buy their dogs from 'puppy mills,' wholesale factories where dogs are confined to cages and denied exercise and companionship."[19] That's a good working definition of puppy mills. However, the practice, if not the term, predates this defining quotation by several decades. My *National Geographic Book of Dogs* from 1958 mentions the "puppy mills" that emerged as early as the 1920s to meet the spike in demand for Chow Chows, one of the most popular breeds of that decade:

> It became too popular, in fact, for reputable breeders to supply the demand. Operators of "puppy mills" took over to provide cheap pups.... As a result, many "Chows" bore only faint resemblance to the fine old Chinese breed. Many were sold without registration certificates or were given forged pedigrees. Obviously, the unscrupulous breeders paid no attention to the breed's temperament. The result was a wave of unfortunate incidents in which unsuspecting children and adults were bitten by these misfit dogs.[20]

The term "puppy mills" was new enough in 1958 for author Arthur Frederick Jones to estrange it with quotation marks. Jones seems to regard these puppy mills as shady fringe elements of the dog trade in the late 1950s, but they were already proliferating.

Today the practice flourishes. The term itself generally applies to facilities designed to mass-produce puppies purely for profit. Of course facilities may do so ethically, but it's very hard, even with economies of scale, to break even, much less make a profit, while still giving the puppies and their mothers adequate time and space for regular socialization and exercise, complete veterinary care, and quality food and supplements. In some cases, dogs may be confined to chicken-wire cages, which hurt their paws and restrict movement. At their worst, these facilities treat their adult female dogs as reproductive machines. Some of these dogs spend their entire adult lives pregnant or birthing, often stuck in cages stacked on top of each other, with little exercise or human contact. Even the possible satisfactions of motherhood are denied to them; as infants the puppies are separated from the mothers and shipped across the country to pet stores, sometimes with brokers as middlemen. Often these breeding dogs are killed when they're no longer reproductively useful.

As for the puppies, they may, in the worst puppy mills, be forced to linger in their own or their litter-mates' feces. This can sometimes cause them to develop the habit of eating the residue, out of curiosity or boredom or even hunger. (The poop-eating habit can be very hard to break even after the caged puppies relocate to their more ample "forever homes.") These puppies would then be sent to independent pet stores. In mid-century, these puppies might also get shipped to general goods stores such as Sears Roebuck, which once sold pets.

Once at the pet stores, the puppies are displayed as if they magically appeared from scratch, bearing no signs of their production. They appeared without mothers or siblings or prior history. Although these dogs sometimes come with a pedigree, a "doggie in a window" seems to come to its viewer as a fresh new product without a past.

Puppies from mass-producing facilities are notoriously inbred, since they're the result of a limited stock of breeding dogs. The dogs are also, often, overbred—bred in large numbers without regard to the quality of the resulting dogs. Undesirable traits that emerge, affecting temperament and anatomy, may be re-bred for generations, ultimately degrading the quality of the breed.

Cockers, as the most popular dog of the era, were particularly overbred beginning in the 1950s, and the breed was a staple of puppy mills. In response, in part, to the rise of unsavory pet stores and puppy mills, as well as to animal cruelty on factory farms and in laboratories, the Animal Welfare Act would pass in 1966, as we will explore further in Chapter Two. The AWA would stipulate minimal acceptable standards for animal treatment, commerce, and research. Additions to the AWA in the 1970s would further improve the standards for treatment of dogs in puppy mills, at least on paper.

As the animal rights movement grew, puppy mills and pet stores would come under public scrutiny. This came a little too late for the reputation of Cocker Spaniels; the breed had already reached its peak of popularity and subsequent overbreeding by irresponsible mass breeders. By then, the Cocker's Lady-like reputation was irretrievable. The United States would treat this breed as it does so many other things it no longer has use for—as disposable. As of this writing, the Cocker sits way down at number thirty in the AKC rankings of the United States' most popular dog breeds. Americans would go on to embrace Beagles, Huskies, Golden Retrievers, and especially Labrador Retrievers as their new love objects and cultural mascots.

Coda: A Confession

Lest I sound too high and mighty in my condemnation of pet stores and puppy mills, it's high time for me to make a confession. I, too, bought a Cocker Spaniel puppy from a pet store supplied by a puppy mill. I bought a "doggie in the window."

I have an excuse. My life-partner of thirteen years, Rajiv, had stage IV colon cancer and had just "failed" his third round of chemo. Because he was losing muscle mass, his oncologist told him to take regular walks. In late December in Colorado, though, it was too cold outdoors for Rajiv's now-skinny frame, especially now that the oxaliplatin (a chemo drug) numbed his fingers. That's how we ended up roaming the indoor mall. Rajiv hunched over like an old man at thirty-seven years old. A week later an MRI would reveal metastases in his spine.

One day, we passed the Pet City display, where a little Cocker wiggled in the window. Rajiv smiled for the first time in weeks as he held the puppy. When we returned several smile-less days later, he asked again for the same puppy, and again he smiled. What else could I do? I bought the smile in the form of a puppy.

My own Cocker story follows that of American culture with uncanny faithfulness. Once we brought the puppy home, Rajiv and I soon saw that the little Cocker wasn't quite right, especially compared to our two older mutts, Pretzel and Chaplin, both likely Cocker mixes. For a while, though, the puppy's quirks kept Rajiv smiling through his nausea and pain. Although the pup seemed absurdly dumb in some ways, he found his way into impossibly tight spaces, so we named him Houdini after the brilliant escape artist. Our Houdini, however, could only get *into* things, but not *out of* them. He pawed open drawers and nosed into the pantry, quickly snapping up whatever he smelled and then vomiting back up whatever wouldn't pass through him.

In short, Houdini turned out to be the stereotypical puppy-mill puppy. By 2002, I should have known better. The Cocker had long since turned, in the American imagination, from precious innocent to bratty numbskull. It was already widely recognized that some of the unscrupulous puppy mills stocking pet stores would overbreed without regard to the long-term health or happiness or either the breeding bitch or her future pups. (When I later sent off for Houdini's pedigree, I learned that he came from a breeder in Missouri, and that his great-grandmother on both sides of his lineage was the same dog.)

Fortunately, Houdini didn't crab or bite children, as some puppy-mill Cockers were rumored to do, but he had his share of behavioral disorders. He constipated himself by eating the toilet paper, ultimately leading to mummified bowel movements. He ate the bandages and tissues that increasingly filled the garbage bin until I figured out how to bungee-cord it closed. He chewed through shoelaces and purse straps. He gnawed at Pretzel's legs to make the older dog play, when all Pretzel wanted to do was tend to Rajiv, and he baffled Chappy, our four-year-old spaniel mix, whose escalating disciplinary snarls left Houdini unfazed.

In the early hours of June 2, 2002, in a bed that hospice had set up three days earlier, with me and his mother at either side of his bed and Pretzel curled up at his feet, Rajiv died. My life was supposed to end then, too, but somehow it didn't.

In the days and weeks following, I roamed in a daze. Pretzel, who'd loved Rajiv above all, refused to eat and hid under the bed. (Nobody can convince me that dogs don't grieve.) Chappy appointed himself my protector, and velcroed himself to me. Houdini, clueless, chattered happily to himself, snatching at the mound of tissues always growing at my side.

Then came the daily "explosive diarrhea" (a term Rajiv's oncologist had used for a side effect of one of the chemotherapies), leaving stains all over the carpet, and forcing me to crawl on my knees, wet-vacuuming as I cried into the piling. This was rock bottom. The love of my life had just died and I was creeping among the feces of a disastrous dog who wouldn't even respect my mourning. As I cursed my Cocker, Houdini clambered over to lick up his splatter before I vacuumed it. "Why couldn't you have died instead," I growled at him. He lowered his head, and something broke in me. I sobbed into his fetid, puppy-soft fur until I exhausted myself, and then I called my veterinarian's office for an appointment.

It was just a "sensitive stomach," common to inbred Cockers, and was easily resolved with special dog food. The house took longer to heal, and eventually I had to tear out the carpet and install easy-clean laminate.

I healed even more slowly. The dogs helped, and of course I grew to love Houdini. Still, it's hard not to see Houdini's troubles as karma for my buying a puppy mill puppy. I didn't know anything about puppy mills when Rajiv and I bought our Cocker puppy, but perhaps that was because I didn't want to know. Now that I do, though—now that I've seen photos of conditions at some of these puppy mills—I can't un-know it.

Perhaps having a disastrous dog on my hands is what kept me going. The death of Rajiv was a trauma too big to face, and it would be months before the protective shock wore off. Meanwhile, Houdini provided a mini-trauma that I could handle. A psychoanalyst might speak of my projections onto the hapless puppy. It's clear to me now, looking back, that Houdini served the needs of my individual psyche, similar to the way that, on a larger scale, dogs of various breeds serve the needs of the American cultural psyche. In my case, Houdini's constant GI-tract crises and trips to the vet filled the emptiness. I fought the daily fight to keep him alive. Maybe having such a high-needs dog saved me at a time when I needed to be needed.

Houdini would go on to show a number of health and (let's be honest) mental problems throughout the rest of his life—most seriously, a congenital heart defect—which none of my other four dogs, all rescue mutts, ever did. I adored Houdini, and he'll always have a special place in my heart. But Oh My Dog, what a "special" dog he was.

For years, his puppy breath long gone but his immaturity intact, Houdini sprung into laps or leaned against human legs in the dog park, presenting himself for adoration before running off to eat some inedible or other. As he flirted with them, people often reminisced about the Cockers they had as kids—but then noted that they would never get another Cocker again. Like me, they knew that the era of Butch, Lady, and Spot has passed.

Chapter Two

Thousands of Howls

Beagles in the 1960s

The Great Ear Lift

On April 27, 1964, then-president Lyndon Johnson lifted one of his year-old Beagles by the ears to make the dog vocalize. He'd done so many times before, but this time the act was caught by an AP photographer and posted in newspapers across the country. When asked by a reporter why he performed what would soon become known as "the Great Ear Lift," Johnson replied, "To make him bark…. It's good for him. And if you've ever followed dogs, you like to hear them yelp." The title of the ensuing article summarizes the results: "President's Two Beagle Pups Sound Off for Guests; Johnson Lifts Dogs to Hear Them Yip; Action Is Criticized."[1]

Although he was enjoying a period of popularity at that time, LBJ's misguided act of affection spurred massive outcry. Many readers seemed to yelp along with the Beagle. The President insisted that "handling them by the ears was not painful, and that any resultant yelps were yelps of joy," but the title of the article quoting him—"Johnson Lifts Dogs by the Ears Again to Prove They Enjoy It"—casts doubt on LBJ's belief. Indeed, many veterinarians, dog handlers, and breeders disagreed. "If someone pulled you up by the ears, you'd yelp too," an angry ASPCA spokesman commented. (That, I'll admit, was my first reaction when I learned of this incident.)[2]

Audiotapes released in the 1990s show Johnson "stung" by the criticism of the Ear Lift and "worr[ied] about how it would affect his image," even though his Press Secretary assured him that the incident was a "one-day sensation."[3] Disgruntled that Senate GOP leader Everett Dirksen "said he wouldn't treat his dog like I treated mine," Johnson said, "It's none of his damn business how I treat my dog. I'm a lot better to dogs, and humans too, than he is…. But they got every dog lover in the country thinking I'm burning 'em at the stake."

Chapter Two. Thousands of Howls

At exactly one month younger than the Beagles, I was still an infant at the time of the ear lift. My parents would have heard of the incident, but I doubt they would have stood among the vociferous objectors. They would have seen Johnson's pup as "just a dog," whose suffering, even as a symbol, was unimportant, a mere distraction from more important human affairs, such as the bombing of a black church in Alabama, Soviet advances in the space and arms races, and tensions in Indochina. My parents liked dogs just fine, but would have found it absurd to fuss over pets as if they were people. In fact, my dad, who grew up in a small town, saw the confinement of pet dogs as the greater cruelty. They should run free in the vast fields with the other animals; it was wrong to keep one as a pet in the confines of our suburban home and meager lawn. So in spite of virtuoso pleading by my brother and me, we never got a family dog.

Had we done so, we might well have gotten a Beagle, among the most popular breeds for family dogs in the 1960s. According to the American Kennel Club (AKC), the Beagle was not the very most popular breed of the 1960s in the United States, or at least not the most numerous of pure-breed registries, having been edged out of that position by the Poodle and the German Shepherd. At a solid third place, though, the Beagle, I would argue, most captures Americans' various and contradictory attitudes toward dogs in that decade of change.[4] I sense, too, that in the 1960s, the Beagle, perhaps more than any other breed, served as America's Geiger counter. It was the breed through which we expressed our contradictions, if not our hypocrisies, in our treatment of sentient animals (including ourselves). Through the image of the Beagle, we represented and reimagined ourselves as humans and as Americans. At the same time, the Beagle represented our changing and increasingly conflicted ethos of human-dog relations. The 1960s marked both a definite turning point in our concept of pets and, possibly, the time of most inconsistency concerning our moral obligations to other creatures, and particularly to domesticated animals. We see these shifting tensions play out with the Great Ear Lift.

Johnson later apologized for his rough treatment of his Beagles (named Him and Her), but the backlash clearly baffled him. He later commented, "I've been pulling Him's ears since he was a pup, and he seemed to like it." Johnson, a Texas ranchman, brought to the White House a model of human-dog relations more like that of my father, one quickly waning in the (sub)urbanizing country.

Like many dogs, Beagles were bred for hunting. As scent hounds, they tracked small game animals such as hares and rabbits. By the 1960s, however, their original purpose yielded to their newer role as pets. At the same time, the very status of pets was being redefined. Pets no longer existed simply for their owners' amusement, but increasingly bore some degree of autonomous dignity in their own right. Indeed, Americans had begun not only to sympathize with, but actually identify with, their dogs. Dogs were moving toward the status of humans, which some would nearly reach in later decades. The Great Ear Lift highlighted the tensions between these two attitudes of dogs-as-subordinates and dogs-as-equals.

President Johnson's Beagles Her and Him on the *Life Magazine* cover June 19, 1964 (photograph by Francis Miller/The LIFE Premium Collection via Getty Images/Getty Images).

At stake in the infamous ear lift photos (later parodied in a *Simpsons* episode) was not only the actual human-dog relationship, but also its political significance. The "dog incident" threatened Johnson's upcoming reelection in November of 1964, requiring the president to do significant damage control in order to win back the dog lover vote. In addition to apologizing, Johnson granted journalist Francis Miller access for a cover story on the White House dogs for the June 1964 issue of *Life Magazine*. Published on June 19, 1964, the issue's cover features Him and Her on the White House Lawn, with Her's head tucked under a more dominant Him. This perfect American couple look both regal and adorable. Through his Beagles, posed as the perfect heterosexual American couple, Johnson rectified his image. These non-howling Beagles spoke to the nation's voters. LBJ was reelected.

In the underlying debate about the place of dogs on the continuum from things to people, the vote seemed to swing toward personhood.

The Character of Snoopy

LBJ would choose not to run for the 1968 election, his popularity waning with the escalation of the Vietnam War. By contrast, another Beagle, even more ubiquitous in the media than Him and Her—one who was known, on occasion, to tuck his ears under a World War I-era fighter jet pilot's headgear and curse his enemy, the Red Baron—was a write-in candidate by a significant number of voters in the 1968 and 1972 elections. In fact, the extent of Snoopy's write-in popularity "prompt[ed] the California legislature to make it illegal to enter the name of a fictional character on the ballot," according to David Michaelis in his biography of Snoopy's creator (*Schulz and Peanuts: A Biography*).[5] Perhaps the capper to Snoopy's political career came in 1968 when NASA named the command module of Apollo 10 after this comic strip dog. As a lunar module, Snoopy blazed the trail for Apollo 11, which put a man on the moon. Instead of Laika, the Soviet dog killed in space, Americans had Snoopy.

This Everydog served a role that no human could, reconciling conflicting subcultures of the era of a controversial war in Vietnam, a Civil Rights movement, inchoate women's and gay rights movements, and a countercultural hippie movement culminating in a "Summer of Love." Snoopy served as a kind of canine inkblot test, taking whatever form we imposed onto him. He spoke to both war veterans and anti-war pacifists, to conservative Christians and to iconoclasts. It's possible to see Snoopy as a Buddhist, an atheist, a hedonist, an idealist, or a pragmatist.

At a time when the pluralism of the country, its divisions into seemingly irreconcilable factions, was becoming undeniable, no single (human) person could stand for the zeitgeist, so it makes sense to me that we turned to animals to represent us. We found ourselves in Snoopy; every subculture seemed to find him mirroring their deepest ideological beliefs back to them in the form of a Beagle. The Beagle served our country by reflecting our projected desires back to us. Snoopy created a compromise formation, giving a temporary if unstable resolution to America's conflicts. He could manage to be both "the cuddliest dog on the planet" and a military symbol, even appearing on American fighter planes.

Snoopy could be all things to all people because he was without human identity. In addition to being both hawk and dove, both warrior and pacifist, Snoopy smoothed over additional fissures in American identity. Those elements of human American identity that seemed fundamental in the 1960s and created fundamental rifts in any possible American identity—particularly race, religion, gender, and sexuality—were meaningless when it came to this blank-slate dog figure. At a time when the implicit but unstated norm was straight, white, Protestant Christian, and male, Snoopy was too, but without restricting himself to these assumed identity markers or excluding other possibilities. By remaining ambiguously open to other possible projections, Snoopy both revealed while simultaneously concealing the tensions, exclusions, and prejudices of the era. This was especially the case in tandem with his human companion, Charlie Brown. Reminiscing in 1970 on the development of the *Peanuts* strip in the 1950s and its rise to national popularity in the 1960s, Schulz collaborator Lee Mendelson observed that "anxiety" became a central psychological ailment for Americans in the 1950s and 1960s, with Charlie Brown as the exemplary *Mr. Anxious*. Further,

> in the late sixties *identity be*came important to the man-in-the-street—in the struggles between blacks and whites, parents and children, teachers and students, husbands and wives, flower children and the Establishment.
> And who was our greatest seeker of identity in the 1950's and 1960's???
> In short, Charlie Brown has become *the* symbol of mid-century America ... because Charlie Brown is ... a basic reflection of his time.... [W]e struggle with "anxiety," "identity," and "self." Who leads us in this fight? We believe it is poor old Charlie Brown.[6]

Charlie Brown may be the paradigmatic figure of our nation's anxieties, identity crises, and struggle against insurmountable problems, but Snoopy is the flip side of Charlie Brown. Snoopy offered an image of someone who has found himself, who lives in the moment, and who follows his bliss. I suspect, too, that the relationship between Charlie Brown and Snoopy models an emerging relationship between human and dog, in which people look to their dogs for psychological models of the sense of freedom and joy they feel they've lost.

In one strip, Snoopy launches himself into his iconic "happy dance," which he continues for all four panels. In the fourth, he says (or thinks— he always "speaks" to the reader in thought bubbles), "Who else do you know who can do the 'Beagle'?"[7] Through Snoopy, Americans vicariously "did the Beagle," allowing him an exuberance that we ourselves could no longer own (if we ever could). In an era of assassinations, of Civil Rights protests and boycotts, which were met with a backlash and police brutality, and of a military quagmire overseas, we gave a dog, our alter ego, the unmitigated optimism we still longed for but were finding it harder to feel for ourselves. A 1960 strip shows Snoopy engaged in a full-on "happy dance" while Lucy says, "Stupid dog! The whole world could get blown up any minute, and all **you** think of is **dancing**." Snoopy continues dancing through the third panel and then thinks in the fourth, "I **could** think of eating, but it's too early in the day."[8]

Peanuts might well have been the most popular comic strip of the 1960s, and Snoopy was arguably the most popular character. While Americans identified with Charlie Brown, recognizing his inveterate persistence amidst chronic defeat, we identified perhaps even more with Snoopy, who, with dogged optimism and vast imaginative capacities, could constantly reinvent himself. Here was a character who could become a fierce vulture one day, a World War I flying ace the next, and a pre–Homer Simpson hedonist the day after. (Even the young Calvin Cordozar Broadus, Jr., in the 1970s, would watch and identify so extensively with Snoopy that his mother said he started to look like the cartoon dog and his family nicknamed him Snoopy. When he began his hip hop career, he retained his nickname, becoming first Snoop Doggy Dogg and then Snoop Dogg.[9])

This Beagle's primary transformation, of course, was into a human, and not just as an anthropomorphized cartoon character. The comic strip documents the changing role of the dog in American society. Though he was still kept outdoors (infamously sleeping on top of his dog house rather than within its shelter), he belonged increasingly to the human world. When the strip began in the 1950s, Snoopy was still mostly walking on four legs (even if he was being summoned by telephone call rather than dog whistle). Over the course of the 1950s, though, he increasingly rose to his back two legs, with his front appendages positioned more like arms than legs. Tracking the rise of Snoopy is almost like looking at those evolutionary charts of the Ascent of Man, where early hominids gradually stand erect. It's as if Snoopy, like other dogs in his era, ascended to near-human status.

This shift in the dog's status from sub-human servant to personhood was new enough to be fodder for humor. In a 1955 strip, Schroeder asks if Snoopy is a hunting dog, and whether he hunts "animals or birds." The final panel shows Snoopy asleep on the sofa while Charlie Brown answers, "What he hunts for mostly is an easier way of life."[10] This four-panel strip nutshells the dog's twentieth-century path from hunting trail to sofa.

In an ongoing storyline, a new girl named Frieda tries to get Snoopy to chase rabbits. "You got it wrong, kid," the dog's thought bubble says, "Chasing rabbits is 'out' … lying on top of doghouses in 'in'!" In another attempt, Frieda tells Snoopy that on such a nice day he should be chasing rabbits. "If it's such a nice day," Snoopy thinks, "why spoil it for the rabbits." Later, he confesses, "I guess it must be heredity. My dad used to run with the hounds, but his sympathy lay elsewhere…. He used to run on ahead to warn the rabbits." In yet another attempt, Frieda tries to get Snoopy to imagine he's following a trail in the woods. "Suddenly, you spy a rabbit! What do you do?" she asks him. The final panel shows him walking—on two legs—toward the rabbit with an open-mouthed smile and a hand outstretched for a handshake.[11] In the 1960s, a Beagle's refusal to hunt was still remarkable, and still funny, but also recognizable. Snoopy identified as man (or child), not beast. Humans now looked to their dogs more for companionship than livelihood. We didn't need our dogs to help us track down dinner, when it was so much easier to buy it pre-packaged in the grocery store. Dogs served humans by providing surrogate happiness rather than by offering the hunting and tracking prowess of previous eras. The happy dance was replacing the hunt.

Snoopy also became a marketing opportunity. As the *Peanuts* franchise developed, Snoopy's icon was used to sell consumer goods (such as insurance) while becoming a consumer good in its own right. This dog modeled the capacities of a culture of commodification, even as he celebrated the little, non-consumerist, things in life. I remember buying the book *Happiness Is a Warm Puppy*, one of the few books my librarian mother allowed me to own rather than borrow. I treasured its colorful pages, its simultaneously wise and child-like adages, and especially its magenta cover depicting a contented Lucy embracing an ear-raisingly startled Snoopy. According to Mendelson, when *Happiness Is a Warm Puppy* was published in 1963, it "topped both the adults' and the children's best-seller lists." Many books followed on its heels. By 1970, sales figures of Peanuts hardback and paperback books had passed the

55 million mark, and in the previous year, "of the top fifty-eight paperbacks sold ..., sixteen were Charlie Brown editions."[12] The marketing of Snoopy previewed the commodification of dogs in decades to come. Dogs would make both extremely effective images for selling merchandise and the ultimate consumer-by-proxy, in addition to being consumable commodities themselves.

Just the other day I picked up a pamphlet at my veterinarian's clinic for HomeAgain pet microchips, a product I've already purchased for all of my dogs. It featured a worried Charlie Brown seeking an errant Snoopy and ended in a passionate reunion of the boy and his dog.

Beagle Colonies

Many real Beagles far less visible than Snoopy, though, were not doing the happy dance in the 1960s. Much as we didn't want to see ourselves as heartless animal abusers or even ear-pulling dog owners, we regularly and systematically caused a lot more suffering than an ear lift. At the very time that we staged an outpouring of sympathy for poor Him, LBJ's howling Beagle, we subjected animals, including dogs, to behind-the-scenes product testing. The Beagle presented itself as the ideal dog breed for the enterprise, partly because of its small size, docility, and loyalty—the very characteristics making it such a popular breed as a pet. (The AKC lists the three outstanding characteristics of the breed as *merry*, *friendly*, and *curious*.) As FDA regulations for the testing of food and medical products increased—particularly following the Elixir Sulfanilamide scandal of 1937 and the Thalidomide scandal of the early 1960s—"Beagle colonies" emerged.

Animal research is, of course, all kinds of controversial, but even more so in animals that we know, from our deep bonds with them, are capable of suffering. Indeed, Animal Rights advocates so often quote Jeremy Bentham's famous utilitarian principle guiding the ethical treatment of other species that it's become something of a cliché: "The question is not, Can they *reason*? nor, Can they *talk*? but, Can they *suffer*?" Every dog owner I know now believes that dogs can and do suffer. In the 1960s, however, as in previous decades, the majority of Americans, or at least of American scientists, did not believe that dogs suffered pain, or in any case not to the degree that humans did. Amidst the outpouring of disapproval toward LBJ's Ear Lift, many of his defenders said that howls indicated not pain but merely activation. Indeed, the animal behaviorist models dominating our understanding of animals in this era treated dogs as machines without feelings. (If that sounds incredible, it's worth noting that a prevailing medical belief was that [human] infants, too, did not feel pain, and so babies would receive invasive medical treatments without anesthesia.)

Most people feel more ethically comfortable with testing on rodents rather than on dogs. (The question of whether dogs are more worthy than rodents of humane treatment is one I can't begin to deal with here, and continues to vex animal ethicists.) However, dogs are much better models of human physiology than are lab rats, mice, and the proverbial Guinea pigs. For the benefit of saving human lives, we decided that some canine lives could be "sacrificed." Researchers borrowed this word from religion; its etymology—"to make sacred"—points to an ethical anxiety about deliberately killing innocent animals and a need to justify it. This was the new version of animal sacrifice, with the god of scientific advancement taking the place formerly occupied by earlier gods of more "primitive" religions.

And so we began to raise dogs on a mass scale for laboratory research. Jeremy Beckham, writing for the Beagle Freedom Project, a group associated with PETA, traces the first "colony" of Beagles bred specifically as research subjects to the University of Utah.[13] In 1951 the university acquired its first eight dogs from a Beagle breeder in West Virginia. More dogs came from backyard breeders in Utah, at a time when Beagles were popular and widely available. By 1952, with 61 Beagles in stock, the breeding program was underway. According to Beckham, the female dogs "were bred after their first estrus, and laboratory personnel performed cesarean sections on the Beagles the moment the in utero puppies were viable. This allowed the mothers to be quickly re-impregnated 'in order to obtain a maximal yield of puppies.'" In that year, the *Salt Lake Tribune* ran a jaunty story titled "The Hounds of Beagleville" and subtitled "They May Save Your Life."[14] By 1955, 671 Beagle puppies, all bred from just 32 breeding pairs, underwent radioactive toxicity experiments. Funded by the Atomic Energy Commission and known as "The Beagle Project," these tests documented the effects of plutonium on dogs, including "bone tumors, gross skeletal disfigurations, tooth loss, and 'spontaneous' fractures." Such experiments spread to other research institutions, including one close to home for me.

Only a few miles northwest of my dog park in Fort Collins, on Colorado State University's Foothills Campus, one such Beagle colony existed from the 1960s to the 1980s. The Collaborative Radiological Health Animal Research Laboratory (CRHARL), nicknamed the "Charlie lab," tested the long-term effects of radiation on mammalian bodies. The Charlie Lab may well exemplify the best of laboratory dog research of the era. Here, some two thousand Beagles were irradiated and observed for several decades. Radiation was relatively new, both as a weapon and as a medical treatment, and its long-term effects were still uncertain. The data gleaned from the dogs helped predict what human victims exposed to radiation (such as in the Hiroshima and Nagasaki bombings) might expect over the coming decades. The Beagle data also applied to the emerging use of radiation therapy to treat cancerous tumors. Dr. Stephen Withrow, a pioneering surgical oncologist at CSU's College of Veterinary Medicine and Biomedical Sciences, told me that this research, particularly by Drs. William Carlson, Robert Phemister, and Ed Gillette, led to a vast increase in our understanding of radiation's effects on the body and laid the foundation for therapeutic uses of radiation on humans today.[15]

The research complex included some 1300 dog pens covered with wire mesh screens to keep the environment as sterile as possible. These indoor/outdoor pens of roughly eight feet by eight feet offered culverts for cold weather.[16] Beagles are especially social dogs, so the isolation of research conditions must be especially hard on them. At least these Beagles could see, hear, and smell each other, and were sometimes even paired in their pens.

This Beagle colony is legendary in Fort Collins. As its former director Dr. C.W. Miller told me, "everybody knew when it was feeding time."[17] The foothills were alive with the sound of two thousand howlers. Several people I talked to from the "Charlie lab" days remembered showering down before entering the pens and washing all the dog food in formalin to keep the setting clean. Countering these attempts, though, skeins of geese regularly flew over the open-topped pens, leaving their droppings behind. Sometimes gaggles of geese tried to snatch dog food. I imagine a cacophony of Beagle howls and goose honks. Maybe the geese even aroused in the Beagles a genetic memory of the hunt from long ago. The dogs did not, however, get to run, much less hunt. Nor did their long ears flap in the chase to wave ground scents into their eager noses. Dr. Miller told me that from the pool of two thousand dogs, only one ever escaped. The Beagle bit down on Dr. Miller's forearm while the gate was still open. "I knew I could either save him or save my arm," Dr. Miller told me. "I chose my arm." The last he saw of the Beagle was his running up into the foothills of the Rockies.[18]

Animal ethicist Bernie Rollin, a young CSU professor at the time, remembers people calling him to report on the constant howling of the Beagles, which sounded like proof of some horrendous torture experiment.[19] In truth, the Beagles probably howled because Beagles howl, and possibly out of loneliness, frustration, and boredom. Knowing how stir crazy my own dogs get if we miss even one day of free running in the dog park, I imagine an earthquake of canine anxiety in those foothills pens.

Dr. Rollin tells me that the living conditions for these Beagles were much better than those for most laboratory dogs. In fact, when I sat down to interview him and told him I was researching the "Charlie" dogs, the animal ethicist told me, "There's no story there." The Charlie lab merely irradiated dogs (some of them pregnant) and then monitored them and their offspring. Conditions were probably as good as they get for research Beagles; I've been impressed with the pride all the Charlie lab researchers I talked to still feel not only over the research produced but also over the care and treatment of the irradiated dogs. (Then again, the Soviet scientists on the Sputnik project loved their space dogs, but they still sent Laika into orbit knowing she would never return.)

Other research Beagles used for other experiments, even at the Charlie lab, were not so lucky. Much as he believes that the research justified the sacrifice, Dr. Miller, a fellow dog lover (with whom I bonded over mutual Border Collie love), told me that after years of overseeing lab Beagles, "I could never keep a Beagle as a pet."

Although the researchers I spoke with at CSU were proud of the data their research on irradiated Beagles yielded, Beckham claims that little scientific data of any use emerged from any of the Beagle radiation studies. Their true and lasting legacy proved to be the use of Beagles as research dogs. By 1970, Beckham says, "there were at least 56 commercial Beagle breeding facilities, marketing their dogs specifically to the research industry." That same year, a manual entitled "The Beagle as an Experimental Dog" was published. Drawing on practical observations from experiments in the 1960s, the manual begins by noting, "The dog has long been a favorite animal in medical research, partly because of its size and docility but also because of the availability of large numbers of stray and unwanted dogs at low cost." Beagles, bred to be especially docile, small, and trusting, made especially good research subjects; they would often continue to love their abusers.

A former Colorado State University police officer told me that one time when she patrolled the Beagle colony grounds, she saw that a little puppy had gotten out of the fencing. "He was just a little thing, all soft and silky." She didn't know what the laboratory experiments entailed, but she certainly didn't want him to be eaten by a coyote. "It broke my heart, but I had to push him back in," she told me. "His tail kept wagging the whole time."

Pepper Mills and Animal Welfare

As the use of animals for scientific research and product testing expanded in the 1960s, questions about animal ethics bred like rabbits. I imagine ethical beliefs about animal rights as a spectrum. At one end is the belief in the inherent worth of all animals and in their right to live free from human-induced suffering. At the other end, any human interest (however trivial) trumps any interest of animals (however substantial). In the 1960s, the balance of opinion had been tipped toward the latter pole, but times were changing. Today, I would imagine, most Americans would place themselves somewhere in the middle of the spectrum. They would condemn animal torture in principle, and might grant that some animals, such as dogs, should have some legal protections from cruelty, but they would still privilege (most) human needs and desires over other those of (most) animals.

I admit I'm among this majority of Americans who are uncomfortable with needless animal cruelty in lab experimentation and testing but who also see a need for some degree of animal testing, even if I can't logically justify my privileging of humans over other sentient, suffering beings. I'm also one of the people who has benefited greatly from such uses of animals. (Nearly all of us do on a daily basis, every time we consume food with artificial additives or take a medication or wash our hair or apply make-up). I, too, probably would have called Dr. Rollin to help me with the ethics of the Charlie lab's two thousand penned Beagles. However, the Charlie lab work seems to me reasonably justified and, well, "humane" (a term animal ethicists rightly challenge for its anthropocentric bias). Of course it's convenient for me to think so. Since my own husband benefited from oncological radiation treatments (albeit only palliative), which were enabled in part by Charlie lab and related research, I can only thank those two thousand Beagles for their involuntary service.

However, in other labs here and across the country, much worse was happening to research dogs, most often Beagles. It was common to perform multiple surgeries on a single dog—even as many as nine surgeries—sometimes without painkillers. Dr. Rollin described to me the "Frankendogs" he saw—dogs whose bodies bore more scar tissue than fur.[20]

Today such research wouldn't be done on "normals" (normal, healthy dogs whose illness was artificially induced for the purpose of research). However, "justified" research and testing of lab dogs, especially Beagles, continues. There are still Beagle colonies throughout the country, including in my own city of Fort Collins, where pups are produced for laboratory testing. As a dog lover, I have to admit to feeling rather horrified by such treatment of dogs. I also have to admit to hypocrisy. I expect my consumer goods to be safety-tested. I want better drugs, such as more effective chemotherapies. I just don't want to know about how they were achieved. I didn't want to know about these Beagle colonies.

Such contradictions (let's call them that, shall we, rather than the un-euphemized *hypocrisies*) abounded throughout the America of the 1960s. It was in this contradictory climate that the Animal Welfare Act emerged, an act that itself is rife with the contradictions of its day. With dogs increasingly seen as pets and companions and even family members, rather than the workers and service animals and hunters they were bred to be, some dogs became individuals, obtaining what we might now call "personhood." At the same time, colonized Beagles (and other breeds) faced rampant abuse, euphemized as "sacrifice." All it took was a vivid incident to dramatize the contradiction.

That happened in 1965, when *Sports Illustrated* reported on a Dalmatian named Pepper.[21] This family dog was dog-napped and then sold to a laboratory, where he died before his distraught family could recover him. With Pepper's story, the use of animals in lab research became personal. Then, in the following year, *Life Magazine* published an article on research pups titled "Concentration Camp for Dogs."[22] Reading it, Americans identified with the laboratory dogs and cats, who could easily have been family members. This article, along with Pepper's story, may have provided crucial impetus for the Animal Welfare Act (AWA), which passed in 1966. In fact, the Act opens by acknowledging this motivation:

> Be it *enacted by the Senate and House of Representatives of the United States of America in Congress assembled.* That, in order to protect the owners of dogs and cats from theft of such pets, to prevent the sale or use of dogs and cats which have been stolen, and to insure that certain animals intended for use in research facilities are provided humane care and treatment, it is essential to regulate the transportation, purchase, sale, housing, care, handling, and treatment of such animals by persons or organizations engaged in using them for research or experimental purposes or in transporting, buying, or selling them for such use.[23]

After the AWA of 1966 (Public Law 89–544), life got a little better for research dogs, and increasingly so with subsequent amendments (see *United States Code,* Title 7, Sections 2131–2156). According to the USDA's explanation on its website of the 1985 addition, referred to as the "Improved Standards for Laboratory Animals Act," conditions of "sanitation, housing, and ventilation" had to meet specific standards of "humane care." The amended Act also required "exercise for dogs and an adequate physical environment to promote the psychological well-being of nonhuman primates." It ruled "that pain and distress must be minimized in experimental procedures and that alternatives to such procedures be considered by the principle investigator." Further, it restricted research to "one major operative experiment with recovery" per animal (with exceptions). No longer could dogs be operated on repeatedly or without adequate anesthesia, for example, and their use had to be justified by the experiment's potential benefits. That was the ideal that the law strove for, anyway. (My veterinary school and researcher friends tell me that this ideal diverges wildly from actual, on-the-ground practice.)

Currently, scientific experiments on dogs at research institutions are overseen by a committee, the IACUC (Institutional Animal Care and Use Committee), consisting of a veterinarian, a scientist, a nonscientist (someone unaffiliated with the institution), and a chairperson. Any project receiving NIH (National Institutes of Health) or other government funding (which covers nearly all university studies) must follow *The Guide for the Care and Use of Laboratory Animals*, or *The Guide*. *The Guide* advocates for "the three Rs" (as they're colloquially referred to): refinement, reduction, and replacement. It states that alternatives to whole-animal testing should be used when possible. When animal testing is required, NIH and FDA guidelines advocate "that research and testing derive the maximum amount of useful scientific information from the minimum number of animals and employ the most humane methods available within the limits of scientific capability." Needless to say, such language leaves lots of room for interpretation and debate. While clear improvements in animal welfare have been made with regard to laboratory research, millions of animals are still subject to laboratory experimentation and product testing today. The vast majority are rodents, who have not achieved the legal status of "animal," much less of "personhood," but a fraction consists of dogs, especially Beagles. Even today, over sixty thousand dogs, primarily Beagles, are used each year for testing. That could make for a lot of howling. (The estimate of sixty thousand dogs comes from 2016 data, as reported by Glenn Greenwald and Leighton Akio Woodhouse in their 2018 *Intercept* article "Bred to Suffer: Inside the Barbaric U.S. Industry of Dog Experimentation." They note that more recent data is difficult to obtain because, almost immediately upon appointment in 2017, Donald Trump's head of the USDA, Sonny Perdue, removed all such reports from the USDA website.[24])

(The AWA also protects non-human primates, cats, guinea pigs, and hamsters along with dogs—but not livestock, and not birds, fish, rats and mice. With 90–95 percent of animal experiments performed on rats and mice, somewhere around 12–25 million mice and rats are experimented on every year, though we can't be certain of the number because the AWA does not require researchers to report this data. The rodent exclusion from the Animal Welfare Act makes for a fascinating ethical debate as well as a complex historical narrative, both of which are way beyond the scope of this book.)

The decade of the 1960s was an era in America when multiple emerging, dominant, and residual ideologies concerning the status of dogs in relation to humans were in play, making it seem an era full of contradictions. It was a time when lifting one Beagle by the ears caused national uproar while the much greater suffering of thousands of research Beagles went unnoticed. We recognized ourselves in the image of a cartoon Beagle, but this recognition of a dogs' similarity to humans also justified their subjugation to medical experimentation. Beagles bore our conflicting capacities to create joy and inflict pain on others simultaneously. Dogs in the 1960s were our companions but not (yet) our equals, and served us by being models and surrogates for ourselves.

Either as pampered pets or as confined research subjects, Beagles of the 1960s modeled a new understanding of the status of dogs and their roles in relation to humans. Although their bodies were bred to be finely tuned for rabbit hunting, they were rarely used for that purpose anymore in the United States.

Instead, as dogs were domesticated even further, their in-bred instincts were silenced.

Coda: Silencing the Dog's Voice

I write this to the sounds of quacking. Not from ducks or from Fort Collins' ubiquitous geese, but from the three Beagles and one Basset Hound who live in the backyard catty-corner to mine. These dogs have been "debarked"—they've had vocal cordectomies to "soften" their vocalizations. It's a controversial but still relatively common surgery performed on dogs, usually because they can't adapt to the needs of the residential environments they now occupy. The baying and howling breeds, such as Beagles, are most prone to this surgery. (Greenwald and Woodhouse claim that such "devocalizations" are regularly performed on research Beagles to keep the barking from disturbing lab technicians.)

The neighbor who lives behind me and next door to these debarked dogs cannot stand any barking whatsoever and calls Animal Control

Chapter Two. Thousands of Howls   53

without hesitation. In contemporary suburban America, dog barking is one of the most common causes of disputes among neighbors.

Though I try to be a good neighbor, dogs gotta bark. I don't have Beagles—my backyard has sported an array of spaniel, Collie, and Husky mixes, but no hounds—so I haven't had to deal with baying, just barking. When issued my own citation, I pled my dogs' barking charges down to an embarrassing "public nuisance" charge, which thankfully has disappeared from my record after a year of good behavior and hundreds of dollars of additional training (far more in cost than the barking ticket). At one point I nearly resorted to shock collars, thinking that hurting my dogs when they barked would be preferable to losing them. Fortunately they got off unharmed.

The Beagles and Basset Hound behind me were not so lucky. Beagles gotta howl and bay. It's in their genes, and their throats stretch forward in the joy of the sound's release. These quacking Beagles sadden me almost as much as the story of the Border Collie of my neighbors to the east. She had to be put down because she went neurotic in the confines of her backyard and became aggressive. Her name, ironically, was Liberty.

I don't write this to condemn my catty-corner neighbors for debarking their dogs. If I were faced with a choice between debarking my dogs or having to relinquish them to Animal Control, I'd probably choose the surgery. The real ethical issue at stake is a larger one. When we brought dogs into our houses and hearts, a move that took a critical turn in the 1960s, many humans clearly benefited. But what about dogs? They gained an easier life, one with regular meals and temperature-controlled shelter, but they lost their voice. They became humanized at the cost of their barks, their freedom to run and roam, their liberty. I keep my own dogs in the house when all they want to do is run. Their cage—my house—is a little bigger than those of Beagle colonies, but my dogs are still captive. It's way too late to first begin questioning the ethics of pet-keeping altogether, but back in the 1960s we might have done well to expand our definition of animal "welfare" from the physical into the mental and emotional realms, and to expand its application beyond the laboratory and into the suburban household.

Even the First Dogs of the 1960s did not escape the confines plaguing their middle-class suburban counterparts. Though they weren't debarked (and in fact had their ears pulled to make them vocalize), they suffered other consequences that arose from forcing dogs to live as humans. Soon after the Great Ear Lift, Her died from swallowing a stone. (I, too, have had dogs eat inappropriate substances, usually out of boredom or frustration or anxiety, and only surgery saved my Cocker

Spaniel from fatal intestinal blockage after he ate synthetic pillow stuffing.) Two years later, chasing a squirrel across the White House driveway, Him was hit, fatally, by a limousine. No matter how domesticated, dogs gotta run.

One legacy of the 1960s is the humanization of dogs, which we see so graphically in the bipedal Snoopy. With the Animal Welfare Act and other changes both legal and cultural, we began treating dogs more "humanely." Perhaps, though, we should also have striven to treat them more caninely.

CHAPTER THREE

Rewilding
Dogs as Wolves in the 1970s

As a child in the 1970s, my favorite book was *Julie of the Wolves*. I made it my world. In the real world around me, the Vietnam War and anti-war protests flared, inflation in the United States was highly variable and twice rose into double digits, cars lined up for blocks at gas stations amidst an oil crisis, and Richard Nixon told our nation, "I am not a crook." But although I was aware of these tensions, and although I watched Nixon announce his resignation on the same TV screen that gave me weekly episodes of *Little House on the Prairie*—a series that nostalgically mythologized an earlier, more wholesome, pre-industrialized lifestyle—my imaginative world was filled with Julie and her wolves. When I played with my next-door neighbors' Collie, I looked for signs of the wild inside her.

Without knowing it, I was very much in line with at least one strand of the zeitgeist of 1970s America. The unintended consequences of the urbanized American lifestyle were starting to show. Pollution and contamination were slowly rising into mainstream consciousness. Anti-pollution and conservationist efforts of the previous decades were moving from the margins to the center of American politics and culture, urging us to re-value nature at the point of its disappearance, and to look back in nostalgia at greener times. As writer Barry Lopez wrote of our approach to nature in this decade, "deep appreciation and a sense of loss have arrived simultaneously."[1] Appreciation of nature on the verge of its loss materialized in environmental legislation in the 1970s, including the establishment of the Environmental Protection Agency (1970), the Clean Air Act (1970), and the Endangered Species Act (1973). The first Earth Day took place on April 22, 1970. People began to purchase through the newly available Whole Earth Catalogs (begun in 1968). Suburbanites took up biking and camping, ironically inflicting further injury on the natural landscapes they now wanted to preserve.

This re-valuation of nature as it disappeared before us shaped the way we saw dogs in America. So much so, indeed, that I have nominated the wolf—or the wolf-in-the-dog—as the "breed" of this decade. Changing mythologies about wolves bind inextricably with changing mythologies about our domesticated canines in the 1970s.

A wolf is not a dog, you may already be objecting, and certainly not a breed of dog. Indeed, the wolf isn't even a breed of wolf. There are many species or subspecies—"breeds" bred by nature, not humans—within the category of wolf, none of which are dogs. So what is the wolf doing in a book on dog breeds?

That "a wolf is not a dog" is an obvious statement. Like so many obvious statements, though, it bears further scrutiny. That was definitely the case in the 1970s, when beliefs about wolves, and about the relationships between wolves and dogs, changed wildly. I chose to include the wolf as the "breed" of the 1970s because in that decade we radically revised our view of wolves, and correspondingly revised our view of dogs. Some of the beliefs about dog-wolf relations that emerged in the 1970s have since been disproven, but their cultural influence remains powerful, as does the revaluing of wolves. It was a decade that bred new mythologies about wolves, and about the wolfiness of dogs.

Below, I will look first at the revaluation of wolves and of wildness

Wolves in a heated body-language conversation (photograph by Guillaume Archambault via Unsplash).

in the 1970s, and then at how that revaluing takes shape in our mythologies of dogs. After that, I'll look at Americans' embracing of the more wolf-like dogs, particularly the Husky, as well as (unfortunately) the wolf-dog hybrid.

The Great Wolf Metamorphosis

Many cultures have generated mythologies about wolves as shapeshifters. In the 1970s United States, the lycanthropy was metaphorical; wolves transformed in the American imagination from evil monsters to signs of health.

Before the arrival of Europeans, wolves had occupied most of North America. But when these humans discovered their "manifest destiny" they encroached on wolves' natural habitats (as well as on Indian lands). By the nineteenth century, as farmers and ranchers pushed westward, they radically displaced wild bison with domesticated cattle, so the wolves adapted by hunting cows instead of buffalo. This put wolves in direct competition with humans for ungulates. Now, wolves threatened settlers' very survival, and so became vilified. Even the naturalist John James Audubon, famous for his meticulous naturalistic drawings of wildlife, which taught so many people to appreciate nature in its most minute details, thought that wolves should be eradicated. Bounties for wolf pelts were offered by private citizens, states, and the national government. As the United States Fish & Wildlife Service reports on its "biologue" of the gray wolf,

> Wolves were trapped, shot, dug from their dens, and hunted with dogs. Poisoned animal carcasses were left out for wolves, a practice that also killed eagles, ravens, foxes, bears, and other animals that fed on the tainted carrion.[2]

Although wolves were nearly exterminated in all forty-eight states by the 1930s, "[b]ounty programs initiated in the nineteenth century continued as late as 1965, offering $20 to $50 per wolf."[3] That is, the extermination campaign lasted almost until the moment wolves were listed as an endangered species and protected from hunters by threats of fines and incarceration. By the time we officially recognized wolves as endangered in 1974, "only a few hundred" of this species, whose members had once numbered around two million across the United States, "remained in extreme northeastern Minnesota and a small number on Isle Royale, Michigan."[4] By then, a cascade effect was already beginning to disrupt ecosystems.

Many nature writers in the 1970s cried wolf—and rightfully so.

They called for a reviewing of wolves and of their role in the ecosystem. Such writers included environmentalist Barry Lopez and children's book writer Jean Craighead George. They were preceded by important writers from the decades leading up to the environmental breakthrough of the 1970s.

Aldo Leopold, "Thinking Like a Mountain"

One of the figureheads of the conservation movement in the twentieth century began his career in wildlife management by exterminating wolves. In a very brief but famous essay in his collection *A Sand County Almanac*, published posthumously in 1949, Aldo Leopold writes of seeing a mother wolf and her pups "in a welcoming melee of wagging tails and playful maulings." This was back in the days when "we never heard of passing up a chance to kill a wolf." After "pumping lead into the pack," Leopold and his companions

> reached the old wolf in time to watch a fierce green fire dying in her eyes. I realized then, and have known ever since, that there was something new to me in those eyes—something known only to her and to the mountain. I was young then, and full of trigger-itch; I thought that because fewer wolves meant more deer, that no wolves would mean hunters' paradise. But after seeing the green fire die, I sensed that neither the wolf nor the mountain agreed with such a view.[5]

Without wolves to keep the deer population in check, the deer will ravage the plant life of the region. Leopold realizes in this moment that "a newly wolfless mountain" and eradication of wolves from the plains result in overgrazing by a swollen deer population, which results in "dustbowls, and rivers washing the future into the sea." This effect is referred to as "trophic cascade." Leopold "now suspect[s] that just as a deer herd lives in mortal fear of its wolves, so does a mountain live in mortal fear of its deer" and speculates that "[p]erhaps this is the hidden meaning in the howl of the wolf, long known among the mountains, but seldom perceived among men."[6]

The essay gives us the rise of the modern ecological movement in the form of an origin myth, and locates that origin in the wolf. It mythologizes the howl of the wolf as a cry against trophic cascade. Leopold learns from the wolf and her mountain to think systemically, in terms of a whole habitat or ecosystem, rather than in terms of individual species. He calls this systemic approach "Thinking Like a Mountain" (which he also titles his essay). In this mountain's-eye view, we see an ancestor to the eco-systemic thinking that blossomed in the 1970s. As he represents it in what would become a cornerstone essay for ecological thinking, Aldo Leopold stages the moment of looking into a wolf's eyes, with their "fierce green fire dying," as the catalyst for his epiphany. Although there's nothing inherent in the moment itself that would promulgate systemic thinking, the wolf becomes the key representative of wildness and the wilderness. Her fiercely green light causes Leopold to shift from seeing the wolf as a destructive predator to understanding her as an enabling and integral component of ecological health. As an "apex predator," the wolf is newly valued. (It's also no mere coincidence, I suspect, that this paradigmatic wolf is refigured as female and a mother, who plays with her pups as dogs do, rather than as the lone male wolf of previous eras.)

Leopold's ideas about eco-systemic thinking were even more influential posthumously than in his life, and formed the backbone of the rising ecology movement. The idea of nature as a network of relations rather than a collection of individual species was not new by any means. Indeed, Darwin's theory of evolution through natural selection depends on it. Rather, the 1970s renewed this idea of putting systemic relations at the absolute center of our concept of nature, and then went on to pursue its implications. When you look at nature as a collection of individual species, it's easier to conceive of picking off the troublesome members (such as wolves) and keeping the good (songbirds, for example). Thought of as an ecosystem, a complex, nature becomes more difficult to manipulate.

Leopold had a big influence on perhaps the most prominent nature writer of the 1970s, Barry Lopez, whose 1978 book *Of Wolves and Men* is now a classic in the environmentalist canon. Thanks to Leopold (and others), the metamorphosis of the wolf from monster to environmental caregiver was so much in place that by 1978, Lopez noted, "I write now in a country and at a time when man's own brutal nature is cause for concern and when the wolf, whom man has historically accused of craven savagery, has begun to emerge as a benign creature."[7]

Farley Mowat, Never Cry Wolf

Another precursor of the 1970s environmentalism and the metamorphosis of the wolf in the American imaginary was Canadian Farley Mowat. In 1963 he first published *Never Cry Wolf*, a somewhat fictionalized account of his research on wolves in the Arctic in the late 1940s. When he began his research, Mowat, like Leopold, had been schooled in the belief that the wolf was destructive if not downright evil. As Mowat's guidebook stated, the wolf is "a savage, powerful killer. It is one of the most feared and hated animals known to man, and with good reason."[8] But the tide was turning, and Mowat (following Aldo Leopold) is credited with being a major influencer in the wolf's metamorphosis from a savage predator to a necessary, and even noble, link in the ecosystem.

Never Cry Wolf developed a huge fan base among members of the developing environmental movement in the United States and elsewhere. Indeed, the book was so popular that it went into a second printing in 1973. By then, wolf and human were beginning to change places in some cultural mythologies, to the extent that it was the human who was the savage predator and the wolf who was, in the words of Mowat's 1973 Preface, "an extraordinarily highly evolved and attractive animal which was, and is, being harried into extinction by the murderous enmity and proclivities of man."[9]

Although Mowat published the book as nonfiction, its factual status is dubious. Its myth-making impact, however, is beyond doubt. It has sold at least fourteen million copies worldwide (with a large portion in the United States), and Penguin Modern Classics Edition now calls it "a brilliant narrative on the myth and magic of wild wolves and man's true place among the creatures of nature." Indeed, Mowat's book works to actively create a counter-myth to the one currently haunting the popular imagination.

(There was, of course, great pushback to this acceptance of wolves, and still is. It's a lot easier to call for the return of wolves when your livelihood isn't at stake. It's much harder for small-scale farmers and ranchers, who lose livestock to wolves, to step back and appreciate their value to the ecosystem. I would speculate, too, that it was only after United States agriculture largely shifted from family farms to factory farms—a shift well underway in the 1970s—that the presence of wolves could be appreciated as a sign of environmental health. Factory farms do not suffer the same losses from wolves as free-range farms do. It was easier for us to respect wolves when they no longer threatened our food supply.)

This change in attitude toward wolves bred a change in attitudes toward dogs. People began seeing wolves as close relations of dogs—so similar, even, that they could be mistaken for each other. An early chapter in *Never Cry Wolf*, titled "When Is a Wolf Not a Wolf?," shows the still-ignorant researcher arriving in the subarctic region. Mowat hasn't yet established contact with "the study species" of his "lupine project" when he hears a sound that he identifies as "unmistakably the howling of a wolf pack in full cry" and coming in his direction.[10] Terrified, he takes refuge under his upturned canoe while hearing the pack rush his canoe and crowd around it. "A terrific chorus of howls, barks, and yelps very nearly deafened me."[11] Then he hears a man's voice, scuffling, and then silence. When Mowat peers out from under the canoe, he sees "the bewildered and rather apprehensive face of a young man clad all in caribou furs."[12] Even more startling than the appearance of another human was this: "Scattered around him, and staring at me with deep suspicion, were the fourteen large and formidable Huskies which made up his team. But of bona fide wolves ... there was not one in sight."[13] A wolf is not a wolf when it's a dog.

What Mowat perceived as his first encounter with wolves was actually an encounter with huskies; so similar are wolves and huskies that they can easily be mistaken for one another (in Mowat's account). I draw attention to this story because it illustrates that in the second half of the twentieth century, the similarity between dogs and wolves became emphasized over their differences. This had two corresponding consequences: on the one hand, more sympathy for wolves along with a re-evaluation of pre-existing mythologies about them; and, on the other hand, more respect and appreciation for the "wild" side of dogs. We began to see anew the wolfiness in dogs and the dogness in wolves, and to value their shared traits.

Soon after the anecdote above, Mowat the young researcher hears "a weird medley of whines, whimpers and small howls." He notes, "If there is one thing at which scientists are adept, it is learning from experience; I was not to be fooled twice. The cries were obviously those of a Husky, probably a young one."[14] As you've probably guessed, this time the Husky was a wolf, with whom Mowat comes within six feet of. They even "stare hypnotically into one another's eyes" before the wolf leaps away.[15]

As Mowat studies the wolves over the course of *Never Cry Wolf*, he comes to see that the myth of the rapacious wolf is wrong. Indeed, a "wolf never kills for fun, which is probably one of the main differences distinguishing him from man."[16] Mowat repeatedly notes the resemblance of wolves to dogs, for example, in the way they play, or in the way they prepare to sleep: a wolf will turn around two or three times, "as a dog will," before setting, "nose under tail."[17] In his observations on the wolf pups, he notes (as did Aldo Leopold in "Thinking Like a Mountain") how much they resemble dogs—or, put another way, how much dogs are like wolves suspended at the puppy stage. (This notion of dogs as paedomorphic or neotenized wolves reappears in the dog origin theories concurrently emerging, as I discuss below.) Mowat begins to realize that the myths attributed to wolves were more accurately projections of humans. We were the invaders, the rapacious savages who killed indiscriminately, whereas the centuries-old and universally accepted human concept of wolf character was a palpable lie. On three separate occasions in less than a week I had been completely at the mercy of these "savage killers"; but far from attempting to tear me limb from limb, they had displayed a restraint verging on contempt, even when I invaded their home and appeared to be posing a direct threat to the young pups.

This much was obvious, yet I was still strangely reluctant to let the myth go down the drain.[18]

Earlier myths about wolves (and about the wilderness in general) put humans in the role of protagonists, a particularly tough myth to overturn. Mowat recognizes that cultural mythologies are such powerful things that they direct even our objective observations. Only through great effort can we see past what our cultural mythologies direct us towards and observe what those mythologies work to obscure.

Mowat was sent to the Arctic to supply objective proof supporting hunters' complaints that wolves were killing off all the caribou. What he finds instead is the opposite: that it's the hunters and other humans who are killing the caribou (in part to keep their Husky teams fed, in part for hunting trophies), whereas almost half of the wolves' diet is mice. It's the humans who have acted in ways we call "beastly" and the wolves who have been what we sometimes call "humane"—restrained, disciplined, and rational. Also, Mowat's Native informant convinces Mowat that wolves keep caribou healthy by culling the weakest of the herd—as opposed to humans, who pick off the best ones.

The ending scene of *Never Cry Wolf* presages the ending of wolves in the near future. In a reversal of the opening scene, in which the human is hiding from the wolves, the ending scene shows wolves hiding in their den, "scrunched hard against the back wall, ... motionless as death."[19] When Mowat enters their tunnel with a flashlight, he sees "four green lights" reflected back, reminiscent of Aldo Leopold's green fire dying. The book ends on the howl of a wolf across the wasteland, which Mowat understands as the voice of a "lost world which once was ours before we chose the alien role."[20] Nature is a world we fell from, and a paradise we may soon pave over and lose completely.

Never Cry Wolf was part of the big move to de-mythologize wolves as monsters but also to re-mythologize them as cousins of dogs. The book has been accused of both romanticizing and fictionalizing the lives of wolves. But it's the myth, more than its scientific validity, that I'm interested in here. Both Aldo Leopold and Farley Mowat broke the trail, in the 1940s–1960s, for what would become an emergent mythology about wolves that would flourish in the 1970s. That new appreciation of wolves would very much affect the way we saw and valued dogs.

After its publication in 1963 and its reprinting in 1973, *Never Cry Wolf* was made into a major motion picture in 1983 by Disney (Amarok Productions, Ltd.) directed by Carroll Ballard and starring Martin Cruz Smith. By then, other books had emerged throughout the 1970s to de- and re-mythologize wolves. This new reverence for wolves was becoming so mainstream, in fact, that even children's books were promoting it.

Jean Craighead George, Julie of the Wolves

I was nine years old when the children's book *Julie of the Wolves* was published in 1972. It would be years later before I read Leopold, Mowat, or Lopez, but when my mother gave nine-year-old me the book, I immediately loved Jean Craighead George's tale of a girl in the Alaskan wilderness, and got my friends to read it so we could play Julie-and-the-wolves together. Sometimes I was Julie, sometimes a wolf.

The author was already a well-known nature writer for children, perhaps most prominently from her 1959 book *My Side of the Mountain.* Her book on the Eskimo girl and her adopted family in the arctic tundra went on to win the prestigious Newberry Award in 1973.

(A note on the term *Eskimo*: commonly used in Alaska to refer to the Inuit and Yupik people, the term did not arise from these aboriginals themselves; it was introduced from the outside, and sometimes bears pejorative undertones. In Canada, the term "Inuit" is currently preferred, but since this term does not include Native Alaskans of the Yupik culture, and since George specifies that her protagonist speaks the Yupik language, I will, for the remainder of this discussion of *Julie of the Wolves*, continue to use the term Eskimo, as George does, however problematically.)

The book opens with Miyax (also called Julie) on her stomach, watching wolves awaken. As often happens throughout the novel, her body language mirrors that of the wolves she's observing. (Mowat also found himself, lycanthropically, "becoming wolf.") Julie/Miyax is a thirteen-year-old orphan (or so she believes) and a child-bride whose twelve-year-old husband tried to rape her, initiating her flight from her in-laws' home in Barrow, Alaska. At the novel's opening, Miyax has been lost on the Arctic tundra. Looking to the wolves for survival, she studies the communication signals of their ears, tails, and spatial positioning. Thinking about the alpha wolf, whom she's named Amaroq (Yupik for wolf), she asks herself:

> Why had he bared his teeth at her? Because she was young and he knew she couldn't hurt him? No, she said to herself, it was because he was speaking to

her! He had told her to lie down. She had even understood and obeyed him. He had talked to her not with his voice, but with his ears, eyes, and lips; and he had even commended her with a wag of his tail.[21]

Observing and reasoning like a naturalist in this naturalistic novel, Miyax learns how wolves communicate. She adopts their methods for signaling deference, affection, and hunger, and manages to get the elders to regurgitate meat for her nourishment (as they do for the other pups). She even learns to sniff messages in the scent of urine, though she recognizes that her sense of smell is not nearly as sensitive or intelligent as that of the wolves.[22]

Amaroq seems to adopt Miyax as his would-be wolf pup, and Miyax, in turn, adopts the lead wolf as her surrogate father. Indeed, "he walked like her [human] father, Kapugen, with his head high and his chest out."[23] She comes to see the wolves as individuals, with distinct personalities and subjectivities, and names them accordingly. Throughout her observations of them and her eventual integration into their pack, Miyax heeds what her father has told her of these creatures: "Wolves are brotherly.... They love each other, and if you learn to speak to them, they will love you too."[24] With the word "love," George may seem to romanticize, even anthropomorphize, the wolves. However, she has been at pains to expand the concept of "love" in her observations of wolf relationships, rather than limiting the term to mere human incarnations. Miyax learns, through the example of wolves, to think (and feel) differently.

For me as a child, the book offered the first positive view of wolves. It proposed a counter-narrative to the ones I was used to, those rapacious Big Bad Wolves of fairy tales who wanted to eat me. In fact, though, as George points out in the book, wolves are very unlikely to attack humans. What's more, *Julie of the Wolves* may also have been my first book that had animals as significant characters communicating in their own language. The book attempts to treat the wolves respectfully, as animals, without reckless anthropomorphizing or even sentimentalizing. I was used to talking Disney dogs and comic strip Beagles who walked on two legs and whose thought bubbles contained clear English. Or the opposite: menacing monsters that blew houses down and devoured protagonists.

Indeed, literature had generally presented non-human animals to me in one of two forms: either (1) they were completely "other" to (and implicitly inferior to, or at least less intelligent than) human beings, sometimes even posed as the antithesis of human beings, or (2) they were basically the same as human beings, with the same basic needs and desires, but without our ability to articulate them; we could appreciate them to the extent that they resembled us. That is, nonhuman animals were either "othered" or subsumed. It's true that there was already a body of literature treating animals neither as the same nor the opposite of humans, but instead as distinct creatures within an ecosystem (the novels of Jack London come to mind here). Nevertheless, the emergence of such approaches within children's books is notable. Previously, most children's books animals had been either human impersonators or without personality. Here, though, was a children's book in which wolves were characters in their own right, compared to humans but also assuredly distinct from humans.

Like Aldo Leopold and Farley Mowat before her, Miyax learns from the wolves to think systemically, in terms of an ecosystem. She laments the disruption to the ecosystem that wolf eradication will wreak:

> When the wolves are gone there will be too many caribou grazing the grass and the lemmings will starve. Without the lemmings the foxes and birds and weasels will die. Their passing will end smaller lives upon which even man depends, whether he knows it or not, and the top of the world will pass into silence.[25]

Miyax's alternative is to live peaceably with predators, and to accept their predations as part of nature's system of checks and balances.

This systemic view of nature suggests the structure of a network rather than a hierarchy. Wolf pack structures today are increasingly being seen as a network of relations rather than a rigid hierarchical structure with a tyrannical alpha male at the top. Nature, too, was being reconceived in the general imagination of the 1970s. This reconception displaced humans from the alpha role at the top of a hierarchy of natural beings, and instead made them members of a network.

The ending of *Julie of the Wolves* seemingly reverses much of the optimism and progressive approach to nature that the rest of the book advocates. Julie reunites with her father, who is alive after all, and has married a white woman and even bought an airplane, which he uses to transport tourist-hunters. Julie realizes that it is her father, Kapugen, who killed her surrogate wolf father Amaroq and shot his son, whom Julie had named after her father. The human Amaroq displaces the lupine one; symbolically, the white hunter is killing a part of himself. On a larger cultural level, humans were displacing wolves. Julie recognizes that the future for wolves is grim:

> Where they had once dwelled all over North America they now lived in remote parts of Canada, in only two of the lower forty-eight states, and in the wilderness of Alaska. Even the roadless North slope had fewer wolves than it did before the gussaks erected their military bases and brought airplanes, snowmobiles, electricity, and jeeps to the Arctic.[26]

In the end, however, Miyax chooses to return to her (human) father and to her role as the Americanized Julie, leaving both wolves and Eskimo ways in her past.

Leaving Eskimos and wolves in the past is troubling for ideological reasons, as well as the ecological ones. Although George's depiction of Eskimos as living in harmony with nature, or even as being one with nature, may seem laudatory, it mystifies these Native Americans and, worse, naturalizes their disappearance. Given our history in America of vilifying the land's native inhabitants by casting them as savage, animal-like, and closer to nature than the more "civilized" colonists, the novel's characterization of Eskimos as animal-like, even when portrayed as a positive thing, inevitably calls up earlier discourses. The problem, I think, isn't individual to George, nor is it a problem that could have been avoided. Rather, it's a paradox widespread in the 1970s, as non–Native Americans sought to rethink our relationship to the land and to the original inhabitants from whom European colonizers stole it. So George's depiction of Eskimos as closer to nature remains, for me, uncomfortable. It's not reducible to an earlier racist discourse, but neither is it entirely separable from that discourse. Still, at least for me as a child, the book offered a preview of an alternative model of human-animal relations, one which would become mainstream in 1970s America.

The novel's penultimate line, "*the hour of the wolf and the Eskimo is over*,"[27] warns against the destruction of the ecosystem, even as it presents that destruction as a foregone conclusion. This is perhaps the most problematic aspect of the alignment of Eskimos with animals: wolves and Indians/Eskimos occupy the same spot as Other in American mythology, even when that Other goes from despised to romanticized, from needing to be eradicated to needing to be saved.

This linking of wolves with Indians extends back to the earliest days of the colonization of (what would become) North America. Mark Derr, in his book *A Dog's History of America*, observes, "From the start, Indians and wolves were discussed in much the same language, as wild, brutal, savage, uncivilized creatures blocking the advance of Christian civilization."[28] In fact, the colonists used their European-derived dogs to hunt both wolves and Indians. "Their rationale, in part, was that Indians were wild, cunning, and predatory, like wolves and bears, and thus had to be hunted like them—with dogs."[29] In the early cultural imagination, dogs aligned with white colonists, while wolves aligned with Indians. That alignment haunts our cultural imagination even to this day. However, while I'm uneasy with the parallel between wolves and Native Americans in American cultural mythology, it's hard not to notice the eerie parallel between the official United States treatment of Native Americans and that of wolves. They share a similar trajectory from vilification, deracination, and displacement to a revaluing (and concomitant exoticization) at the edges of extinction.

Two decades later after the publication of *Julie of the Wolves*, George wrote a sequel, *Julie*, in which she tried to rewrite this fate by having Kapugen give up his airplane and guns, allowing his musk oxen to graze freely at the risk of occasional wolf predation. But by 1994, this sequel comes off more as a wish fulfillment fantasy than as the credible and naturalistic novel its predecessor was.

Problematic as the depictions of Eskimos are, *Julie of the Wolves'* predominant effect on me as a child was a chance to try on a new view of wolves (and through them, of nature). This book reflects a larger cultural shift underway from seeing wolves as four-legged devils requiring eradication to valuing and even respecting them. Too bad this shift didn't occur until the actual wolf population was nearly wiped out, and many wolf subspecies had already gone extinct. Indeed, a fundamental contradiction in American culture in the 1970s was the revaluing of wildness simultaneous with its accelerated loss. And we started to value the wolf in our dogs as the wolves themselves neared extinction.

Rewilding

Indeed the wolf has become a kind of symbol, a test case, for ecological preservation. As Jason Mark says in his book *Satellites in the High Country: Searching for the Wild in the Age of Man*, "it's easy to love a nature that just looks pretty. It's an entirely different task to live with a nature that is threatening—quite literally, the wolf at the door."[30] As a species that "is actually antagonistic to our [human] interests" (at least for certain individual humans in the short term), it's the wolf who really tests our commitment to ecological health. "More than any other animal," Mark writes, "the wolf tests our ability to live with things out of our control and beyond our understanding.... The wolf makes us ask whether we're willing to share space on this planet."

Aldo Leopold's career shifted from hunting down wild predators to preserving them at the pivotal moment of gazing into a dying wolf's eyes. By the 1970s, it was as if Americans society found itself looking into those eyes and seeing the "green fire dying." The Endangered Species Act, signed by President Nixon on December 28, 1973, can trace its ancestry to Leopold's work. Although the Act's title seems to suggest that it focuses on individual species, the methodology of conservation recognizes the importance of habitats and ecosystems in species preservation. It "thinks like a mountain" when it opens with the finding that "various species of fish, wildlife, and plants in the United States have been rendered extinct as a consequence of economic growth and development untempered by adequate concern and conservation." Further, its primary purpose is "to provide a means whereby the ecosystems upon which endangered species and threatened species depend may be conserved, to provide a program for the conservation of such endangered species and threatened species, and to take such steps as may be appropriate to achieve [these] purposes...." Here and throughout, the Act regularly mentions the ecosystem before the species, literally putting the ecosystem first and then introducing the imperiled species as a part of this larger whole. It takes the holistic view that Leopold represents as "the hidden meaning in the howl of the wolf."

Gray wolves, on the brink of extinction, were listed as endangered in 1974. Official government policy went from eradication to protection and even reintroduction or "rewilding," a process in which wolves from elsewhere are reintroduced into areas where the species once roamed but has since become extinct. Even before we could rewild actual wolves, we had to rewild our imaginations—to train ourselves to think ecosystemically and to appreciate the importance of an apex predator (other than ourselves) within our ecosystem. This process began in the 1970s with the recognition not only that wolves were endangered, but also that their endangered status was dangerous to the health of our land at large.

Since the 1970s, many nineteenth- and early twentieth-century policies on wolves in the United States have reversed, going from eradication to preservation and rewilding. More recently, for example, wolves have been reintroduced to regions in the northwestern United States, such as Yellowstone, as described by Rick Bass in his 1992 best-seller *The Ninemile Wolves*. While bans on killing wolves remain controversial among ranchers, they have helped preserve the gray wolf. According to the most recent report from the U.S. Fish and Wildlife Service, the "gray wolf has rebounded from the brink of extinction to exceed population targets by as much as 300 percent. Today, there are at least 5,510 gray wolves in the contiguous United States. Wolf numbers continue to be robust, stable, and self-sustaining."[31] Still, wolves keep their "endangered" status throughout most of the United States. The fate of gray wolf preservation remains in the balance.

Wolf to Dog

The new respect for wolves in the 1970s interbred with our understanding of dogs. For one thing, it affected our hypotheses about how wolves and dogs related to each other, and about how dogs evolved in relation to wolves.

By the start of the 1970s, several different models of how dogs evolved were in play. Apart from the science of dog evolution is its cultural mythology. We told ourselves stories both about how dogs emerged from their ancestors as well as about the start of the human-dog relationship.

Models of Wolf Ancestry

Over the past half-century, conflicting hypotheses about the origins of dogs have emerged. All recognize that there is some relationship between dogs and wolves, and that the two can interbreed, but that dogs and wolves are also distinct, and that their divergence occurred thousands, if not tens or hundreds of thousands, of years ago. However, these origin stories themselves diverge.

Models of dog ancestry from earlier in the twentieth century prior to the 1970s often emphasized the distinction between dogs and wolves, and spoke of them as distinct species (even though they were known to interbreed). Indeed, the evolution of dogs from wolves was still being debated, and many hypothesized or imagined a much greater mixture of different types of canid in the dog's origins. Animal behaviorist Konrad Lorenz, for example, writing in 1954 in *Man Meets Dog*, speculated that our dogs were descendants of jackals.[32] Others hypothesized that dogs descended from coyotes, foxes, or an interbreeding of these different canines.

By the 1970s, the attention shifted more singularly to the wolf as ancestor, and the emphasis shifted from distinctions between wolves and dogs to their remarkable similarities. Dogs came to be seen fundamentally as domesticated wolves. Correspondingly, the era saw renewed attraction to a mythology of the sliding continuum from wolves to dogs, of the sort depicted decades earlier in Jack London's novels *Call of the Wild* and *White Fang*. In the former, a domesticated dog joins a wolf pack (becoming "rewilded"), while in the latter, a wild wolf-dog is tamed. Either way, the boundary between wolf and dog appears permeable and reversible, a matter of nurture over nature. This mythology was a favored one in the 1970s, as it aligned with a zeitgeist of rewilding.

Models of First Contacts and Domestication

The twentieth century has also told competing stories about the first relationships between dogs and humans. One dominant and wide-ranging origin story says that wolves and prehistoric humans first learned how to hunt together. Wolves are great at tracking, isolating a large animal (usually an ungulate) from its group, and running it to exhaustion, but less good at the final kill. Humans, with their sharp tools, would have been the opposite. Perhaps early humans learned to follow the ravens that followed the wolves on their hunt for caribou, elk, or bison. Over time, the two species, human and wolf, may have learned to hunt cooperatively and to share the kill. Perhaps over time those wolves most attentive to and comfortable with humans began to live alongside this two-legged species. Thousands of years could have selected for those wolves most compatible with humans. In this hypothesis, wolves joined humans as hunters, and humans played an active role in selecting the wolves to cohabit with them. This seems to have been the dominant myth going into the 1970s.

In another model of dog origins, at perhaps the opposite pole to cooperative hunting, dogs emerged as scavengers of human waste, especially once prehistoric humans turned to agriculture, and created static villages with waste sites. Those wolves least skittish around humans may have begun to scavenge those waste sites, and eventually leaving the wilderness and living beside humans, at the margins of the human world. In this model (most vocally advanced by Lorna and Ray Coppinger starting in the 1970s and laid out more thoroughly in their book *Dogs: A New Understanding of Canine Origin, Behavior and Evolution*), wolves domesticated themselves into dogs, with little input from humans until well down the evolutionary path.

There's also the pet-keeping model, which imagines dogs as pets from the start. Perhaps—as this mythology goes—a wolf pup was abandoned, and perhaps a nursing mother of the human persuasion, evolved to release oxytocin at the sight of a youngster's whimpers and big eyes, suckled the pup. Perhaps taking in abandoned wolf pups became a practice, and perhaps these orphaned wolves began to interbreed. Perhaps over time humans kept feeding the most docile and human-oriented of the wolves, who, in turn, would help alert the humans to approaching danger. Over time, humans would have discovered additional uses for dogs beyond companionship and community.

All of these models are enhanced by the "fox farm experiment" at the Institute of Cytology and Genetics in Siberia, which has been ongoing for the past half-century. In this 1950s, Dmitry Belyayev began breeding foxes selectively for tameness. In just a few generations, the increasingly tamer foxes began to show dog-like characteristics, such as floppy ears and piebald coats, along with behaviors such as tail-wagging, face-licking, and whining. In this process, called "neotenization," some infantile and juvenile characteristics remain into adulthood. Indeed, after a few decades of generations, the foxes bred for tameness could be kept as pets, even coming when called.[33] This extended experiment and others like it offer several important suggestions: that a dog-like tame animal can be bred from a wild one over generations; that tameness is, at least in part, genetically encoded; that tameness is genetically linked with other key components that distinguish the dog from the wolf; and that dogs more closely resemble wolf pups than they do adult wolves.

Our range of models of how today's dog evolved from a precursor wolf already existed in the 1970s, although we didn't have the varied leads offered by, for example, DNA sequencing, to support these models. These different models mostly agree on the dog's evolution from a now-extinct wolf ancestor, but differ on whether emphasis is on continuity or distinction between dogs and wolves. There is no doubt that wolves and dogs are distinct beings; as John Bradshaw suggests, even if their DNA is 99.96 percent identical, their behaviors are radically different. However, without some of the scientific methods we have today, such as DNA gene sequencing, much of this thinking about dog evolution in the 1970s had to stay at the level of speculation. This meant that the favored models reflected the cultural zeitgeist even more than they do today, when some of our more precise scientific technologies might point toward conclusions we might not have preferred. It's my sense that as the wolf rose in estimation in the 1970s from a reviled to a noble creature, models emphasizing dogs' distinctiveness and humans' roles in their creation gave way to models favoring continuity—the similarities of dogs to wolves.

Which hypothesis about dog origins seems most credible within a given cultural moment relates to which dog breed is seen as most representative of the species as a whole. If you spend your time with Cocker Spaniels or Beagles, and make them your model for dogness, then their differences from wolves become more prominent than their similarities. If you spend your time with Siberian Huskies or other working dogs (such as my intense, tireless Border Collie), and see these dogs as the essence of dogness, the similarities between dogs and wolves rise to the fore, and in a positive way. (Folks in the latter group sometimes say that the best aspects of working dogs come from wolf instincts redirected, such as the "prey drive.")

We still don't have a clear answer to the origin of dogs; in fact, we have clearer but also more contradictory evidence than we did in the 1970s. Most researchers—but by no means all—now agree that dogs and the modern gray wolf shared a common ancestor, now extinct, from which they both diverged, making the wolf more a distant cousin than a direct ancestor to the dog. When that divergence occurred, though, is up for debate. While archeological evidence suggests that dogs have existed for 12,000 years (plus or minus a few thousand), mitochondrial DNA evidence suggests much longer. Conflicting evidence has long suggested that dogs arose in Eastern Asia—or in central Asia—or in Europe. The most recent evidence suggests that dogs may have emerged at least two distinct times, once in Europe and once in Asia—or possibly three times, or even more. Informed speculation points to multiple points of emergence. Also up for debate is how much cross-breeding among dogs, wolves, and coyotes may have happened over the ensuing millennia.

Whatever the truth of dog evolution actually is, my point here is that different eras seem to favor different models—or mythologies—of the relationship between humans and dogs, and of the relationship between dogs and wolves, reflecting the needs of the day. By no means am I suggesting that the truth of dog evolution is just a matter of opinion; rather, different eras sensitize researchers to look for, focus on, and discover different things. Beyond the science, different mythologies of dog origins take hold at different times. In this way, different theories themselves have reflected the cultural needs of the era creating them. The model most popular in the 1970s seems to be the cooperative hunting one, in which humans bonded first with wolves as wolves, rather than as already nascent dogs. This model put the wild wolf back into the dog at a time when our culture envisioned putting our endangered wilderness back into the American landscape. More recently, as we'll see in future chapters, we've returned—with a difference—to putting the emphasis on the crucial differences between wolves and dogs.

Rewilding Mythologies in the Popular Culture of the 1970s and Beyond

Cultural critics have noted that images of things sometimes proliferate in a culture as the thing itself disappears. In the 1970s, images of wolves, especially in howling-at-the-moon pose, began appearing on sweatshirts, picnic blankets, belt buckles, and posters taped to wood-paneled walls. They not only appeared in best-selling books, including award-winning children's novels, they threatened to push aside their human narrators in the role of protagonist.

While the era of the wolf's metamorphosis in the popular imagination may be past its peak, the legacy of dogs-as-wolves continues. New discoveries and models of dogs in relation to wolves may have emerged, but earlier ones keep hold in residual and tenacious forms. The dog-as-wolf model of dogs may have peaked in mythological power in the 1970s, but it didn't disappear; its effects have lived on into ensuring decades. We can see the dog-as-wolf model's legacy, for example, in dog training and in dog food marketing.

Training Like a Wolf

Models of dogs and their relationship to wolves show up in dog training practices. Popular training techniques of the 1970s commonly invoked the "wolf pack" model and advised dog owners to be the "alpha" of the pack. This often involved inflicting physically aggressive corrections of bad behavior. For example, in *Good Dog, Bad Dog: Dog Training Made Easy*, a best-selling book first published in 1971 and then revised and republished in 1991, Mordecai Siegal and Matthew Margolis advocate for the use of the "corrective jerk," which they call the "most effective communication technique" in dog training.[34] They recommend using a metal-link training collar. "As the jerk is performed, the training collar tightens slightly around the dog's neck, giving a mild tightening sensation."[35] They warn their readers that

> [t]he dog may whine or cry out after the first few corrections. Do not be upset by this. The sensation of the training collar is a startling surprise for most dogs. In this situation, the dog's whimpering is more like a complaint rather than an expression of pain. Your dog may be trying to manipulate you into letting him maintain control over the situation. Some dogs are criers and will emit a shrill squeal to force you to stop making them do what they don't want to do. This is a ploy and does not indicate that the dog is experiencing the slightest bit of pain. Maintain a firm attitude and never let the dog control the situation.[36]

Disciples of this approach to dog training, in which the human needs to be the alpha of the pack, have continued in ensuing decades. Celebrity dog trainer Barbara Woodhouse, too, in her 1978 book *No Bad Dogs: The Woodhouse Way*, and in subsequent books in the 1980s, advocates the use of corrective jerks with a choke chain. More recently, the Monks of New Skete, in *How to Be Your Dog's Best Friend* and subsequent books, believe that dogs are so much like wolves that "many books on wolves help you to understand and appreciate your dog's behavior better than some of the dog-training manuals currently available."[37] These approaches to training draw on a model of dominance based on the beliefs about the alpha dog's behavior in a wolf pack that have since been debunked. Still, although the alpha-in-the-wolf-pack mythology has been debunked by many scientists, the view of dogs as wolves and of wolves as hierarchical pack animals still thrives, and informs some dog training approaches even today. For example, celebrity dog trainer Cesar Millan understands dogs as domesticated wolves, and it's up to the human to "Be the Pack Leader" (the title of one of his dog-training books). This model of wolf behavior depends on a long-standing idea of wolf packs requiring one dominant alpha.

Earlier studies of wolf packs had been based on observations of wolves in artificial conditions. However, as we began to study wolves in the wild (starting in the 1970s), wolf ethology has shifted away from this model of linear ranking with its "paramilitary descriptions" (as Barry Lopez called them[38]). In the wild, new evidence suggests, wolf packs are not so rigidly hierarchical as we once thought, and the idea of an alpha in a constant state of domination is being displaced by more complex models of wolf communities. Indeed, the very notion of the "pack" is being displaced by the concept of "family," with "alpha male" and "alpha female" replaced by "father" and "mother."

In newer models of how power operates (among humans as well as among wolves), power isn't so much a matter of hierarchy, of positions of dominance or submission, as a network of relations. Power is not so much a solid substance that an individual either has or lacks as it is a liquid, or perhaps a circulating electric circuit. This model of power, too, is reflected in our dog training techniques. As we revise our model of wolf behavior as based less on competition and hierarchy than on cooperation and mutuality, and as we at any rate distance dogs from wolves in our imagination, our techniques of dog training have corresponded with our re-visioning of wolf behavior, and reflect a less hierarchical model based on positive reinforcement rather than correction. What's more, newer dog training models emphasize the fact that dogs, unlike wolves, can communicate with humans quite well and generally want to please their humans. These days, the dog-human bond, rather than the human-over-dog hierarchy, underlies our popular approaches to training. (More on this in Chapter Five.) The popularity of dog training techniques (and their underlying philosophies) are as variable as the models of dog origins, and themselves reflect (and also mystify) the changing worldviews of the culture producing them.

Rewilding Kibble

The dog-as-wolf model so popular in the 1970s lives on in the pet store, where you can buy some of this aspirational wildness. The wolf-in-the-dog is alive and well in the marketing of dog food (which may be one of the best measures for gauging how a culture sees its

A Siberian Husky on the watch (photograph by Erik McLean via Unsplash).

dogs—if not itself). For example, Blue Wilderness features a blue-eyed gray wolf on its package, which also states "Natural Evolutionary Diet." Although the marketing does not outright claim that our dogs descend from these gray wolves, it certainly leads us to that impression. The dog food, "inspired by the diet of the wolf," comes in such varieties as Bayou Blend (with alligator and catfish), Denali Dinner (with wild salmon, venison, and halibut), and Rocky Mountain Recipe (with bison, rabbit, or other kinds of red meat). A marketing video offers the free-standing dependent clause, "Because inside your dog lives the soul of a wolf."

The wolf motif is often invoked for the high-end, high-protein and grain-free ("meaty") versions of a brand. Natural Balance makes a Wild Pursuit line "with freeze dried raw pieces," and Nutro makes a Wild Frontier line featuring a gray wolf on the package; both are high in protein and grain-free. Wild Frontier comes in such habitat-themed "recipes" as "Open Valley Recipe," "Rolling Meadows Recipe," "Cold Water Recipe," and "Woodland Trail Recipe." The appeal to rewilding your pet also animates Taste of the Wild brand's packaging. Each of its "formulas"—such as "Appalachian Valley Small Breed Formula with Venison and Garbanzo Beans" and "Pine Forest Canine Formula with Venison and Legumes"—features an image of wolves in some stage of hunting.

While the quality of this food or its appropriateness for dogs is a matter I'll leave to veterinarians, I'm interested in its appeal to the lingering desire of contemporary dog owners to put the wolf back into the dog. Residual 1970s fantasies of running with the wolves, and of reviving your inner wildness by feeding your dog's inner wolf, still trek through our current cultural imagination. Putting aside the irony of buying wildness in a mass-produced package, it's as if, having lost a connection with natural wildness, we're using our dogs to fill the gap.

Huskies and Malamutes: The Rise of Wolfy Dogs in American Mythology

One way we see the revaluing of wolves and the wolf-in-the-dog is the rise in popularity of dogs that are most evocative of wolves in appearance and habitat, such as the Siberian Husky. While not necessarily closer to wolves according to DNA evidence, they were so in the popular imagination. Remember Mowat's first mistaking huskies for wolves at the beginning of his wolf study, and then mistaking his first wolf for a Husky. They were symbolically interchangeable. (More recently, John Bradshaw and his research team have concluded that of all the common breeds, the Siberian Husky is "the most wolf-like" in terms of "visual signaling" [ear and tail positioning, facial expressions, etc.] as well as appearance.[39])

AKC registries, while not an absolute measure of breed populations at large, since most American dogs are not registered with the AKC, can nevertheless give us an index to this rise in popularity of wolf-looking dogs. According to AKC registry placings, the Siberian Husky slowly rose in popularity in the years leading up to the 1970s. In the early 1950s, the breed placed in the sixties and seventies (#67 in 1950; #76 in 1951). Then it slowly rose in the 1950s, reaching #49 in 1958. In the 1960s, the Siberian Husky rose slowly from being in the top 50 most popular breeds to being in the top 40. By 1970 it was the 28th most registered breed, and then rose to a peak at #14 in 1976. In ensuing decades, the Siberian Husky fell slightly in popularity, residing in the upper teens to lower twenties in popularity following its peak.

The Alaskan Malamute, another breed evocative of wolves in its appearance and original habitat, followed a similar path. In 1950 the breed had the 96th most registries in the AKC. In the early 1950s, it rose in popularity to spots in the eighties, and then kept rising. By the late 1950s, the breed took spots in the 50s, and by the 1960s the forties. In 1970, '71, and '72 it was the 40th most popular breed, and rose to the thirties over the rest of the decade, peaking in 1980 at #30. Since then, it's steadily fallen in placement rankings, sitting in the high thirties by the end of the 1980s, the forties in the 1990s, and the fifties in the 2000s.

Again, most dogs in America are not registered with the AKC, and some types of dogs (as well as mutts) are not recognized by ACK breed classifications. Still, AKC registries give some indication of the trends in popularity of breeds. Popularity of both Siberian Huskies and Alaskan Malamutes grew through the 1970s and then declined. They seem to agree with something in the spirit of the 1970s—not only its environmentalism, but also its appreciation of dogs' relationships with their environment. Huskies figured symbolically into this revaluing of nature and nostalgia for origins both because they were bred by indigenous Alaskans and because in the popular imagination Siberian Huskies (and Malamutes) are closer to their wolf roots than other dogs. Because they seemed to resemble wolves, they became an emblem of an earlier, more natural era. The Husky symbolized a more natural, rugged, undomesticated dog, one closer to nature. We saw in the Husky our own values. In truth, of course, the way of life that huskies symbolized—putting the wolf back into the dog and ourselves back into nature—was more aspirational than actual.

The desire to put dogs (and ourselves) back into nature, to move dogs from the indoors back into the outdoors, and to celebrate their endurance and survival skills in the harshest of wilderness environments, is particularly evident in the rejuvenation of dog sledding.

The Iditarod

The re-valuing of both wolves and Native American traditions (albeit as symbols more than in actuality) came together in 1973, the same year the Endangered Species Act passed, when some folks up in Alaska held a sled race.

The race commemorates and re-enacts the 1925 Serum Run, in which an antitoxin for a diphtheria outbreak in Nome was delivered by sled when weather conditions made flight impossible. Nearly a hundred dogs ran over 670 miles from Nenana to Nome and delivered the diphtheria antitoxin in time to save lives. Such a narrative lends itself naturally to myth, and this myth lives on. The lead dog of the last run, Balto, is still commemorated by a statue in New York, and a 1995 animated movie was very loosely based on his legend. (I've also met several dogs in my dog park named after Balto.)

The run was resurrected in the 1970s, in part "to save the sled dog and Alaskan huskies, which were being phased out of existence due to the introduction of snowmobiles in Alaska."[40] Sled dogs, and the indigenous breed they comprised, were themselves seen as endangered along with the purpose that created them. The revival of sled dog racing met the cultural zeitgeist of rescuing what was on the verge of extinction. Like the actual Balto, the most common sled dogs were huskies, both Siberian and Alaskan Huskies, with the latter sometimes called "Indian Huskies" or "Eskimo dogs." In fact, according to the Oxford English Dictionary, the name "Husky" itself comes from a conflation of the people with their dogs. The word "Ehiskimo," another word for "Eskimo," was shortened to "Hiski," and then "Hiski dogs" became shortened to Husky. While European Americans' equating of the dogs with their human counterparts in the name of the breed seems to harken back to an ideology that bestializes Native Americans, it is true that these dogs were integral to Ehiskimo society. The Native Americans of the Arctic used these medium-sized, thick-coated, hearty dogs for pulling sleds and carrying packs across vast distances, and, secondarily, for help with hunting.

It was widely believed at the time that huskies were originally bred from gray wolves. Recent DNA evidence suggests that the earliest human settlers of Alaska (the "Paleo-Indians"), many thousands of years ago, brought their dogs with them on their trip across the Bering

Strait from Asia—that Siberian Huskies did, indeed, originate in Siberia and are related to Spitz-type dogs of Japan and the Asian arctic, such as Akitas, Shiba Inus, Chow Chows, Samoyeds, Siberian Laikas, and Elkhounds. Unlike Cockers and Beagles, which were originally bred primarily as hunting and tracking dogs before their transition into indoor pets, huskies were bred for centuries as working dogs. When European Americans arrived in the Arctic regions, often as fur traders and gold miners, they quickly realized that no other breed was more ideal for sled-pulling. With their compact power, strength, agility, endurance, and intelligence, as well as a double coat that keeps dampness out and heat in, and, of course, their astonishing will to pull, they were the Arctic working dogs of choice.

(I've experienced that Will to Pull first-hand; it drives my own Husky mix, Tiger—and sometimes drives me—nuts. He wins every game of tug we play [unless I cheat] even though I'm more than twice his weight, and he would happily play tug all day long, stopping only to slurp water as the rope absorbs his saliva. He sports the neck muscles of a weight lifter, muscles that cry out for expression. They seem to double in size when they bulge. He's never so fulfilled as when he's towing me. That's when, while his muscles strain, his body relaxes into its calling.)

The Iditarod (and the larger sport of long-distance sled-racing, an extreme outdoor sport) represents a very different relationship between humans and dogs than the ones we've seen in previous chapters. Both species are athletes in the race, and both are valued equally as members of a team. This race celebrates the athleticism of dogs and their ability to work collaboratively with humans, offering a vision of humans at one with creatures of nature in the natural world. These rugged dogs and their mushers symbolized a larger cultural project of revaluing "the wilderness." (That's the ideal, of course. In recent years, the Iditarod has seen charges not only of animal abuse but also of doping dogs with most *un*-natural performance-enhancing drugs.)

Alaska itself was a literal expansion of American identity, having become a state just fourteen years earlier, in 1959. It also expanded the possibilities for America's vision of itself. Long before 1970s and the Iditarod's becoming an annual sled race, the Iditarod Trail itself originated with the Inupiaq and Athabaskan people hundreds of years ago. It was later used by European fur traders and, later still, gold miners. The trail has served as one of those mythologies that holds cultural contradictions together. By reaching back to Native American traditions and linking them with the rugged individualism of their colonizers, Iditarod mythology "mystifies" (in Barthes' sense) a history of depredation, both of the land and its inhabitants. The Iditarod race's website states as much: "The race pits man and animal against nature, against wild Alaska at her best, and as each mile is covered, it is a tribute to Alaska's history and the role the sled dogs played."[41]

The trend of whites appropriating Indian mythology for pseudo-progressive ends further made the Iditarod legend perfect for revival in the 1970s. Because those most at risk in the 1925 Nome diphtheria crisis were Native Alaskan children (lacking immunity to "white man's diseases"), the legend portrays European Americans as rescuers rather than destroyers, an image particularly needed to counter-balance those coming out of Vietnam. In the face of increasing anxieties about America's national power and natural resources, this northern sled race offered an alternative image through which Americans could understand their cultural identity.

The Iditarod race has only grown as an annual event taking place every March. In recent years, however, due to rising temperatures, snow has had to be brought in to cover parts of the trail. The thick-coated sled dogs are beginning to overheat on the run, thus serving, now, in a new way as a bellwether for their era.

Coda: Wolf-Dogs

Unfortunately, this mythologizing of dog as wolf and its minimizing of the real differences between the two—a blurring of dog/wolf differences characteristic of the 1970s—has resulted in a problematic trend toward breeding wolf/dog hybrids and keeping them as pets, a trend that seems only to have increased since the 1970s. I've seen quite a few wolf-dogs in my dog park. Some are wonderful, and make me long for one in my life. Others don't work out so well, and many end up in rescue sanctuaries, unable to thrive in either dog or wolf realms.

I understand the pull of the wild—that fierce green fire—that the wolf seems to represent. When I adopted my Husky-Terrier mix Tiger, a wolfy-looking beast, he was an unsocialized stray found roaming a six-lane highway in Texas. He bounded into my life with a delightful and terrible wildness. The first three times I took him to the dog park he jumped the fence and ran into the woods. When he did stay inside the fence he grabbed the scruffs of other dogs' necks and pulled, swinging his powerful neck to and fro, a move wolves use to break the spines of prey. He was just playing, but his behavior dismayed other dog owners (and some dogs). Tiger jumped up on tables and countertops, knowing no bounds. When winter came he grabbed people's mittens off their hands and raced through the dog park as if showing off his loot. He especially liked to gnaw on human arms like a puppy does, but with two-year-old teeth. I slathered Neosporin over my arms and began clicker training. Within a few months, Tiger settled into a "good dog," obeying all my commands and walking solicitously at my side, with only an occasional lunge at an unneutered male or an extended howl at the living room window. By then I missed his wildness. I even tried to train some of it back into him, but there's no going back.

For a time, I was even tempted to adopt a wolf hybrid, which seemed like the next step into wildness, even though most of the wolf-dog hybrids I've encountered in the dog park have been so gentle, so reserved, almost the opposite of Tiger's kind of wildness. They don't want to be touched, and disappear from under you when you go to pet them. They have no dog body language whatsoever—no relaxed-jaw dog-smile, not even a play bow past early puppyhood—and don't heed invitations of the frolicking dogs around them. These are canines whose eyes can never be met. If you look directly at them, either they turn away, as if in submissive deflection, or they accept your challenge. I've only seen the latter happen once, and fortunately the owner grabbed the leash and pulled hard before his canine launched.

Once, though, a muscle-bound man brought his hybrid puppy. "Seventy-five percent wolf," he said proudly. He also brought his adult wolf mix, but never let that canine off the leash despite its determined straining. The six-month-old pup, already more self-sufficient than the adult versions of his paedomorphic dog counterparts, tore through the park without sound, reached the gate, and rammed his way under it, digging as he ran, still soundless. People in the dog park shook their heads as the man charged into the woods to retrieve him. "Never keep wolves as pets," they agreed, and I joined them. Part of me, though, admired the 75 percent wolf pup. *There's the real deal*, I thought. *He makes my tough Border Collie and Husky mix look like Toy Poodles or shivering Chihuahuas. Of course it's wrong to keep wolves and wolf hybrids as pets, and this owner is in over his head. Still, if I were to do it, I'd be a whole different kind of owner. I'd be so much better....*

...and that's how it begins.

Indeed, while wolves remain endangered, animal sanctuaries are full of rescues who don't fit in the human world but can't survive in the wild. In my home in Northern Colorado, the W.O.L.F. (Wolves Offered Life & Friendship) Sanctuary is full of wolf and wolf-dog pets gone awry. Southeast of us, in Keenesburg, Colorado, is The Wild Animal Sanctuary, or TWAS, "the world's largest carnivore sanctuary," which houses "more than 400 rescued lions, tigers, bears, wolves, and other large carnivores," and currently holds about twenty-six Timber and Arctic wolves and wolf hybrids. Most of these come from individuals who got these creatures as cute pups but then quickly found themselves in over their heads as the pups grew and grew. Such sanctuaries remind us that much as we may re-value the "nature" of dogs—their powerful instincts, their athleticism, their drives—they are not wolves, but a mostly domesticated, super-complicated hybrid of ancestral wildness and evolutionary adaptation to the human world.

Perhaps putting the wolf back into the dog was a useful correction for the treatment of dogs as humans, which led to practices like de-barking, as we saw in Chapter Two. But in overcorrecting for the penchant to humanize our dogs, we expressed our own cultural needs and desires as much as the dogs.' While we model our dogs either on our own image or our images of nature, dogs themselves remain stubbornly resistant to clear classifications, their "true natures" seemingly as malleable as the many shapes and sizes we've modeled them into.

CHAPTER FOUR

Breeding Bullies
Pit Bulls in the 1980s

Canine Jaws

On the *Sports Illustrated* cover for July 27, 1987, a Pit Bull threatens to lunge out of the frame and bite the faces of his viewers with his gaping maw.[1] Photographed so close-up that his canine teeth, hanging like fangs beside jagged incisors, appear far larger than his eyes, he might evoke for some readers the jaws of the infamous shark that menaced pop culture consumers of the 1970s. These jaws could easily devour "Homer Hero Don Mattingly," whose image appears in miniature in the upper right corner of the cover, small enough to fit easily into the dog's ready oral cavity. So monstrous is this dog that his image threatens to take over the whole magazine cover, as if crowding out Mattingly to the margins. Capital letters above the dog's image decree, "BEWARE OF THIS DOG." Although "this dog" is labeled "The Pit Bull Terrier," he represents something more than a breed, or even a dog. He's a mythic creature, a monster. For 1980s' America, the Pit Bull served as our Grendel, our gremlin, our jaws. He became the new werewolf.

It's worth noting, too, that on this *Sports Illustrated* magazine cover, the Pit Bull's coat is a black-and-brown brindle, while the hero of baseball, that most American of sports, is a white man in a white uniform. The story this cover lay-out tells (accidentally, I assume), is of the brown/black brute displacing the white man. Race in America is complicated, and racism pervasive, working most powerfully when it balances at the edge of consciousness, such as in mythological forms. Its codes and substitutes mark the world of dogs as surely as they do almost every other aspect of American culture. The Pit Bull, in particular, bore a racial significance. I'm not saying that the *Sports Illustrated* cover is racist in any simple sense, or that it was intended to bear racial coding, but that it replicates the racial coding rampant in American culture in

83

the 1980s. If only racism were so simple as a matter of a few individual pop culture producers who could be handily condemned and eschewed, rather than being an insidiously systemic and structural phenomenon. More likely, the cover lay-out must have "felt right" to its composers. When a creation "just feels right" to its creator, that's often a sign that it fits into an invisible cultural mythology. This cover makes that mythology (or what I'm calling "breedology") visible.

The article inside, "The Pit Bull: Friend and Killer," asks, in its subtitle, "Is the Pit Bull a fine animal, as its admirers claim, or is it a vicious dog, unfit for society?" The writer, E.M. Swift, leans heavily toward the latter option of this either/or question, while also casting much of the blame on the Pit Bulls' human counterparts. Swift tells of how Pit Bulls are being both bred and trained as hyper-aggressive killing machines to be used in dogfighting rings and as guard dogs for drug dealers. The Pit Bull has become a "weapon"—or, in today's parlance, we might say that the Pit Bull was "weaponized."

The article goes on to tell of Pit Bulls killing or maiming small children and even turning on their owners. The jaws are as monstrous in prose as they are in the visual image of the cover: "the Pit Bull doesn't merely bite man—or, most horribly, child—it clamps its powerful jaws down and literally tears its victim apart." While the article concedes that a Pit Bull can also be a "friend," and is so in 99 percent of the cases, the proportion of the article spent on Pit Bull as killer comes closer to 99 percent than the actual 1 percent, aggrandizing the clamping jaws and fighting spirit of the breed-type.

What's more, this article identifies the Pit Bull as a sign of a larger cultural ill: "[S]omething has happened to the Pit Bull in the last decade that says as much about the nature of American society as it does about the nature of this aggressive animal," the article states. It's right. The Pit Bull had become a monster. The word "monster" comes from the same root as "demonstrate," and a nation's monsters of choice demonstrate its warring identities far better than the flag it waves. Monsters make flesh a culture's spiritual crises, its fears, and sometimes its guilty conscience, if not its unconscious.

This chapter looks at how race and class issues in the 1980s were projected onto and dramatized through Pit Bulls. The "breed" was demonized alongside the demonization of the (presumed) races of people associated with these dogs. In actuality, Pit Bulls may not have been the disproportionately active killers these articles imply. My concern here, though, is not with the true numbers of Pit Bull bites relative to other bites and other dogs, but with how Pit Bulls were characterized in the 1980s (and beyond) and with the mythological work they enacted.

The *Sports Illustrated* article exemplifies a spate of articles in the 1980s alerting readers to Pit Bull aggression. Suddenly "the Pit Bull" or "the dog" popped up everywhere, usually in the singular, as if one dog could represent a whole breed, or as if it were one omnipresent satanic essence attacking innocent children. Even the American Bar Association ("Murder by Dog," *ABA Journal*, June 1989) and the American Medical Association ("Dog Bite-Related Fatalities from 1979 Through 1988," *JAMA*, September 15, 1989) weighed in on the Pit Bull. *Time* magazine offered such articles as "Battling Over Pit Bulls" (August 11, 1986) and "'Time Bombs on Legs': Violence-Prone Owners Are Turning Pit Bulls into Killers" (August 27, 1987). The latter article says the Pit Bull, "has seized small children like rag dolls and mauled them to death in a frenzy of bloodletting." Further, "maladjusted owners" are training their dogs for an "orgy of pain and violence."[2] Criminals to the core, Pit Bulls are purported to disobey the rules of dog behavior: "When other dogs submit by showing their bellies, Pit Bulls have been known to disembowel them."[3]

Pit Bull hysteria demonstrates a particular fascination with the dogs' jaws, which acquire the status of other mythic menaces. *People* magazine, in its 1987 article "An Instinct for the Kill," quoted an animal control officer's comment that Pit Bulls "grab hold and keep shaking like a shark. They tear huge chunks of meat out of you."[4] A *US News and World Report* article claims, "While other dogs usually bite and back off, the Pit Bull will clamp its viselike jaws on a victim and continue biting, shaking and tearing, like a shark in a feeding frenzy...."[5] The *Sports Illustrated* article quotes a Humane Society field investigator's observation that while most breeds don't multiple-bite, a "Pit Bull attack is like a shark attack: He keeps coming back."[6] And it wasn't just the mythic shark menacing beaches of the 1970s that the Pit Bull evoked; "[t]hese animals can be canine crocodiles."[7] They're regularly referred to as "creatures" and "brutes" rather than as animals or dogs, and to inanimate "weapons" and "machines." An article referring to these dogs as "time bombs on legs" noted that teenaged boys in Chicago's West and South sides were "brandishing their fierce Pit Bulls just as they would a switchblade or a gun."[8]

It wasn't just Pit Bulls as *actual* dogs that suddenly pervaded the urban landscape of the 1980s. More significantly, the *image* of Pit Bulls as an icon of aggression pervaded the cultural landscape. In the same decade as the Pit Bull became vilified as "the most dangerous dog in America" (in *US News & World Report*), it also came to be used with grudging admiration for politicians. The Pit Bull as a metaphor for an aggressive, relentless fighter is a well-worn trope now, but it was fresh in the 1980s, when *Time* magazine called the 1980s an era of "Pit Bull politics"[9] and labeled Newt Gingrich "the Republicans' Pit Bull" for his "attack-dog rhetoric."[10] A *New York Times Magazine* article described ultra-conservative Jesse Helms as a "Pit Bull Politician" (in an article of that title) for his negative attack ads.[11] The 1980s became the decade of "Pit Bull politics," an era when it was becoming the norm, if not desirable, for politicians (or at least for conservative white politicians) to fight in the way that a Pit Bull allegedly fights.

Some of the Pit Bull toughness on the part of these politicians involved defunding social services for the very demographics associated with Pit Bull ownership, as well as deregulating the safety measures in place to protect the labor conditions and physical environment of this demographic. Meanwhile, dog fighting—both real and imagined—became an arena in which not just party politics but also the politics of race, class, and gender were staged. How did Pit Bulls become both scapegoats and mascots? What do we make of this seeming contradiction, where Pit Bulls are both vilified and appropriated as metaphorical role models? What does the Pit Bull of the 1980s *mean*?

Troubling Pit Bulls

To treat these questions properly, we need to back up and appraise the very category of the "Pit Bull," first as a zoological fact and then as a cultural artifact. The Pit Bull has been a troubling "breed" for a number of reasons, starting with its very definition. The contention over the identity of this "breed" is itself a microcosm of cultural identity debates. In fact, though it's commonly referred to as a breed in colloquial parlance, experts consider it a "type." This type is generally understood to include the American Pit Bull Terrier, the American Staffordshire Terrier, the American Bulldog, the Staffordshire Bull Terrier, and even the Bull Terrier (the breed of Bullseye, the Target mascot). In some circumstances, English Bulldogs and even Boston and French Terriers have been referred to as Pit Bulls. The "Pit Bull type dog" might also include mixtures of these breeds, or mixtures of one or more of these breeds with other breeds, such as Boxers and Labs.

All of these breeds, like all breeds, are the result of human engineering, carefully selecting and combining for specific genetic traits (or absence of certain traits). The Pit Bull type dog is a relatively recent arrival in the pantheon of breed-types. According to Bronwen Dickey in her book *Pit Bull: The Battle Over an American Icon*, the Pit Bull type dog originated on one side from the large, sturdy working dogs called "mastiffs" in medieval England. Farmers found that if their mastiffs would "worry" the cattle before slaughter, the resulting lactic acid surge in the cows and bulls would soften their meat. Over time, this "worrying" of bulls, or "bull baiting," became sport. The dogs were further refined into "bullying" or "bully type" dogs (thereby giving rise to the term "bully" as a verb meaning "to intimidate"). To add to the "sport," such dogs were also pitted against bears, and later each other. Around 1800, these sturdy Bully dogs were combined with Terriers to produce a more agile fighter and vermin hunter. This produced a range of Bull-and-Terrier mixes from an open gene pool, producing a range of dogs referred to as "Pit Bulls."[12] That is, until recently, the Pit Bull was defined by function rather than by phenotypic appearance.

That heritage of breeding the dogs for function rather than appearance, generally from an open gene pool, not the closed one that purebred status requires, makes the Pit Bull type dog notoriously difficult to identify visually. It can be indistinguishable from Lab and Boxer mixes. Often dogs with neither Bully breeds nor Terrier breeds in their genes get labeled Pit Bulls, particularly if their owner fits the stereotypical profile of the Pit Bull owner (poor, African American and/or Latino, and "ghetto," as I'll discuss below). In truth, the classification of "Pit Bull" is a matter of perspective and often has more to do with the race and class of its human owners than with the dogs' genetic lineage.

Given its complicated history and genetic make-up, many of its advocates insist on referring to this breed-that-isn't-a-breed as "Pit Bull type dogs" (or "American Pit Bull type dogs," abbreviated to APBT dogs) rather than Pit Bulls. I'm sympathetic to their argument that referring to the "breed" as a Pit Bull only validates the existence of such a breed. In addition, some argue, the term "Pit Bull" comes with so much cultural baggage that it can never be unburdened from its false attributions. I've chosen to use the term "Pit Bull" anyway, since the general understanding of the Pit Bull as a breed has already stuck, however falsely, and has had a very real presence as a breed in American culture. Like race in America, it exists both as an idea and a lived reality, even if it's not actually a genetic-based reality. Rather than putting annoying scare quotes around it each time I use the already scary term "Pit Bull," I'll trust my readers to understand its inherent instability. The Pit Bull is a creature of American mythologies.

Breeding Trouble: Pit Bulls' Bad Raps

Pit Bulls did not always connote blackness, the ghetto, and the underclass, nor were they always seen as dangerous. For decades, the

Pit Bull played the role of quintessential family dog in America. Defenders of the Pit Bull often point to Petey of *Our Gang* (later known as *Little Rascals*), the epitome of the friendly family dog. Other examples of Pit Bulls in American history include Pal the Wonderdog of early motion pictures, Helen Keller's beloved dogs, the childhood dog of Laura Ingalls Wilder mentioned in *Little House in the Big Woods*, Billie Holiday's Mister, and James Thurber's Rex, about whom he wrote lovingly in *The New Yorker*. Indeed, Dickey writes, Pit Bulls'

> widespread popularity among people of all ages, races, and classes owed much to their reputations as plucky, unfussy sidekicks and hardy all-purpose workers. More than that, however, "the dog with the patch over his eye" was seen as quintessentially American: good-natured, brave, resilient, and

Billie Holiday and Mister, Downbeat Club, New York City, William P. Gottlieb Collection, February 1947 (photograph by William Gottlieb, Music Division, Library of Congress).

dependable. By World War I, Pit Bulls were so beloved as national symbols that we literally and figuratively wrapped them in the flag. We even called them "Yankee Terriers."[13]

By the 1980s, however, the Pit Bull had slipped from the super-American Yankee Terrier to the country's Enemy #1 domestic terrorist.

According to Dickey, it wasn't until the 1970s that things began to go terribly wrong for Pit Bulls. This coincided with things going terribly wrong for both urban industrial centers in the United States and for rural agricultural enclaves. The 1970s' recession disproportionately affected the most economically vulnerable, and the "trickle down" Reaganomics of the 1980s benefited the top economic tier while passing down mere trickles to the lowest tiers. With globalization, many factories moved overseas, and major industrial cities took big hits. Middle-class blue-collar jobs slipped away just as African Americans were beginning to reap the benefits of their hard-won civil rights.

With the loss of quality blue collar jobs and increased inner city unemployment came a loss of the hope of previous decades, as inner-city communities (over-represented by African American and Latino residents) devolved into ghettos. Long-standing historical inequities became re-entrenched. Cornel West, in a critical essay of 1991 looking back at the previous decade, called this loss of hope and meaning "Nihilism in Black America." These communities, distrusting a police force that seemed to serve the property interests of the rich, were unable to count on adequate police protection, and sometimes turned to guard-dogs.

Poverty and nihilism provide great breeding grounds for drugs and crime. Even greater than the rise of drugs and crime were the fears it spawned. These fears further led people to acquire dogs for protection, which led to a rise in the market for "aggressive dogs." Fear aggregated in a feedback loop as stories of vicious attack dogs churned through the media. At the same time, breeds that had previously occupied the structural role of "demon dog" gave way to the smaller Pit Bull, whose popularity made it readily available and whose size fit better with urban dwelling.

I do want to note that in my research I could find no evidence (other than anecdotal) that people of color were over-represented among Pit Bull owners. The association of Pit Bulls with people of color is metaphorical, and bears all the power that metaphors on a culture-wide scale—that is, mythologies—can wield.

I also want to note that a culture's candidate for "demon breed" has varied in different eras and places. In nineteenth-century America, the Bloodhound held that title. The United States later replaced this role with Rottweilers, Dobermans, German Shepherds, and even Saint Bernards. Other cultures demonized other breeds. Laura Schenone notes in *The Dogs of Avalon: The Race to Save Animals in Peril* that in mid-twentieth-century Ireland, it was Greyhounds who occupied the place of "the other": "They were big, muscular animals, most often seen wearing Hannibal Lecter–style face masks as they sped around the track. Clearly they would kill and eat your children."[14]

A study in *JAVMA* (*Journal of the American Veterinary Medical Association*) in 2000 seems to confirm that Pit Bulls became the "dangerous dog" of the 1980s.[15] In a study of dog bite-related fatalities (DBRFs) in the United States from 1979 to 1998, Pit Bulls and Rottweilers together accounted for about 60 percent of deaths. The raw numbers are complicated by a number of factors, including the subjective classifications of breeds, the expansive definition of a Pit Bull, the reporting of gross numbers rather than DBRFs per capita (or per breed), the unreliability and incompleteness of the DBRFs recorded, and the failure to factor in such variables as sex and reproductive status of the dogs, whether they were leashed or unleashed, whether the bites occurred on or off the owner's property, and, most importantly, how the dogs were trained. Even so, the breakdown shows that the most fatal dog bites in the United States came from Pit Bulls, peaking in 1987–88 at 11 (with 10 in 1983–84 and 9 in 1985–86). However, from 1975 to 1980 the most DBRFs came from German Shepherd Dogs, followed by Husky-type dogs and Saint Bernards. From 1991 to 1998, the most DBRFs came from Rottweilers, with 10 per year from 1993 to 1997. These numbers suggest that breedology is at much in play as anything inherent to these breeds or types. People wanting dangerous dogs, for whatever reason, will obtain the dog breed or type reputed the most dangerous in their era.

At any rate, in the 1980s, reports of dogfighting increased, particularly among communities of African American and Latino men. Urban people of color soon became equated with dogfighting. It was easy for mainstream, middle-class Americans to condemn dogfighting and then to let the transitive property of the equation do its work. While in reality only a small number of Pit Bull owners fought their dogs, dogfighting became part of the breed's image. These fears added a "gangster" status to both the Pit Bulls and their owners. All of these factors coalesced into a perfect storm for the Pit Bull. Dickey nicely summarizes this perfect storm:

> The crime of dogfighting exploded in the headlines, and the well-intentioned, well-publicized crusade to stamp out a barbaric but moribund form of animal torture unwittingly made it more popular. Once reporters and misinformed activists cast the dogs as willing participants in their own abuse, Pit

Bulls were exiled to the most turbulent margins of society, where a cycle of poverty, violence, fear, and desperation had already created a booming market for aggressive dogs. Headlines about Pit Bull attacks on humans multiplied. Within a few short years, America's century-old love for its former mascot gave way to the presumption that Pit Bulls were biologically hard-wired to kill.[16]

It's hard not see, in the rhetoric both demonizing Pit Bulls and proudly reappropriating them, the legacy of a racism once applied overtly to people of color, and now diverted through indirect means onto their dogs.

While Pit Bulls were overtly racialized in the 1980s, the racializing of different dog breeds has long occurred and continues to this day. Usually the racializing is more subtle than that of Pit Bulls, particularly when dog breeds connote whiteness, the "unmarked term" of race in America. As Meisha Rosenberg puts it in an intriguingly titled article, "Golden Retrievers Are White, Pit Bulls Are Black, and Chihuahuas Are Hispanic."[17] We can find multiple examples to back up this racial coding of canines throughout American media. While we can never ultimately prove that dogs are racialized, it's hard, at least for me, not to recognize the truth of Rosenberg's title.

Indeed, it's hard to ignore the way the stereotype of African American and Latino men shares language with the stereotype of the Pit Bull. These dogs were characterized as angry, aggressive, brutish, predatory, bloodthirsty. Their violent tendencies were innate, "hard-wired"; therefore they were incapable of reform—not just uncivilized but uncivilize-able—and at best in need of constant monitoring if not incarceration. They were even more dangerous because they were irrational and impulsive. One magazine article from the 1980s notes their "treacherous Jekyll-and-Hyde unpredictability." They were solid muscle, matter over mind, and they would "fight to the death," holding their victims with a "death grip." They were said to feel no pain, or to feel pain differently from other dogs, an echo of the widespread but false belief that Black people feel less pain than white people, resulting in Black Americans' being "systematically undertreated for pain relative to white Americans."[18] A 1991 article in *The Economist* ("Killer Genes Ate My Dog") even suggests that Pit Bulls are addicted to pain: "The dogs may be junkies, seeking pain so they can get the endorphin buzz they crave."[19] A *Time* magazine article of the same period declares, "the dogs should be demoted to the rank of 'man's worst friend' and the world's 'most obnoxious minority group.'"[20]

It's also hard to ignore the incorporation of misogynist attitudes into this discourse. Feminine humans were "pussies," whereas real men, tough men, were Bulldogs. Pit Bulls (whether male or female) were often characterized as macho or hyper-masculine or even testosterone-fueled. A 1986 article in *Newsweek* referred to them as "The Macho Dog to Have,"[21] and *People* magazine observed in 1987 that "inner-city teenagers have begun to adopt them as symbols of manhood."[22] Owning a Pit Bull was "a macho thing, like carrying a weapon."[23] (Note that in the opening to this chapter, describing the *Sports Illustrated* cover, I assumed the pronoun "he" for the dog depicted; whatever that dog's actual sex, the iconography of the image asserted his maleness.) Such a characterization drew on and augmented a cultural presupposition that both men and Pit Bulls are inherently violent, and their extreme versions all the more so. They are powerful because they are feared.

Dreaded Metaphors

"[H]ow we think about breed and how we think about race inform each other," writes Bronwen Dickey in her study of Pit Bulls.[24] Before I continue looking at America's displaced discussion of race through the image of Pit Bulls in the 1980s, I want to step back and note that this terrain has already been marked and re-marked by American history. In the last chapter I discussed this idea with wolves and wolf-like dogs in relation to Native Americans of the north in the 1970s. How we thought about "Eskimos" and how we thought about the wolf-in-the-dog informed each other. In 1980s' America, Pit Bulls came to be associated with men of color. So what we thought about Americans of color—in particular African American and Latino men— informed what we thought about Pit Bulls, and vice versa. Any discussion of analogies between breeds and races in the United States (which I discuss further in Chapter Six) needs to first acknowledge America's history of treating non-whites as non-humans. Paralleling men of color with Pit Bulls did not come out of nowhere; this dreadful history of comparing certain humans to other animals pre-existed the 1980s by centuries.

Since before the United States became a country, colonists from Europe characterized the continent's non-white inhabitants as subhuman, and in particular as animal-like. We have a particularly impressive history of rhetorically bestializing Native Americans and Africans in America. Native Americans were seen—sometimes positively but more often negatively—as "one with the land," members of a natural ecosystem that white people stood outside of and above. Such discourse enabled European settlers to see Native Americans, along with America's native animals, as natural resources. Somewhat similarly, Africans in America—and, later, African Americans—were described as bestial and animalistic, with predatory instincts (a clear instance of projection). Black men were referred to as "bucks," a term drawing from the animal kingdom. By the 1980s, groups of young black men were referred to as "packs" that went "wilding." (I suspect that a similar metaphoric structure underlies the references to guides bringing Mexicans across the United States border as "coyotes.") Characterizing non-whites as instinctively predatory creatures of nature "fits" unspoken cultural mythologies and serves to naturalize racism.

If only these metaphors, which turn certain kinds of humans into animals, were "merely rhetorical." But they're not. They're the linguistic residue (and sometimes, also, the reinforcements) of actual, physical oppression—oppression of both people of color and animals. In her book *The Dreaded Comparison: Human and Animal Slavery*, Marjorie Spiegel argues that "the oppression of animals, which was being honed to a clumsy science centuries before black slavery in America began, was in many cases used as a prototype for the oppression of blacks."[25] More controversially, she argues that the "suffering animals must endure today in laboratories, on 'factory farms,' as 'pets,' and in the wild, sadly parallel those endured by black people in the antebellum United States and during the lingering post-bellum period."[26] Enslaved people in past centuries, like animals now, have endured parallel treatments, "from the disruption of self-regulated reproduction, to birth and the consequential destruction of the familial structure," and other cruelties through their lifespans.[27] Like animals today, black people under slavery were separated from their families, bound, caged, forced to labor, and whipped for insubordination.

Rhetoric comparing certain groups of humans to (nonhuman) animals almost always serves to bolster racist ends. I suspect it goes even deeper; the comparison of humans with animals provided a "condition of possibility" for racism. Such a comparison made racism possible and conceivable. Present at the creation of racism, the "dreaded comparison" made both race and racism thinkable. American culture inherited an ancient legacy, or "discourse," of such comparisons, from which it developed its own special idiolect.

American culture has struggled to move beyond this rhetoric, and some progress has been made. It's no longer acceptable to publicly and outrightly equate Black people with dogs (or other nonhuman animals) in support of an ideology of white supremacy and black inferiority. Sadly, though, such bestializing rhetoric still permeates American culture just below the surface (and, increasingly, above it), and so we need to continue to call out this bestializing rhetoric wherever it appears and to insist on its falsity. Sadly, in this era, when some politicians are not willing to say that "Black Lives Matter," we still need to insist (invoking a strategic humanist rhetoric) that Blacks are equally human and occupy an equal level on the hierarchy of species.

Comparing nonwhite humans to animals is clearly derogatory in intent, and we should condemn that intent. At the same time, though, we might ask *why* it's insulting to compare a human to a (nonhuman) animal. Why do we accept the invisible "speciesism"—the assumed supremacy of humans—underlying the insult? (I ponder speciesism and human supremacy further in Chapter Seven.) Spiegel observes that the very structures of thought underlying both racism and speciesism need to be challenged, and not just the position of individual groups within these structures. Indeed, says Spiegel, both systems of oppression—the oppression of animals by humans and the oppression of some humans by other humans—reinforce each other. Spiegel notes further that "any oppression helps to prop up other forms of oppression. This is why it is vital to link oppressions in our minds, to look for the common, shared aspects, and fight against them as one, rather than prioritizing victims' suffering."[28] So Spiegel argues that we not only recognize the faulty alignment of Black people with nonhuman animals, but that we dismantle both systems—white supremacy and human supremacy—together. Spiegel critiques forms of anti-racist activism that "continue to actively struggl[e] to prove to our oppressors, past or present, that we are *similar to our oppressors*, rather than to those whom our oppressors have victimized." Doing so says "that we would rather be more like those who have victimized us, rather than like those who have also been victims."[29] Or, to put it crudely, comparing people of color to dogs (especially to Pit Bulls) is abhorrent, but the reason it's abhorrent is *not* that dogs are inherently inferior to humans.

It's also important to acknowledge that, while people of color have been aligned with animals—and particularly with canines—in American history, the reality shows something very different: animals (particularly dogs) have been used to preserve white supremacy and to commit violence against Black insubordination. From this perspective, dogs acted on behalf of white people. In one infamous example, the Fugitive Slave Act of 1850 was colloquially referred to by abolitionists as "the Bloodhound Act" because it allowed (human) citizens in free states to become tracking dogs—to find and return to their "masters" any enslaved people who escaped to "free" states. From the dogs used to savagely attack

Native Americans to "Bloodhounds" used to track and capture escaped slaves to the German Shepherds employed by police against nonviolent Civil Rights protesters of the 1950s and 1960s to the police dogs used in the drug wars today, the rhetorical alignment of people of color with dogs is diametrically opposed by the violent reality.

Reclaiming Pit Bulls

At any rate, Pit Bulls became more powerful as symbols of terror than they ever were as fighters in the pit. When people have very little access to legally recognized forms of power, they tend to gravitate to the forms they can get. In yet another feedback loop, dog fighting became an expression of power, and the people who were unfairly equated with the negative traits unfairly attributed to Pit Bulls began to identify with the Pit Bull image, and to re-appropriate the image and make it their own.

It's a commonly known phenomenon for denigrated groups to "reclaim" and "reappropriate" the language of their denigration. Terms like "gay," "queer," "bitch," and "crip" (as in "crippled") have undergone or are undergoing such transfers of ownership. The most notorious example, of course, is "the N-word," which has been asserted with counter-cultural pride and affection by people for whom the term was previously used to denigrate. In addition to negative terms, groups may appropriate and reclaim negative imagery—often wryly, with tongue in cheek, as with the "pussy hats" worn in the Women's March the day after Donald Trump's inauguration in 2017. When, in the 1960s, Huey Newton and Bobby Seale named their group for Black empowerment the "Black Panther Party" (drawing on a name previously used by another group), they appropriated the power of the racist image of black people as animal-like, savage, and dangerous. Recontextualized, the bestial image becomes a figure of pride.

Hip hop culture, arising amidst the post-industrial hopelessness of the 1980s, did a similar thing with the imagery of dogs and particularly of Pit Bulls. 1980s hip hop culture has been characterized as, simultaneously, a reflection of, a reaction to, and a counter-cultural defense against the larger cultural forces that devastated large manufacturing cities. Hip hop scholar Tricia Rose notes that the centrality of economic conditions of the 1980s—post-industrialization, deep cuts in social services, a housing crisis, and an increasingly unequal distribution of wealth—manifests itself in rap music's "ghetto specificity." Specific sites and details of post-industrial urban dwelling appear in lyrics and music videos. Also appearing are the material objects of these urban environments, such as fences, chains (sometimes reappropriated as jewelry), and yes, Pit Bulls.

Rose notes that rappers tended "to craft stories that represent the creative fantasies, perspectives, and experiences of racial marginality in America."[30] Pit Bulls embodied the potential power within marginality. Indeed, Pit Bulls came to signify a kind of ghetto authenticity. Members of hip hop culture began to call themselves and each other "dog" or "dawg." (This epithet seems to have displaced the cool "cat" of the 1950s and 1960s, a vocabulary that had made the black panther its logical culmination). This colloquial canine epithet is perhaps most obvious in the (doubly redundant) name Snoop Doggy Dog, which appropriates Snoopy, a cartoon character that the rapper enjoyed as a child. and puts him into a gangsta setting.

As I've discussed earlier, discourses that are dominant in one era may linger residually in later times, sometimes even maintaining significant power. We can see this with the case of Armando Perez, who would become a major hip hop artist a little later than hip hop's golden years of the mid–1980s to early 1990s. In a 2004 interview, he explained why he had chosen to name himself Pitbull. He asserted that Pit Bulls

> bite to lock. The dog is too stupid to lose. And they're outlawed in Dade County. They're basically everything that I am. It's been a constant fight.[31]

Pit Bulls became the burgeoning hip hop movement's "unofficial mascot," says Dickey, noting that these dogs appeared in the lyrics of rappers such as Big Daddy Kane, Salt-N-Pepa, and Ice-T, and that Pit Bulls were regularly pictured on album covers or music videos for artists like Snoop Dogg, Dr. Dre, DMX, and Missy Elliott, and Jay-Z.[32]

So Pit Bulls are complicated and ambiguous signifiers; they can mean different, even opposite things at the same time. They embody both a kind of nihilism and the fight against that nihilism; they signify both despair and protest; they make overt the toughness of underclass survival even as they represent pride in that toughness.

This was as true for ghetto-dwellers as for the rural underclass, which may have preceded the ghetto in popularizing both Pit Bulls and dogfighting. The most prominent case of dogfighting in the United States was the Michael Vick case. This is another example of a phenomenon whose ideological meanings were codified in the 1980s but remain active in residual forms decades later. Jim Gorant describes the agricultural version of this underclass identification with Pit Bulls in America. These dog men saw themselves in the dogs. In the exterior toughness and bravado, to a degree, but even more in the animals' willingness to take on any challenge, to endure pain and injury, to never give up despite long odds and great difficulty [...] and that is how these men view their own struggle against the disadvantages they've had to contend with. Even more, there is a certain godlike feeling that comes with knowing that these creatures of superior toughness and strength and will are a product of their own making [...], perfect symbols of their own triumph.[33]

Similarly, Dickey quotes actor Michael B. Jordan as saying, "Black males, we are America's Pit Bull."[34] Both are labeled "vicious, inhumane and left to die on the street." And so some urban rappers, like their rural counterparts, identified with Pit Bulls as outcasts, survivors, fighters, and tough guys. They drew on the Pit Bull image to represent such characteristics in their art.

This strategy of appropriation is fraught with dangers. For one thing, it can seem to reaffirm, rather than undermine, the stereotypes both about Pit Bulls and about the humans they represent. That is, it can be seen to maintain this black-as-bestial structure supporting white supremacy. It also accepts the gendered model of power of the dominant culture: power is a matter of toughness and masculinity, whereas femininity means weakness. The macho image of Pit Bull toughness accepts the idea that power is masculine. Powerless men assert their masculinity to achieve (or simulate) power rather than displacing the conceptual framework altogether.

Policing Pit Bulls

As reports over Pit Bull attacks on innocent children rose, these narratives took the form of one already pre-scripted for their human counterparts. Angela Davis has called this narrative "the Myth of the Black Rapist."[35] Active from the beginning of American culture (and even before), this myth says that black men, left to their own "natures," will rape or murder innocent white women, and so white men need to police black men in the name of white women (and other vulnerable members of white society). The reverse situation—white men raping black women—was the more common actuality in United States history, but it's the myth that held the most power on both official and unofficial public policy. Valerie Smith succinctly describes this central myth or pre-scripted plot as

> a cultural narrative in which the rape of a frail white victim by a savage black male must be avenged by the chivalry of her white male protectors ...

instances of interracial rape constitute sites of struggle between black and white men that allow privileged white men to exercise their property rights over the bodies of white women ... [while] black women represent the most vulnerable and least visible victims of rape....[36]

Similarly, some of these Pit Bull attack stories recrafted the "myth of the Black rapist" into "the myth of the Pit Bull." In this narrative, the black attacker works by proxy through his dog, a kind of canine id. Or the dogs may be represented as "weapons in the criminal's arsenal," as in the case cited in a 1986 *Newsweek* article in which an interviewee "just testified in a rape case where one of these dogs was used as force."[37] Such Pit Bulls, proxy symbols for their owners, must be incarcerated or they will attack, and they "often can't be kept with other dogs" because "Pit Bulls have been know to disembowel" other dogs submissively showing their bellies.[38]

Many of these stories of Pit Bull attacks tend to emphasize the innocence of the victims. In the tragic case of James Soto, a two-year-old boy killed by his neighbor's chained Pit Bull, *People* magazine writers Michelle Green and Dirk Mathison make space in their short article to include such All-American details as the family's "celebratory stop for ice cream" and James' "newly acquired Tonka truck" prior to the attack.[39] Such attacks, horrible as they were, could have been seen as individual aberrations of a breed-type that has long co-existed happily with children. Instead, the attacking Pit Bull stood for a whole type—a casebook example of stereotyping. The myth of the Pit Bull fed a hysteria demanding that vulnerable, innocent children (coded white) be protected from these bullying, vicious, rapacious attackers. Pit Bulls became a dog-whistle code for Black men.

Some cities began to institute breed specific legislation (BSL) banning or restricting specific breeds. Such legislation continued into the 1990s and 2000s. More recently, some of these laws have been repealed, but new ones continue to arise. The breeds banned almost always include Pit Bulls or Pit Bull type dogs, and often include related Bully breeds or other breeds used for fighting or guarding, such as Rottweilers. The ban in Denver, Colorado, instituted in 1989, comes closest to home for me. A product of the 1980s, it still persists. The ban's language is typical. It covers "any dog that is an American Pit Bull Terrier, American Staffordshire Terrier, Staffordshire Bull Terrier, or any dog displaying the majority of physical traits of any one (1) or more of the above breeds, or any dog exhibiting those distinguishing characteristics which substantially conform to the standards established by the American Kennel Club or United Kennel Club for any of the above breeds."[40]

Chapter Four. Breeding Bullies

Many of the bans have been challenged and mostly upheld in higher courts. To the charges that such laws unfairly discriminate against a "breed" that can't even be defined or proven, the courts' reasoning often suggests that common-sense understandings of "Pit Bull" are sufficient. They may also posit that the danger such dogs pose outweighs the problems with discrimination. For example, in *Vanater v. Village of South Point*, in 1989, the Ohio federal district court stated in its ruling that

> [t]he breeding history of Pit Bulls makes it impossible to rule out a violent propensity for any one dog as gameness and aggressiveness can be hidden for years. Given the Pit Bull's genetic physical strengths and abilities, a Pit Bull always poses the possibility of danger; given the Pit Bull's breeding history as a fighting dog and the latency of its aggressiveness and gameness, the Pit Bull poses a danger distinct from other breeds of dogs which do not so uniformly share those traits.

This case ruling cited characteristics often attributed to Pit Bulls, such as "the propensity to catch and maul an attacked victim unrelentingly until death occurs" and "a history of frenzy, which is the trait of unusual relentless ferocity...." In this stance, voracious aggression has been bred into the Pit Bull's nature.

Even admirers of APBT dogs sometimes take the nature side of the nature/nurture debate when it comes to the dogs' temperaments. Carl Semencic, in his 1982 book celebrating dogfighting breeds, *The World of Fighting Dogs*, says that "gameness," or tenacity in fighting, is inherent to them and should be admired, even if dogfighting itself is condemned. He worried that fighting dogs' admission into purebred kennel club status would come at the cost of their inherent nature, and that unless gameness were recognized in the judging criteria, that trait would be lost. Further, "to destroy (by selectively breeding against) those qualities that are the essence of the fighting dog—i.e., gameness and the ability to fight on a grand scale—is tantamount to aiming a genocidal effort at the breeds in question, in this case the American (Pit) Bull Terrier."[41] Affirming "gameness" as the "essence" of a Pit Bull reinforces the ability to stereotype these dogs and then to selectively police them. It justifies a kind of "breedal profiling" that parallels "racial profiling."

Indeed, it's hard to ignore the overlap of language used in the policing of Pit Bulls to that used in racism. Defending Pit Bulls from such unfair policing, some people talk about discrimination and stereotyping, and call the activity "breedism," in a clear parallel to racism. Some anti-breedist activists even refer to "the P word," in parallel to that other unspeakable, "the N word." An Ontario inspector for the SPCA has noted that

A Pit Bull–type dog taking a dip in the pool (photograph by Anthony Duran via Unsplash).

throughout Ontario, the "P" word prevails ... and as a result, hundreds of these misunderstood dogs have died needlessly. Ontario politicians couldn't identify a Pit Bull in a photo lineup when they imposed the ban, but that didn't stop them from making the decision to put them on death row after a few high-profile dog-bite cases.[42]

The metaphoric language of "a photo lineup" and "death row" makes clear that the policing of Pit Bulls works in the same ways as the policing of humans. (This Canadian shelter accepts dogs from areas in the United States with high euthanasia rates, so policies in Ontario also affect the treatment of American Pit Bulls.) Pit Bull bans have even been called "racism by other means" and "Jim Crow for dogs." In a famous *New Yorker* article, social critic Malcolm Gladwell has compared breed bans to racial profiling.[43]

It's not merely a matter of language, or structural parallels; a ban on these dogs effectively keeps out "undesirable elements" who might depend on such dogs for protection as well as cultural identity. Often, if the municipality itself doesn't ban APBT dogs, individual rental units and apartment complexes do. The ones that don't ban Pit Bulls outright may ask for (expensive) liability insurance for the dogs, which can be financially prohibitive, and will most affect people below the home-owning income bracket. Breed bans have very real and material effects on cultural geographies.

Rescuing Pit Bulls

Some fans and defenders of Pit Bulls fight "breedism" by invoking a nature/nurture framework. They argue that Pit Bulls aren't "naturally" vicious; if they are vicious, it's because they've been trained into their aggression. Change their environments and you change the so-called nature of the dog. This argument pits nature against nurture in its own kind of staged dogfight. This argument, too, parallels a related argument about race and criminality. If prisons are disproportionately filled with people of color, some have argued, and if we take that as evidence that people of color commit disproportionately more crimes (a huge "if" for another time), it's because they were "bred" to a life of crime due to poverty and lack of opportunity in a racist society. Human "nature" has nothing to do with skin color, this argument goes; human nature is deep within, whereas skin color is superficial, and affects how we're treated (nurture). It may seem like an anti-racist argument, whether applied to humans or dogs. However, it often takes the form of saying that Pit Bulls aren't bad dogs, they're just dogs raised by bad people. Pitted against their owners, the Pit Bulls' moral status rises as their owners' proportionately falls.

The countermovement to rescue actual Pit Bulls themselves as well as their reputations has been growing in recent years. Probably the most visible proponent of the Pit Bull in American culture presently is Cesar Millan, the "Dog Whisperer," best known for his *National Geographic* television show of that name. Millan, himself a compact, muscular Latino man, parallels himself with his beloved Pit Bulls. Millan markets his story as a rags-to-riches and illegal-immigrant-makes-good narrative, a story he wants to hold for Pit Bulls as well. His television show is devoted to showing how "bad dogs" (what he calls dogs in "the red zone"), if given the proper environment, can make good. Millan's most famous canine success story is that of Daddy, the "calm assertive" Pit Bull whom Cesar acquired from rapper Redman. As he rehabilitates "red zone" dogs, many of whom are Pit Bulls, Cesar (and Daddy) model the idea that there are no bad breeds (or races), only bad environments. It's nurture, not nature, that makes Pit Bulls go bad. (It should be noted that Millan, while praised for his work on behalf of Pit Bulls, is condemned by "force free" dog trainers for his use of aversive punishment, which some see as bordering on abuse, as I discuss in Chapter Five.)

In another more positive spin on the negative co-stereotyping of underclass men with Pit Bulls, the television show *Pit Bulls and Parolees* also adopts the "second chance" and "rehabilitation" discourse modeled by Millan. In this television show, Tia Torres, who runs the Villalobos

Rescue Center, matches parolees (who are disproportionately men of color) with Pit Bulls so that each can rehabilitate the other. The show operates on a model of animal and human behavior in which nurture predominates over nature, an assumption underlying all notions of reform. The center's website offers the mottos "Saving man & man's best friend" and "Every dog deserves a second chance."[44] Tough, nurturing, and loving, Torres (at least as she's depicted on the show) believes in the inherent goodness of her stray dogs and wayward men, who were wronged by society, not bad by nature. Given the right nurturing environment, seeming "bullies" can be reformed.

In a more cynical and Foucauldian vein, I might trouble the concept of reform, with its coercive inclusion, as well as the talk of "redemption," a term used on the show's website, and one which often signals an unstated but compulsory morality tale. In essence, reform can be a kind of ideological incarceration, more effective than the bricks-and-mortar version both because it's invisible and because the inmate (or out-mate) polices himself. (Likewise, is a highly trained dog, who's internalized rules commanding all his behavior, "free"? But that line of thought, important though it is, is for another time.) For now I want to appreciate *Pit Bulls and Parolees*' creation of a narrative in which both condemned dog and convicted human can share the role of protagonist simultaneously, instead of being pitted against each other.

More commonly, though, the "optics" of Pit Bull rescues show well-meaning middle-class-ish white people rescuing victimized Pit Bulls from bad nonwhite abusers. In spite of the intentions of these rescuers, they often take the structural form of well-bred, privileged (white) people rescuing the dogs from the ill-bred, shady (dark) people. The dogs aren't bad; they just have a Bad Rap (as an important Pit Bull rescue group in Oakland, California, is named, short for Bay Area Dog-lovers Responsible About Pit Bulls). Unfortunately, the racial structure of rescues—white, middle-class people using their white privilege to rescue underprivileged dogs—can have the inadvertent effect of scapegoating African American men even as these rescuers attempt to disentangle dogs from the scapegoating. As the Pit Bull narrative gets rewritten, it still echoes the "myth of the black rapist," but instead of Pit Bulls playing the role of black rapist/abuser in that mythology, they shift to the victim role of white women (and children), with black men returned to the role of rapist/abuser. Rescuing the innocent Pit Bulls from the bad black man becomes a noble cause, coded white.

Another problem with the white-middle-class rescue and rehabilitation of Pit Bulls is that it gives the impression that white people care more about (nonhuman) animals than about people of color. While I think it's a false dualism to pit caring about people in opposition to caring about (nonhuman) animals, and while I agree with Spiegel that racism and speciesism *ultimately* support each other, I also recognize that animal rescue often ends up unintentionally reinforcing the structural racism of the culture in which the animal abuse arose in the first place.

I want to be very clear here that I'm not accusing individual white Pit Bull rescuers of racism. Far from it. I really do believe that Pit Bull rehabilitation is a noble cause, and one of the better uses of white, middle-class privilege. Having "rescued" a Border Collie bordering on what Cesar Millan calls "the red zone," I have an inkling of the hard work, as well as the drain on energy and material resources, it takes to "rehabilitate" an abused dog—and my dog was not anywhere near as traumatized as some of the Pit Bulls rescued from dogfighting rings. (I also suspect that people who believe in rehabilitation for dogs are also likely to favor rehabilitation over punishment for humans, and to be both liberal and anti-racist.) What I'm suggesting instead is that the race and class structures in America, and the narratives that support and naturalize them, are incredibly resilient, resistant to radical change. In more academic language, we might say that ideology absorbs and reconstitutes resistance to it. Individual attempts to treat the results of structural racism and classism in America often end up seeming to confirm the racism and classism themselves.

The Bad Newz Dogs

The casebook version of this rewritten narrative was that involving football player Michael Vick in 2007, which I referred to earlier. I want to spend some time on this case; although it's anachronistic to this chapter, it shows how the racially coded mythology of Pit Bulls, which became entrenched in the 1980s, is still alive today, and is able to be reactivated when the right moment arises—as was the case with the NFL quarterback.

Michael Vick grew up in an impoverished neighborhood in Virginia, in a town people called Bad Newz. As his football career took off, and Vick joined the Atlanta Falcons, he launched his dogfighting operation with family and friends, perhaps as a way to stay grounded in his culture. He even named his kennels in Surry County, Virginia, the "Bad Newz Kennels," as if recalling his origins. In 2006, Virginia law enforcement was tipped that Vick was operating an illegal dogfighting operation. When agents arrived on the scene of Bad Newz Kennels, they found over 50 dogs, many chained, scarred, and underfed, as well as "a blood-stained fighting area," a "rape stand," and performance-enhancing drugs regularly used in dogfighting.[45] Witnesses spoke of executions (including hangings and drownings) of inadequate dogs, and further investigations unearthed six-to-eight dog carcasses. Vick was subsequently tried, convicted, and sentenced to twenty-three months in prison and three years probation for funding the dogfighting and engaging in unlawful interstate commerce associated with it. He was fined $5000 and required to pay another $928,073 in restitution for the fifty-three dogs seized from his property in order to pay for their rescue and rehabilitation. This prosecution and sentence set a new precedent of concern for Pit Bulls.

This concern for Pit Bulls continued in the ensuing efforts to save as many of the dogs as possible. Specialists in Pit Bull rescue wanted to save both the dogs themselves and the reputations of Pit Bulls, to show that they've had a "bad rap" and have been undeservedly stereotyped as inherently vicious. In the end, the majority of dogs were "rehabilitated," and some even became therapy or ambassador dogs. A representative 2013 reunion party of the "Vicktory dogs"—the Bad Newz Kennel dogs who went to the Best Friends Animal Society—shows the happy ending for some of these dogs. It also shows primarily white rescuers replacing the dog's former abusers, all African Americans.

Why did this story of Vick and his dogs get so much press at this moment in history? It's a powerful story, for sure, involving a high-profile celebrity, in an era when dogs are becoming family members and citizens. But it also falls readily into a pre-scripted narrative (or mythology). The Myth of the Black Rapist storyline that Americans have internalized readily adapted itself into the Myth of the Black Abuser, in which Black men, instinctually vicious no matter how much success they achieve, need to be kept in check and corrected by white humanitarians. Such a storyline had both the ring of familiarity and the lure of newness. For many Americans, it fit a worldview long in the making, confirming our unconscious ideology back to us, while giving us a hit of self-righteousness.

An added irony in the Michael Vick case is that while dogfighting is condemned, football is the exact opposite of condemned, even though there are some disturbing similarities between the two. I suspect that even bringing up a comparison between dogfighting and football will raise hackles. But the structural similarities are hard to ignore: football is, to be blunt, a pitting of primarily African American men against each other for the entertainment of primarily white fans. It's a game in which injury is expected and brain damage common, a game in which primarily African American men hurt themselves and each other. Cultural critic Steve Almond, in his self-described "manifesto" against football (*Against Football: One Fan's Reluctant Manifesto*) asks us to think about what it means that "the perverse arrangement by which watching young African-Americans in tight pants engage in mock combat has become our most profitable form of entertainment."[46] He wonders if "it fuels our most insidious and intractable stereotypes about such men: that they are inherently animalistic"[47] and asks why "we think nothing of calling them 'studs' and 'beasts' and 'specimens'? Are we turning them into fetish objects?"[48] He goes so far as to ask, "Can anyone really watch the NFL Combine—in which young, mostly African-American men are made to run and jump and lift weights for the benefit of mostly old white coaches, and us couch potatoes—and *not* see visual echoes of the slave auction."[49] Almond further asks, "Why do white fans react with such shock and horror when African-American players, who are rewarded for ruthless aggression on the field, exhibit these traits elsewhere? Is the obsessive coverage of their violent crimes a public justification for our private prejudices?"[50] Why, we might also ask, do we applaud Michael Vick for being a "Pit Bull" in the football arena when we're so horrified by his pitting of Pit Bulls against each other in the dogfighting arena? Why is his culture of machismo rewarded in football but condemned in dogfighting? Those of us who readily and self-righteously condemn dogfighting—myself included—might do well to ask why dogfighting is worse than football.

But I'm veering into dangerous territory here. The sanctity of the football field is a terrain that its proponents will viciously guard. Besides, it's too easy for me to criticize football, which I've had no taste for in the first place. Unlike Almond, I don't love it or watch it or identify with it, so I have nothing at stake. I spend Super Bowl Sunday watching the Puppy Bowl—and wondering why other people see the puppy version as more ridiculous than the human one.

Almond asks if football "relieve[s] the racial guilt of white Americans to lavish so much money and adulation on a few African-American men" while "provid[ing] white Americans a continued sense of dominion over African-American men."[51] In other words, what cultural mythologies is football both satisfying and masking? I want to ask the same of dogfighting, as well as of the highly publicized condemnations of it. I'm certainly not condoning dogfighting—it still horrifies me—but I also recognize that the phenomenon plays the role of myth in America, and myths do cultural work, both revealing and concealing the culture they serve. What is (or was) dogfighting the decoy for and the distraction from? Who are the real bullies, the ones for whom Pit Bulls serve as symbol and scapegoat?

The Real Pit Bulls

As I mentioned at the beginning of this chapter, even as "real" Pit Bulls were condemned in the 1980s, the term "Pit Bull" gained currency in politics, and it was often applied with barely concealed admiration for the so-called "Pit Bull politicians" who had the chops to bully others. In addition, even as actual Pit Bulls were aligned with people of color (especially African Americans and Latinos) and vilified, they were also used as metaphors for white conservative politicians, such as Newt Gingrich and Jesse Helms. The irony goes even deeper. It was sometimes applied to politicians working against the interests of people of color; the Pit Bull was pitted against African Americans and Latinos. North Carolina senator Jesse Helms, one of the few politicians even whiter than Newt Gingrich, and infamous for his opposition to integration (as well as for voting against making MLK's birthday a national holiday) was seen as a "Pit Bull politician" during his 1990 campaign for Senator, launching ruthless and vicious attack ads against his African American opponent Harvey Gantt.

The Pit Bull as metaphor for tenacious politicians has only proliferated since then. The most famous example is probably the one made by (the wolf-hunting) Sarah Palin, who invoked the metaphor in her bid for Vice President in the 2008 presidential election. After identifying as a hockey mom herself, she quipped, "You know, they say the difference between a hockey mom and a Pit Bull? Lipstick." Because the joke depends on the assumption that Pit Bulls are tough, ruthlessly protective, unrelenting fighters, Palin's calling herself a Pit Bull only reinforces the prejudice against the breed. It also reinforces the Pit Bull's machismo; Palin appropriates and exploits the Pit Bull's image of masculine toughness and gangster bad-ass-ness to legitimize herself as a woman in politics. To some extent, Palin's likening herself to a Pit Bull with lipstick may suggest that the era of Pit Bull-as-epitome-of-evil may be waning. If so, it will likely be replaced by some other dog breed. (Dogo Argentinos and Presa Canarios are already waiting in the wings). At the same time, though, Palin's comment reflects and reinforces not only the idea that Pit Bulls are tough, aggressive, and masculine on the inside (even if decorated with lipstick) but also the strand of American politics that deems it good to be a bully (as long as it's the "us," not the "them," being the bully). Pit Bull imagery helped politicians give form to the emerging credo that bad-ass, no-compromise bullying should replace civic discourse. (Personally, I'm more inclined to elect a Border Collie politician than a Pit Bull politician.)

The positive claiming of Pit Bullship by conservative white

Chapter Four. Breeding Bullies 107

politicians (I couldn't find any cases of liberal or progressive politicians identifying as Pit Bulls) does not signal a corresponding empathy with the people of color with whom Pit Bulls have been aligned. Actually, the opposite seems to be the case. The conservative and right-wing politicians of the 1980s (and beyond) strove to conserve and strengthen the structures of economic imbalance and white supremacy already in place. As I see it, "trickle-down," supply-side Reaganomics meant that the unequal distribution of wealth already in place became even more entrenched. Corporate profits and CEO salaries soared, while workers' incomes remained stagnant and unemployment rose to 10 percent. Labor unions, which historically helped to protect workers' wages and labor conditions, were significantly weakened in this era, starting with Reagan's uncompromising treatment of the air traffic controllers' union (the Professional Air Traffic Controllers Organization) when they held a strike in 1981. Rather than negotiating with the union, Reagan fired the 11,000 government workers who refused to return to work. Industry deregulations followed, with workers' rights and protections curtailed.

The "War on Drugs," which seemingly justified police brutality, brought on a new Jim Crow effect, and not just for dogs; this was the era in which the phrases "racial profiling" and "driving while black" emerged. Simultaneously, policing became increasingly "militarized" to fight this "war." Peter B. Kraska has shown that the period from 1980 to 2000 saw a striking increase in paramilitary policing, which includes police forces' acquiring military weapons technology and using SWAT teams to perform pro-active military-style raids. The number of police paramilitary deployments during the drug war of the late 1980s and early 1990s increased by 1400 percent.[52] Kraska notes an equivalent growth in the ideology, within police culture, of militarism, "a set of beliefs, values, and assumptions that stress the use of force and threat of violence as the most appropriate and efficacious means to solve problems."[53] A "military special operations culture" developed, "characterized by a distinct techno-warrior garb, heavy weaponry, sophisticated technology, hypermasculinity, and dangerous function."[54] Increasingly, police performed "'street sweeps' in high-crime neighborhoods" and "deployed their teams to do routine patrol work in crime 'hot spots.'"[55] This culture of a militarized, hypermasculine, offensive police force makes Pit Bulls and even dogfighting culture look like a weak after-image. Abroad, the Reagan administration armed anti-communist groups (such as the Contras) to overthrow democratically elected governments in Central and South America. This illegal activity sent a message back home that resistance would be met with violence. Again, who were the real Pit Bulls?

It's no wonder that the sense of optimism and hope for the future among African Americans of the 1960s and 1970s gave way to the hopelessness and "nihilism" of the 1980s. When Cornel West lamented that "post-modern culture is more and more a market culture dominated by gangster mentalities and self-destructive wantonness," he was talking as much about Wall Street as he was about inner-city 'hoods.[56]

When it comes to attacks on the most vulnerable of society, those perpetrated by Pit Bulls are easy to see. There is—or seems to be—a clear bully to blame. Systemic forces baked into the economic and psychosocial structure are much harder to see, and the source of the attack, or even the attack itself, is rarely singular or identifiable. Even so, some of the bullies of the 1980s can be identified. Some of them even bore the epithet of "Pit Bull" proudly, even as they condemned and disempowered the Pit Bull demographic of stereotype. While Pit Bulls became the public face of menace to society's most vulnerable, and while dog fighting among poor rural southerners and inner-city dwellers was condemned, politicians fought viciously in the political ring to cheering crowds while touting policies that would maul the working and even middle classes far more thoroughly than any dog could. In fact, I see the Pit Bull moniker as their "tell," tipping us off to their attempts to prestidigitate our attention away from who the real bullies are, who actually gets mauled, and why a scapegoat is so badly needed.

Coda: The Pit Bull Comes Home

Two things that happened as I was writing this chapter. First, an encounter in the dog park.

The two dogs pulled on either end of the rope. Growl-like sounds leaked from their clamped jaws, as is common when dogs play tug, but their tails were wagging, putting the growls in air quotes. This game went on for a good ten minutes, while we humans in the dog park talked and laughed at the two pups. Susie, a Boston Terrier/Beagle/whatever mix, white with brown Holstein spots, was a dog park regular. Penny, an adolescent black Pit Bull, was a newcomer. They happily pulled and vocalized.

Then with no warning the pittie erupted into a chaos of nails and teeth and frothing saliva as she attacked Susie, who fought back, equally seething. Stupidly, without thinking, I stuck my hand into the mess of snarls and fangs to break up the dogs—and felt teeth sink into my left hand, as other human arms pulled the combatants apart.

The punctures were deep enough to ooze blood from both sides of my hand, and the laceration between my pinky and (ring-less) ring finger probably could have used a stitch or two, but the bite was mild, all things considered (though serious enough, I hope, to have taught my instincts a lesson about how not to break up dog fights).

I don't know which dog bit me, but I'm pretty sure it was Susie, partly because I imagine that if it were the Pit Bull, my hand would be in much worse shape. That's me stereotyping, a practice I would normally condemn.

The bite brings out deeper stereotypes. I instinctively blame the Pit Bull for starting the fight. I've seen Pit Bulls turn without warning (a phenomenon sometimes referred to as the "Jekyll-Hyde syndrome"). They'll be playful and happy one moment, and then suddenly flip into attack mode, just as Penny did while playing tug with Susie. Of course, other dogs do that too, but pits seem to do it more often and with less cause or warning. Or so I sometimes believe. Still, I do wonder if some unacknowledged prejudice I don't want to see is skewing my dog park observations.

I do know that shelters are flooded disproportionately with Pit Bull type dogs, and will often label ambiguous pit mixes as Lab or Boxer mixes to avoid stigma and breed-specific laws. It's well known, too, that shelters disproportionately collect black dogs, who are harder to place than their lighter-furred counterparts. The homeless of the dog population mirror, demographically, the homeless of the human population.

I myself have adopted two black dogs from shelters, but I've never owned a Pit Bull. I don't want to be a breedist any more than I want to be a racist. I want to stand right there along with the righteous pit defenders, whose rhetoric of equality I find so compelling. However, pits and pit mixes give me pause. I've tried to justify my breedism: it's not that pits are any more vicious than other dogs, I say, it's just that when they do bite, their bites are more likely to do severe, even fatal, damage. Those powerful jaws were bred over centuries to lock and tear. It's not their fault; they can't help the power of their jaws. (In other words, it's not prejudice, it's just fact, I want to say.) On the other hand, dog bite statistics are unreliable, argue Pit Bull defenders, because pit attacks are far more likely to be reported than, say, Chihuahua bites. I, myself, didn't report being bitten by Susie, the Boston Terrier/Beagle cross. Had the pittie bitten me, would I have gone to a medical care provider, who would have had to report it?

The stereotype of Pit Bulls runs far deeper in American culture than the gash in my hand.

Later in the day that Susie bit my hand, I graded essays from my creative nonfiction class. Opening one paper, I caught the words "Where was my nose?" next to "Pit Bull" and "paramedics." I remembered my student's face: very pretty, but with light a scar running down it, forehead to mouth. I read, riveted. "Where is my nose?" sounds like a bad joke waiting for a punch line, the student wrote in her essay, but it was what she thought when the paramedics arrived after the Pit Bull attacked her, tearing at her face. They had to carry her nose on ice to the hospital. Not only had the Pit Bull ripped her nose off her face, he also ripped open an eyelid and gashed her forehead skin to the bone. A plastic surgeon sewed the nose back on; it's now half the size it once was. The student is still terrified of dogs, still having flashbacks, still suffering from PTSD.

My student said that she could not identify any triggers for the incident. She'd been in bed, and rolled over to reach for her book on the floor. Her hand touched her housemate's dog, sleeping in a curl, before finding the book. That touch was not what did it. The dog stirred, roused, looked up, caught my student's eye, stared hard for two seconds, and then sprang at her face. (Maybe the dog interpreted the two-second stare as a challenge. But who doesn't instinctively look back at a dog staring at them?)

By the time I'd gotten to this essay in my pile of grading, my hand had already begun throbbing. Every movement of a finger produced lines of pain. I couldn't grip anything. It was miserable—and this was just a mild puncture wound. I couldn't even imagine my student's pain, the agony. Her eyelid had to be stitched back together.

In my student's case, as in my dog park experience, all humans involved, including the pit owners, were white and female, so we could believe that we weren't playing out a racial drama, on top of everything else.

I have to confess, though, that even as I saw my student as the protagonist and victim in the essay, even as I empathized with her pain, even as my own hand throbbed, I couldn't help wondering what happened to the dog. My student's essay never said, but most likely the Pit Bull was "put down." I'm probably the only reader of her essay who would wonder about the pittie's fate, and of course I didn't say anything about this (non-)absence in my comments to the student, which would have been inappropriate in about ten different ways. Still, the question lingers: what about the dog?

I'm not implying that the attacking Pit Bull shouldn't be euthanized. I understand that dogs who've attacked once are more likely to attack again and can't be trusted. But what does it mean that the dog bred in part for the protection of an underclass, one that can't always count on police protection, is the dog breed who is routinely scapegoated, deemed expendable, and sacrificed?

So while I want to champion the Pit Bull as a misunderstood underdog, I end up as ambivalent as American culture. If Pit Bulls serve as a small-scale and covert discourse on race and power in America, and if my own role as player in this racial drama is representative, things don't bode well. It's only as I reach the end of this chapter, in which I have attempted to figure out where I stand with Pit Bulls and breedism—but also, subconsciously, I suspect, have attempted to assure myself that it's not racism underlying my suspicions of Pit Bulls—that I recognize a fundamental irony: although it was the non–Pit Bull who bit me, it's the Pit Bull I've been implicitly blaming. It's the Pit Bull I keep blaming as my gash, inadequately tended, keeps re-opening.

Chapter Five

A Dog for All Seasons
Labrador Retrievers in the 1990s

In 1997, then-president Bill Clinton brought a three-month-old chocolate lab to the White House and named him Buddy. This was in the midst of the Paula Jones sexual harassment charges and just before the Monica Lewinsky scandal went public. We can't know if his getting a dog was a political tactic, or if Clinton was merely feeling the dog urges I did when I got my first dog, Pretzel, in that same year. Cynics saw Clinton as making a Checkers move, a la Nixon's strategy with his Cocker Spaniel. Perhaps it wasn't a tactic; I know that if I were in Clinton's position, I'd need a dog at my side.

If it was a tactical diversion, though, Clinton proved once again his ability to read the pulse of American culture. Whether calculated or not, Buddy was a savvy choice. Labrador Retrievers were to the 1990s what Cockers were to the 1950s. What better way to both distract attention from an impending impeachment hearing and reaffirm "family values" than with America's number one family dog? Who could be so cold as to look at a chocolate Lab puppy and not melt, at least a little? And in a time of "culture wars," what better breed to appeal to culture warriors on both sides of the aisle than a Labrador Retriever? The Lab offered an all-purpose, all-American dog for all identities to celebrate.

It's no accident that the Lab is, as I mentioned in the last chapter, the breed most commonly invoked when people try to pass their Pit Bulls off as something else. While Pit Bulls bear the (inaccurate) reputation of antisocial aggressors, Labs conjure up the opposite. In contrast to the Pit Bull's monstrous jaws, the Lab offered a "soft mouth" (bred for retrieving game without puncturing the bodies). The Barron's *Labrador Retriever Handbook* of 2001 offers a retrospective and representative 1990s view on Labs: "Labs personify what we love most about dogs: they are loyal and gentle, playful and hard working. When it comes to dog breeds, they are the cream of the crop."[1] The Lab's reputation is almost

Chapter Five. A Dog for All Seasons

President Clinton being greeted by Buddy as he arrives at the White House 12 August 1998 in Washington (TIM SLOAN/AFP via Getty Images).

the opposite of the Pit Bull's rap. Labs tend not to make good guard dogs for the same reasons they make great buddies.

There's also a very subtle but palpable way in which Labs connote whiteness without having to say so. This is particularly true of yellow Labs, who, like Golden Retrievers, can, in Meisha Rosenberg's words, "simultaneously display and hide" whiteness "through symbolic absorption."[2] Rosenberg points to advertisements like the Cottonelle commercials, which show a soft little yellow (really whitish) Lab puppy frolicking among soft white toilet paper. The puppy, the softness, and the whiteness all go together and reinforce each other metonymically. Such images are now ubiquitous. "In a culture where explicit racial images and language are taboo," Rosenberg writes, "Golden Retrievers and yellow Labs can safely transmit assumptions about whiteness."[3] Chocolate Labs like Clinton's may be a little less white, but they still connote the opposite of a Pit Bull.

The Labrador Retriever reached the top of the AKC rankings for dog popularity in the United States in 1991 and has remained there ever since. Although it's also a favorite breed in Canada, the U.K., and elsewhere, to many Americans the Lab connotes American-ness at least as much as does the eagle. By the time Clinton brought his Lab puppy to the White House, the breed already served as one of the country's unofficial mascots. Although this all-American dog actually arose in Canada, it did develop on North American shores. At first it served as a supremely practical dog, a sturdy, all-weather swimmer and all-terrain hunter that could retrieve game with a "soft mouth" (that is, without biting into the flesh). By the 1990s, though, this dog was also a buddy, a friend, a companion, even a family member. Above all, the breed represented loving faithfulness, a trait Clinton desperately needed to ally himself with.

Bill Clinton didn't just get the breed right; he also got the name right. Buddy was named after a (human) great-uncle who had recently died. The very fact that a dog received the same name as a human, and in his honor, speaks volumes about changes in the status of dogs in America. The name Buddy also captured dogs' new status as buddies and as kin. Perhaps more than any other breed, the Lab of the 1990s epitomized the promotion of dogs to the status of family members and citizens. Labs, with their adaptability, easy-going temperament, and easy maintenance, made particularly good family members to (otherwise) human families, so it makes good sense that Labs became popular in the era when dogs became family.

Though some Americans had referred to their dogs as family members long before the 1990s, this status still troubled the majority until well into the twentieth century. The 1990s normalized pets' roles as family members. In fact, our biggest pet store chain, PetSmart, which was founded in 1986 as PETsMART and went public on the NASDAQ in 1993, bore the motto "Where Pets Are Family."

But what is a family? That's a radically contested term in the 1990s, and one played out through our dogs as dogs became family members. This contest over the meaning of family is one version of the decade's "culture wars."

The Family of Culture Wars

Finding a dog breed—or anything else—that could appeal to multiple constituencies in the 1990s was quite a feat. Not just any dog would have done. By the time Clinton brought little Buddy to the White House in 1997, the "culture wars" were already unleashed. The term "culture wars" was introduced by James Davison Hunter in his 1991 book *Culture Wars: The Struggle to Define America*, in which he argued that the country was polarizing, and doing so not just over religious or political issues—a kind of polarization the country had long known—but over our entire moral system. What might have seemed to be disagreements about individual issues—including sexuality, abortion, gun politics, affirmative action, religion in the state, and bioethics—could better be understood in terms of two fundamentally different worldviews. We were forming two ways of seeing the world, which fundamentally disagreed about basics: about the nature of human nature; about whose "human nature" counted as universal; about the fixity of truth and the separability of "reality" from the structures through which we represent reality; and about what "American culture" actually meant. These polarized debates sometimes got phrased in terms of "orthodox" vs. "progressive," "conservative" vs. "liberal," "universalism" vs. "particularism," "foundationalism" vs. "relativism," and "the melting pot" vs. "multiculturalism." Some critics at the time argued back that we were not as polarized as the media or "cultural elites" made it seem, that the beliefs of actual people tended fall closer to the middle of the spectrum rather than at the poles, and that Hunter's binary model over-simplified our socio-political alignments. Writing nearly three decades later, however, I believe that the "culture wars" have only become more deeply entrenched.

In 1992 Patrick Buchanan took up Hunter's phrase in his speech at the Republican convention. He argued that the presidential election pitting George H.W. Bush against Bill Clinton was not merely about policies or material things. It was "about much more than who gets what"; rather, it was "about who we are" and "what we believe" and "what we stand for as Americans." Indeed, it was a "struggle for the soul of America."[4] In a speech a month later, Buchanan affirmed that "we Americans are locked in a cultural war for the soul of our country," a war over "[w]ho decides what is right and wrong, moral and immoral, beautiful and ugly, healthy and sick" and "[w]hose beliefs shall form the basis of law." Buchanan rather reductively characterized the side of "the secularists" as having substituted, for the Bible,

> a New Age Gospel, with its governing axioms: There are no absolute values in the universe; there are no fixed and objective standards of right and wrong. There is no God. It all begins here and it ends here. Every man lives by his own moral code. Do your own thing.[5]

Implicitly, Buchanan simultaneously characterizes his own side quite reductively as believing in an absolute God with a clear, fixed, and unchanging morality and a binary understanding of right and wrong. While few people in 1992 would have placed their lived beliefs on either side of these two poles or in these stark terms, Buchanan's characterization of a polarized culture war seems, in retrospect, rather prophetic, if not a self-fulfilling prophecy. In describing this culture war, Buchanan also fomented it.

Other thinkers and commentators noted related forms of radical polarization. It wasn't just a matter of different views on issues or even different religious beliefs but a matter of *identity*, both on the part of the individual and on the part of culture.

In 1996 linguist George Lakoff, in his book *Moral Politics*, put the matter in terms of "frames." He later made this scholarly book more accessible to a non-academic readership in 2004 in his book *Don't Think of an Elephant!: Know Your Values and Frame the Debate*. Looking back at the politics of the previous decade, he argued that although many of the issues of the culture wars—abortion, guns, the environment, same-sex marriage—don't inherently align, their existence as a package deal follows distinct underlying worldviews, including moral systems. Not only do those worldviews inform our expectations for how both a nation and a family should be run, but we actually use our concept of family as a metaphor for the nation. So, to make sense of American politics, we needed to identify their underlying models of family. Lakoff sees, in the 1990s, two distinct understandings of family: "a strict father family" and "a nurturant parent family."[6] I probably don't need to spell out that the "strict father family" corresponds to Hunter's orthodox moral system and the "nurturant parent family" corresponds to the progressive moral system. Ultimately, I'll argue, these conflicting family models affect the ways we experience dogs as family members.

The "strict father family," according to Lakoff, corresponds to a worldview in which competition reigns: "There will always be winners and losers." The moral poles of good and evil are unambiguous and absolute. Children are born bad and have to be made good.[7] This means that children need to be disciplined, often through punishment, in order to learn right from wrong. This model is based on a sense of hierarchy, with a (male) father figure at the top. (Lakoff doesn't address nonhumans, but I would submit that the strict father family model puts humans at the top of the hierarchy of earthly beings; on the Great Chain of Being, men sit just under God.) Parents and children are not equals or friends; their relationship is structured by hierarchy. As are the genders; the strict father family model tends to be a male-centered worldview, one that favors traditionally "masculine" ways of being. This strict father family model has bearing on the place of dogs in the family and the way we should discipline them.

The "nurturant parent model," by contrast, is "gender neutral."[8] In this model, "children are born good and can be made better" and the "the parents' job is to nurture their children and to raise their children to be nurturers of others."[9] The nurturing family model values empathy and responsibility, and structures itself on equality and mutuality rather than hierarchy. This kind of family values trust, honesty, and "open, two-way communication" between parent and child.[10] Again, this nurturant family model has bearing on the place of dogs in the family and how we raise them.

Lakoff's notion of framing describes not just a set of distinct beliefs, but a belief-feedback-loop or network of reinforcing narratives. So the clashing cultures are not just a matter of political differences, but a matter of identity. Lakoff recognizes that few people live their actual lives on either pole, that some people adopt the strict father frame in some aspects of their lives but the nurturing parent frame in others, and that at any rate people operating in one frame have some understanding of the other frame even if they reject it. Still, these frames have a tremendous force in structuring our realities. So much so that they take precedence over facts: "The strict father and nurturing parent frames each force a certain logic. To be accepted, the truth must fit people's frames. If the facts do not fit a frame, the frame stays and the facts bounce off."[11] That's why facts don't speak for themselves. Put another way, a frame is a cultural mythology of the kind that Barthes analyzes in *Mythologies*. The facts speak only through frames or mythologies.

There were "breedologies" to match. Different types and breeds of dogs exemplified—and seemed to confirm—different cultural identities (or frames or mythologies), as I've been arguing throughout this book. The Lab, with its versatility, could fit into opposing mythologies. The different models of family correspond to different beliefs about how humans should relate to dogs. So it will be no surprise to see these competing models of family show up in dog training. The orthodox or conservative frame embraced hierarchy, whereas the progressive or liberal frame embraced mutuality.

Labrador Retrievers in the Strict Father Family

The history of the breed, as recounted in the nineteenth edition of the AKC's *The Complete Dog Book* from the 1990s, lends itself well to the conservative side of the culture war, for whom the breed represented a certain kind of orthodox American patriotism. The breed began on North American shores in the nineteenth century, not in Labrador but in Newfoundland, as water dogs. A traveler quoted in *The Complete Dog Book* said in 1822 that the dogs were "admirably trained as retrievers in fowling, and are otherwise useful."[12] Soon afterward, these American dogs, also called St. John's dogs, caught the eye of the Earl of Malmesbury, who had some imported to England. There they were interbred with other retrievers until the late nineteenth century and early into the twentieth century, when fanciers established this type of retriever as a distinct breed. The breed was recognized by the English Kennel Club in 1903 and the American Kennel Club in 1917.[13]

These were hearty, rough-and-tumble, all-around useful gun and water dogs, used for hunting and outdoor sporting. Consummate workers, their name may actually arise from a Spanish word for "worker" rather than referring to a geographical site in Canada. Their origins associate them with traditionally masculine activities, with guns and hunting, and with North American/Anglo-Saxon lineage. This fits nicely into the "strict father" or conservative model of American politics in the 1990s. What's more, as a breed created to serve humans in hunting, Labs nicely respected their roles in both the father/child and human/nonhuman hierarchies. The conservative view takes as a given that humans are superior to nonhumans. Labs, with their high trainability and generally eager-to-please personalities, could seem to confirm human superiority, at least for the humans who wanted their superiority confirmed. Labs' faithfulness to their master could be understood as confirming the patriarchal order. Even as they became family dogs, they could seem to affirm the strict-farther, traditional model of the American family.

Chapter Five. A Dog for All Seasons

Breed guidebooks from this decade often invoke this framing mythology. Here I'll offer *Labrador Retrievers: A Complete Pet Owners Manual*, written by Kerry V. Kern as part of the Barron's Educational Series as one representative, though not necessarily authoritative or definitive, case. Indeed, in this 1995 manual's account, dogs' very origins mesh with a strict father, leader-of-the-pack family model:

> The dog has succeeded in becoming our most treasured companion due to its adaptability. In the earliest times, the dog's ancestors—wolves, jackals, coyotes—learned to group together for survival, for hunting was easier in this manner. They developed pack behavior, whereby one animal assumed the leadership position and others fell in line behind, each working out its own niche in the line of power. This hierarchy is still found today in domesticated dogs.[14]

We already saw this model of dog origins in Chapter Three. It offers a now-residual belief that the dog's first role with humans was as hunter. This origin story aligns with the training method of the conservative, strict-father family. According to this model, a "successful owner must be a consistent, guiding force in the dog's life—the undisputed leader, the 'alpha.'"[15] This approach, in turn, was consistent with using a "choke" collar—a metal chain to which the owner can apply "a light snap upwards" to make a correction; the dog quickly learns that "the upward tug and the resultant tightening signify displeasure."[16] The emergent dog mythologies of the nurturant family model would offer a different origin story and a different approach to dog training.

The Barron's manual emphasizes the Lab "was unknown as a companion dog for many generations, as Labradors were bred exclusively for work," in particular as fishing dogs first and then as gun dogs.[17] They were bred for their ability to retrieve game in water and in the field, which meant soft mouths, steady temperaments (allowing them to work hard all day but also to be able to wait), athleticism, a lack of territoriality, a great sense of smell, intelligence and trainability, and loyalty with a touch of independence. Even while "gaining a foothold in the American home as a companion pet, the Labrador Retriever was still thriving as a true sporting dog and being bred primarily by knowledgeable owners."[18] The origin of the breed was seen, in this model, as so central to what it is today that to truly understand a Lab you need to acknowledge and respect the dog's hunting and retrieving origins. It retains an American heritage mythology of frontiersmen and pioneer.

The breed still maintains its identity as a hunting dog and an implicitly masculine dog (unlike, say, a Shih Tzu or a Pomeranian, or even a Saluki). Even people who don't themselves hunt might identify with the huntsman's identity, and might see themselves reflected in this gun dog. A strong, hard-working, human-serving breed such as the Labrador Retriever, unafraid of gunshots or cold or rugged terrain, made an apt mascot in the 1990s for the conservative-leaning frame of American culture.

But the Lab could also find fit with a very different family mythology or frame, one embodied to some degree by the Clintons. Since this progressive frame was the emergent one of the 1990s, whereas the conservative frame was already well established, I'll spend the bulk of the chapter on this Clintonian model of dog as family member.

Labrador Retrievers in the Nurturant Parent Family

At the time when he brought an iconically all-American dog into the White House, Bill Clinton's nuclear family, too, was representative of demographic changes in the United States, or at least in the prototypical white, middle-class family. The First Family of three humans, one dog (Buddy), and one cat (Socks), represented the increasing percentage of non-humans in the new trans-species family. The diminishing number of humans in the family coincides with the expanded role of animals within the family, and it can't be mere coincidence that the "family dog" became a true family member at time the American family was reducing its load of human offspring.

I formed one of those families. I got my first dog, Pretzel, in 1997, when I was living in a long-distance relationship with my life-partner. As a childless woman living in a single-human household with one dog and two cats, I formed a more exaggerated version than the Clintons did of the new trans-species family. And the role my new dog filled was, like Buddy's, far from that of hunter of yore.

Perhaps the most famous family dog from the 1990s was Marley, whose owner—or guardian—wrote about him in the South Florida *Sun Sentinel*. John Grogan characterized his dog as a goofy, unruly, but loveable family member. Marley, a yellow Lab, was not the disciplined gun dog of the breed's origins, but an undisciplined companion. When Grogan eulogized Marley in a 2004 column for *The Philadelphia Inquirer*, the volume of emails in response to this column far exceeded that of any other column, and inspired him to send out a book proposal on his life with Marley. The eulogy and its resulting book, *Marley and Me: Life and Love with the World's Worst Dog*, became such a phenomenon, I believe, because it appeared at a moment in American culture when the kind of trans-species relationship embodied by that particular Lab and that particular human—by Marley and Me—was widespread but still undervalued. It recognized the dog's role as family member right when it was begging for recognition. Although the book was published in 2005, it covers the 1990s, the decade of Grogan's thirteen years with his Lab. This book became a runaway best-seller, so ubiquitous that when many Americans hear *Labrador Retriever* the image that immediately arises is the book cover's adorable yellow Lab with his head slightly cocked, almost inquisitively, as he sits atop muddy paws and looks, with suspicious innocence, at the viewer.

Currently the AKC's website summarizes Labs as "friendly, outgoing, and high-spirited companions who have more than enough affection to go around for a family looking for a medium-to-large dog."[19] It's worth noting that these once-working dogs are now characterized, first and foremost, more by emotions and personality traits than by function. Compare that with the Siberian Husky, which the AKC website summarizes as "a thickly coated, compact sled dog of medium size and great endurance, [who] was developed to work in packs, pulling light loads at moderate speeds over vast frozen expanses. Sibes are friendly, fastidious, and dignified."[20] (I have never met a Lab I could honestly call "fastidious.") While Huskies are defined first by function, Labs' primary trait is their friendly personality.

Having "more than enough affection to go around" fits well with the needs of the nurturant family. So it makes sense that Labs rose to #1 in popularity at a time when dogs became family members. At the same time, dogs became increasingly urbanized (or suburbanized), brought into city rather than rural settings, and were subject to increasing leash laws. Unable to roam off-leash, as their fictional predecessors Spot, Lady, Tramp, and Snoopy regularly did, these dogs became all the more confined to the household as they became members of the family.

Making dogs true members of the nurturant nuclear family in relationships of equality and mutuality sometimes took the form of making dogs honorary humans. We turned the dog into what David Grimm, in his book of the same title, called "Citizen Canine." (Anecdotally, it seems to me that this was the period in which dogs were increasingly named with the same names as humans: Sasha, Buddy, and Marley overtook Spot, Butch, and Rover.) This humanization of dogs often failed, though. And so, by the 1990s, we began to learn to respect their canine differences from us, and to adapt to the needs of the other species in the trans-species household. This meant changes in how we cared for and trained our dogs, and resulted in the great irony that the more we make dogs members of hearth and home (and, in that sense, humanized), the more we need to respect their species-specific needs. This led to contradictions still with us today: we both treat the dog as an honorary human and try to respect the dogness of the dog.

When Pets Are Family

We see this contradiction in the pet retail business. Much of the pet retail business in the 1990s was geared toward helping the dog live in the house as family member. As we'll see in Chapter Seven, by the 2010s dogs will have become thoroughly integrated into the economy as both consumers and objects of consumption. Two decades earlier, this transition was still in process. Already, though, the dog market was seeing major transformations.

Take PetSmart as an example. From its start, the quickly growing mega-chain realized that it was far more lucrative to sell goods to dogs (i.e., dog owners) than to sell dogs. Not only does PetSmart not sell dogs, it supports and hosts adoptions through its charity arm. A rescue dog may cost under $100, but a lifetime of dog food and supplies can come to thousands if not tens of thousands of dollars. Indeed, it's common for first-time dog adopters to spend more money on their first trip to PetSmart for collar and leash, dog bowl, kibble, chew toys, maybe a crate, and perhaps training pads, than for the dog himself.

The pet store item that to me most represents attempts to integrate the dog into the human household is the Kong, so it's no surprise to me that it was one of the top-selling dog toys of the 1990s. That iconic red rubber toy, shaped like an ear-stopper for the giant gorilla of legend, testifies to dogs' need to chew, and chew heartily. Originally designed in the 1970s for a rock-chewing German Shepherd named Fritz by Joe Markham, owner of a motorcycle repair center, the Kong has become the go-to toy for orally fixated dogs (which Labs tend to be).[21] Sales really began to take off in the mid–1990s, and have only grown since then. These hollow toys, meant to withstand the toughest of maulings, can be filled with treats to keep dogs chewing. Their large size meets the needs of larger-sized dogs, like Labs, confined in the home. Although a dog probably can't see red as anything other than dark, the Kong serves the purpose of providing a tough chewing texture. It's a no-nonsense chew toy, without the "cute" factor designed to attract the corresponding humans, as you'll find in abundance today. The Kong was designed to appeal to the dog, not the human. The Kong respects the dog's point of view—the dogness of the dog—in an era when dogs are becoming fully-fledged family members. (More recently, the company has

Chapter Five. A Dog for All Seasons 123

branched out into other shapes [balls, tires, tuggers with grips], sizes, and colors [baby blue and pink Kongs for puppies], and even into plush toys [turtles, octopuses, starfish, hedgehogs, rhinos, elephants, and beavers], but the bulk of the Kong toys are still targeted and readable to the dog as their primary audience.)

While these toys seem to respect the dogness of the dog, though, they're still a substitute, a displacement for a dog's true instinct. They accommodate the anxiety of dogs confined to the house or yard all day, rather than changing the conditions of boredom that cause that anxiety. Wolves in the wild, or even dogs who hunt or herd all day long, don't need Kongs. (Who's to say, though, that a wolf in the wild wouldn't mind settling down to a good Kong chew session of an evening?) Much of the pet retail business in the 1990s was, like the Kong, devised to help the dog live in the house as family member. Items such as dog beds, nail clippers, doggie toothpaste and finger brushes, and carpet deodorizer are all geared toward accommodating a dog and his household to indoor living.

Beyond physical goods, PetSmart (and other pet retailers) began to offer pet "hotels" (upscale kennels, allowing families to travel without guilt) and doggie "daycare" and "day camp." I sometimes brought my first round of dogs—Pretzel, Chappy, and Houdini—to day camp on days I worked late; PetSmart stayed open until 9 p.m. I especially made use of day camp with my next round of dogs, when I added a high-energy Border Collie and then a Husky cross to the mix. Day camp allowed hard-core working dogs to live as pets.

And if their freedom of movement was increasingly restricted due to increasing leash laws, off-leash dog parks began popping up to give dogs a separate space to be dogs. Pretty soon, dog people like me were bringing their dogs on daily trips to the park, spending more time there than a human might with her (human) child at a playground. In fact I made my own community of dog people there, with whom I frequently learned dog training tips and exchanged tales of the ongoing war between vacuum cleaners and shedding Huskies.

Beyond basic needs of nutrition and health care, PetSmart-like retailers moved into the realm of socialization and dog training classes, so that dogs could be good citizens in their (human) society. Beginners classes taught dogs to sit and stay, so they wouldn't lunge on walks or run into busy streets. More advanced classes taught even more behavioral refinement, culminating in the AKC's "Canine Good Citizen Test." This test, which started in 1989, certifies the pairing of a responsible owner with a well-mannered dog, recognizing that "dogs with basic obedience training are a joy to live with—interacting well with other people and dogs and responding well to household routines."[22] Passage of the CGC test is also a prerequisite to therapy dog training.

The very title of this test attests to the new status of dogs as potential citizens in human societies. Some dogs were even, slowly, given some of the rights of citizens—along with the responsibilities. Even non-citizen pets were increasingly seen as animals in captivity who deserved better. (I've also wondered if my dogs experience my house, with its restricting walls, as just an extra-large cage.) Indeed, beyond deserving better, they had a right to a better life, one full of intellectual stimulation and emotional enrichment. The 1990s saw the extension of some "basic human rights" to some pets—and to the shift from "pets" to "companion animals." Humans, correspondingly, shifted from "owners" to "guardians." The shift is not merely a semantic, "politically correct" one. It signals tectonic shifts in humans' relationships with their closest nonhumans, who now approached the status of under-age and dependent family members. One no longer needed to be a human to have "personhood," including subjectivity or cognitive and emotional agency.

One way to put this new animal philosophy into practice for dogs was through clicker training. Indeed the whole approach to dog training shifted to accommodate dogs' personhood.

Clicking with Dogs

One day when I was weeding my rose garden, my head jerked up reflexively at the sound of a click—a sound I knew but couldn't quite place. I was still trying to identify it when I heard it again. I stood up. The third time I heard it I started moving toward it, almost as if it had cued me to "come." By then, I recognized what it was: the clicker I'd used in training my dogs Olive and Tiger. Sure enough, the neighbor two houses down was training her new puppy in the driveway. "Watch me," she said, and when the gangly puppy looked at her she clicked and treated. Even without getting a treat, I got my own little shot of happiness at each click. It was fun to watch the little guy working it out. At first, he looked up at the tall lady's face by chance, maybe when he hit the end of the leash and turned his head to see why he couldn't go farther. Quickly, though—you could almost spot the moment—he figured out that the looking led to a click, which eventually led to a treat. Suddenly looking at the woman was far more fun than attending to the smells around him or pulling her forward. He couldn't get enough of her face.

Walk into any dog-training facility today and chances are good

Chapter Five. A Dog for All Seasons 125

you'll hear these clicking crickets. They've been chirping since the 1990s.

Clicker training was introduced to dog obedience in the United States (and beyond) by Karen Pryor, who first developed the approach in her work with dolphins in the 1960s. Her 1984 book *Don't Shoot the Dog* began spreading the word of this approach to dog training, and by the 1990s the approach had become wildly popular. In her 2009 book *Reaching the Animal Mind: Clicker Training and What It Teaches Us About All Animals*, which overviews her development of clicker training, Pryor claims that the approach can work with all animals, including humans. She herself has used it on everything from dolphins, dogs, and horses to hermit crabs to (human) gymnasts and sailors.

Based in the ethology of Konrad Lorenz and the behaviorism of B.F. Skinner, Pryor's method combines classical conditioning with operant conditioning. *Classical conditioning*, the "association of an unconscious physical or physiological response with a conditioned stimulus," offers its most famous example in Pavlov's dog drooling (unconscious response) at the sound of a bell (conditioned stimulus). Classical conditioning generally works unconsciously. *Operant conditioning*, the "reinforcement of conscious behavior deliberately offered by the learner" (whom Skinner called the *operant*), happens when, say, a dog *chooses* to sit because sitting leads to a treat. Operant conditioning usually happens on the conscious level.[23] To her combination of classical and operant conditioning, Pryor introduced a secondary reinforcer—the clicker—which gets linked to the treat, so when the dog hears the click he associates it with an ensuing treat.

Clicker training is now offered throughout the United States in mega-stores such as PetSmart (where two of my five dogs and I got our training) as well as in smaller kennel clubs and clinics throughout the country. Although I refer to the chain throughout this book by its current name, PetSmart, its orthography changed in 2005 from PETsMART to PetSmart, subtly changing its connotations from a marketplace (or mart) where you can shop for your pet to a place where pet's smarts are recognized. This name change reflects how attitudes to pets changed over the previous couple of decades.

I received my first clicker at the start of my beginner's class at PetSmart, when I took my troubled Border Collie mix, Olive, in for training. Soon after adopting her, I realized I was in over my head. Olive, whose previous life was spent tied to a tree all day in the backyard of a dog hoarder, had behavioral problems far beyond my ability to manage: incessant barking, resource protectiveness, and leash aggression, for starters. I was desperate—so desperate that I was tempted to resort to a shock collar, even though I'm pretty much the stereotype of the "nurturant family" person.

The clicker is a small plastic rectangle, just bigger than a thumb drive, with a metal press that, when pushed, makes a clicking sound. Mine fit comfortably in the palm of my hand, where I could rest my thumb over it, ready and waiting to capture good behavior, should Olive happen accidentally to offer any.

"Load up your clickers," Beki told us. It was our most important homework for the first week. The young daughter of one of my classmates looked at both ends of the clicker. "How do you get the treats in?"

We all smiled, though at least one of us wondered the same thing. To "load" a clicker, Beki explained, is to cement your dog's association of the clicker with a treat. That turned out to be the easiest part of dog training. Back home, I clicked with my left hand and gave Olive a treat from my right hand. When I clicked a second time, Olive looked immediately to my right hand, which then opened and dispensed a treat. I took Olive into a different room, because "dogs don't generalize." I clicked with the left hand and she looked to the right, which again dispensed another treat. Then I switched it up and clicked with the right hand. Olive looked at the right hand, then dove in for the treat appearing at the left hand. After that, Olive's clicker was loaded. That quickly.

Next, as Beki had instructed, I walked towards Olive and held a treat just above her head. Raising her head to keep looking at the treat, she found herself sitting. I clicked, then gave her another treat. In two tries she got *sit*. *Down* came about as quickly; I brought the treat under her chin, which automatically made her lower herself. I added verbal cues. Soon Olive was throwing herself into downs. I stopped treating every time, but Olive seemed almost as happy with just the click.

Recent studies suggest that the clicker itself might trigger a dopamine rush. What's more, the pleasure of anticipation might exceed the pleasure of the treat. The anticipatory dopamine rush may be its own reward. Whether or not this is true biochemically, it's consistent with what a trainer experiences. In fact, I think I, too, got a dopamine rush at the sound of the clicker, or at least it's become coded into my neural programming as a happy sound. That time when I'd looked up from my rosebushes to the neighbor's clicker, I'd felt that happy anticipation that a dog might feel. It got my attention, got me focused, and got me to move toward her obediently. I, too, became clicker-trained.

(I can't help but wonder, too, if the experience of dog training clicks is akin to the experience of internet clicking. The happy anticipation of clicking is almost always better than the subsequent screen evoked. Maybe that's why clicking can be so addictive. Perhaps in the internet era, humans have become clicker trained by their computers.)

My introductory experience with clicker training was a revelation. I couldn't believe how easy and effective clicker training was, and how fun. I couldn't stop smiling. This would be a piece of cake.

Little did I know that, for one thing, training a Border Collie was almost cheating, and for another, the training would soon get a lot harder. What was true for the dogs, though, was equally true for the humans: it's good to begin on a few wins, to set the operant up for success and then reward and reinforce her for it before upping the ante.

The clicker allows the trainer to capture not only the exact moment the dog offers the desired behavior, but, even better, the exact moment the dog *decides* to offer that behavior. It's the dog's *thinking* that gets acknowledged and rewarded. The trainer attunes herself to the dog's cognition. In her communication with the dog, she's responding to his thoughts even more than to his actions.

The dog as decider is key. This approach stresses the *mutuality* of the training interaction. It's not a relationship of dominance and submission, but of collegiality and comradeship. The approach, says Pryor, "produces real communication between two species."[24] Pryor's approach stresses that the animal being trained is an operator (or operant), an agent, a player. In describing her interactions with Josephine the dolphin, Pryor even uses the term "colleagues"[25]: "In contrast to Pavlov's dogs," the animal in Pryor's operant conditioning "is aware of what it's doing, and offers the behavior deliberately."[26] The animal being trained has *agency*, and that agency is respected. This granting of agency to animals is consistent with other fields of study in the 1990s.

Because the dog offers the behavior through choice rather than coercion, the term *command* becomes inaccurate. In her dolphin training, Pryor replaced *command* with *cue*: "These cues were not orders to be obeyed. The dolphins were perfectly free to not do them. But they wanted to do them. The cue became more than a discriminator, a name, for this behavior or that: it also became a green light, permission to Go! Now!"[27] The difference is not mere semantics. With a cue, the animal has the right to say no without punishment. "In contrast to a command, which is a veiled threat, a cue is a promise: if you understand what I'm saying, and you carry it out correctly, you will definitely win."[28] Clicker training results in a different temperament of dog: "Dogs that are working for cues don't act like dogs that are working for commands. They are merry and enthusiastic rather than somber and cautious."[29] The animal is not ordered to perform but invited to play.

The Clash of Dog Training Mythologies

As it turns out, clicker training is not only more effective than aversive (punishment-based) training, but also kinder (which we sometimes describe, anthropomorphically and humanistically, as "more humane"). This approach nurtures the dog, rather than punishing him, as does the "strict father family" approach to dog training. In other words, clicker training fit nicely with the nurturant family model of the 1990s.

While Pryor, Donaldson, and others pose the kinder, gentler nature of positive reinforcement as merely a fortuitous side-effect of the clicker approach's effectiveness rather than the goal in and of itself, I think its kindness—its "humaneness"—is an important part of the approach's popularity in the 1990s (and into the present). Pryor and Donaldson avoid gender stereotypes, but it's hard not to notice a gendered facet to this discussion. The clicker training approach is based on mutuality, nurturing, kindness, communication, and gentleness—traits that are traditionally considered "feminine" and that Lakoff aligns with the nurturant family frame as opposed to the strict father, patriarchal frame. The approaches that clicker training displaces tend toward conventionally "masculine" traits based in hierarchical relations, dominance and submission, physical punishment, and even aggression. While I don't want to endorse these stereotypes, I do think that gender is a factor playing into the shift in dog training in the 1990s from aversive training to clicker training. This is happening at the same time that the demographic of dog trainers took a decided turn from being male dominated to having much greater female representation. A similar shift was happening in the veterinary world in the 1990s. Causation is tricky, and I don't want to say that one caused the other, but rather that the shifts in gender representation and in approaches to animals—such as the increasing recognition of animal emotions, the growing preference for mutuality over dominance and submission, the granting of agency to animals, and the rejection of punishment (particularly physical punishment) in favor of positive reinforcement—seem all of a piece. If I were more comfortable with gender stereotypes, I might be tempted to say that dog training was "feminized" in the 1990s.

Readers might reasonably object that the "masculine" mode of dog training remained popular in the 1990s—seen, for example, in the Monks of New Skete, who warn against "unnaturally sentimentalizing our relationship with our dogs."[30] and who take the "alpha dog" approach to training that I posed above as the traditional, "strict father family" model of dog training. However, this approach was already declining and residual in the 1990s. Nevertheless, it has also been tenacious. It has made a comeback in the 2000s, with the popularity of Cesar Millan, and

Chapter Five. A Dog for All Seasons 129

such books as *Be the Pack Leader*. As the title of this book suggests, Millan, though writing in the 2000s, draws on a model of wolf societies as rigidly hierarchical, even though this model was already well outmoded in the ethological scholarship. However, Millan is something of an outlier; indeed, other dog trainers go out of their way to note their disagreement with him. Often, he's not named directly, but it's clear from their rejection of the leader-pack model that they mean him. (As I mentioned in the last chapter, there's sometimes a troubling tinge of [subtle] racism in the [polite] rejection of Millan, a Mexican American who aligns himself with Pit Bulls as his trademark breed. Although I find the arguments against the alpha-dog model compelling, I also find Millan a sympathetic figure, particularly in his commitment to rehabilitating dogs considered unredeemable.)

Moreover, recent ethologists and trainers reject the "wolf pack" model on which Millan's approach is based. As I've been arguing in previous chapters, theories of dog evolution often align with an era's dog training approaches as well as with other attitudes to dogs. Earlier eras, as I've discussed in Chapter Three, favored the dog origin model of dogs as recent descendants of wolves, joining the human race as hunting pack partners. Although scientists were already dismantling this model of both wolves and dogs in the 1970s (and even earlier), the dog-as-wolf myth held sway in the popular imagination, which saw today's dogs as stunted wolves, the "wolf in the parlor." The 1990s, however, gave increasing popularity to the Coppinger model of dogs as self-domesticated scavengers. In this model, dogs domesticated themselves by working among humans at waste sites; they joined human societies at the back end of the consumption process rather than at the front end. This latter model aligns with the granting of agency and personhood, if not subjectivity, to dogs in the 1990s. It gives dogs agency in domesticating themselves; dogs chose us humans, and we are linked through mutual dependency rather than master-servant hierarchy.

Indeed, in the 1990s, the model of a dog as a member of a wolf pack with pack mentality was not only thoroughly dismantled, but also doubly dismantled. First, dogs didn't arise directly from today's gray wolf; both arose from a previous, now extinct, ancestor, and the two subspecies branched apart longer ago than previously thought. Second, even if dogs were basically wolves, our model of wolf society has been flawed. The pack model is based on the behavior of wolves in captivity. But ethological studies of wolves, observing them in their natural habitats, suggest a much less rigidly hierarchal society, one in which mutuality is more the norm. In fact, adherents of gender stereotypes might say that our model of wolves was "feminized" in the 1990s, along with our approach to ethology, our dog training practices, and vet school demographics.

I made this shift in microcosm with Olive, moving from a punitive to a positive approach. I went in for training to fix her bad behaviors. As I said, I was desperate. Olive had been lunging at other dogs; I didn't know what else to do. I soon learned that it was a lot easier—and more fun—to teach Olive to do things than to teach her not to do things. Almost as easy as sit and down came an array of silly tricks: beg, spin, rollover, play dead, say your prayers, high five, high five from behind, and a good fifty more. Even "heel" came with some work, and from there I taught her to weave through agility poles. But to get her to stop barking or protecting her food (or her food source, me) proved harder. Eventually, I figured out that I could replace a bad behavior with a good one. If another dog approached her when she was on leash—one of her triggers—I gave her "sit" and "watch me," which she did with great focus until I released her ("All done!") when the other dog was gone. Sitting still around other dogs was a good thing that led to treats.

In short, for me dog training went from a punitive measure to a positive game. I could tell Olive was having fun too. The alacrity with which she threw herself into downs and roll-overs induced smiles every time. Her temperament went from being a nervous, anxious, fearful dog to a more focused, more purpose-driven one. She might even learn what happiness was. (She wouldn't learn how to play, though, until Tiger came into our lives.) There were no miracles; Olive will always be a somewhat troubled, obsessive-compulsive dog (like her human companion). But clicker training made us both a little happier and more able to live with each other. It helped us to communicate with each other better, to teach each other, and to appreciate each other. I no longer threaten every day to return her to the pound. Post-clicker training, that happens only once a month or so.

I also learned that Border Collies don't make good pets or members of human families—they can't adapt well to household living. Olive still can't mellow out or stay calm; she is always, always on alert, as if in constant watch for the stray sheep that needs to be righted. Labs are much better at the role of family member. However (hyper-)active they are, they understand what it means to chill, and while they have an "on" button, they also, eventually, also have an "off" button.

Dog Culture Wars

To some extent, nurturant dog training, such as clicker training, treats dogs and humans as different cultures. Jean Donaldson, in her

Chapter Five. A Dog for All Seasons 131

1996 dog training book *The Culture Clash*, presents a parable of "the Gorns." To help would-be dog trainers see training from the dog's point of view, she suggests this: "Imagine you live on a planet where the dominant species is far more intellectually sophisticated than human beings but often keeps humans as companion animals."[31] Donaldson calls this intellectual species "the Gorns."

> They communicate with each other via a complex combination of telepathy, eye movements and high-pitched squeaks, all completely unintelligible and unlearnable by humans, whose brains are prepared for verbal language acquisition only. What humans sometimes learn is the meaning of individual sounds by repeated association with things of relevance to them. The Gorns and humans bond strongly, but there are many Gorn rules which humans must try to assimilate with limited information and usually high stakes.[32]

In this extended scenario, some humans can't be "House-Humans" because they get too excitable whenever a Gorn approaches them (probably because they're so lonely and attention-deprived), and so they are chained outside. Other humans are lucky enough to live indoors in a Gorn dwelling, but find themselves punished for urinating in the toilet or for engaging in enjoyable behaviors such as watching TV, eating pizza, sitting on chairs, and talking with other humans. So these humans are kept away from other humans. On the few chances they get to see a fellow human, they go nuts, and are punished for that too.

This, Donaldson suggests, is what we do to dogs when we keep them deprived of other dogs' company and don't even let them greet each other, when we rub dogs' noses in a urine-soaked carpet to try to teach them not to pee indoors, when we yell at them for eating food left on the buffet (or what we understand to be the kitchen counter), and, to top it all off, when we punish them for getting frustrated and showing it.

> This nightmarish world is the one inhabited by many domestic dogs all the time. Virtually all natural dog behaviors—chewing, barking, rough play, chasing moving objects, eating any available food item within reach, jumping up and pawing to greet, settling minor disputes with threat displays, establishing contact with strange dogs, guarding resources, leaning into steady pressure against their chests or necks, urinating on porous surfaces like carpets, defending themselves from perceived threat—are considered by humans to be behavior problems. The rules which seem so obvious to us make absolutely no sense to dogs. They are not humans in dog suits.[33]

I've given so much space to Donaldson's extended allegory here because it so nicely embodies key assumptions underlying the clicker training approach: that dogs think differently from humans; that they have their own distinct points of view, which are neither superior nor inferior to human's points of view, just different; that empathizing with dogs means recognizing this difference; that we humans need to respect the canine point of view and the dogness of the dog; that we need to communicate with dogs clearly and on their terms; and that we would do well to understand dogs' cognitive differences from humans as "cultural" differences.

Donaldson's allegory also highlights that a "culture clash" offers a hot metaphor for her readership of the 1990s. That is, the conspicuous clashing of cultures and of ideologies within the country offered itself as a ready metaphor for her readers. As Lakoff pointed out, politically divided human beings had such clashing worldviews that communicating with each other was almost like communicating with another species. When we see from our own frame, the other's behaviors and beliefs make no sense.

Dog trainers of the 1990s proposed approaches that recognized dog cognition and the difference in how dogs think from how humans do. In the nurturant parent model, as dogs came into households and adapted to us, it was incumbent on us to adapt to them. We had to recognize the dogness of the dog in order to make dogs full family members. And unlike my Border Collie, Labrador Retrievers, the most popular household breed, were able to meet their humans more than halfway.

But while we began to address the dog-human culture clash, the intra-human culture clash in the America of the 1990s proved much more intractable, and seems only to have widened since then. While the nurturant, positive-reinforcement model predominated dog training in the 1990s, the strict father model persisted. Perhaps the real culture clash—or at least the more intractable one—was between conservatives and liberals rather than between humans and dogs. Some ideologically opposed humans in America are finding it easier to communicate with a different species than with each other.

Labrador Retrievers as Service Dogs

Both frames, however, come together in Service Dog, a role predominated by Labs. The service dog role reinforces the strict-father view of dogs as subordinate to humans but also depends on the mutuality and interdependence of the human-dog bond that the nurturant family model values.

Probably the most well-known of service dogs are Guide Dogs or Seeing Eye Dogs. Although accounts of dogs guiding blind humans go back centuries, it wasn't until the early twentieth century that organizations developed formal programs to train dogs. The first Guide Dog

Chapter Five. A Dog for All Seasons 133

program arose in Switzerland under the guidance of American Dorothy Eustis. She used German Shepherds, bred at her Fortunate Field Kennels. Soon afterward, she also co-founded the organization The Seeing Eye in the United States in 1929.[34] The Seeing Eye is now located in New Jersey and provides the majority of guide dogs for the blind in the United States Though they began with German Shepherds, over the years, Labrador and Golden Retrievers joined German Shepherds in this task. By the 1990s, Labrador Retrievers proved the most successful breed of the dog trainees. Today, The Seeing Eye serves around 260 blind or visually impaired people a year, and there are approximately 1700 current Seeing Eye dog users in the United States and Canada. The organization breeds its own dogs, around 500 puppies a year, with a 60 percent success rate. (The other 40 percent are placed with other service organizations such as law enforcement and search & rescue agencies, or are adopted by the public. The majority of these dogs are Labs.[35])

Not only do Labs make great all-around dogs, sturdy and adaptable to all kinds of tasks and situations, and not only do they come in the perfect Goldilocks size—not too small, not too big—but they are temperamentally suited to serving alongside humans. They're generally not as high-strung and hyper-vigilant as, say, a certain Border Collie I could name, who would never be able to chill in a mellow curl at my feet. They can both work hard and chill out, whatever the occasion calls for.

Such a guide dog combines conflicting family values—a synthesis the country itself resisted. Even the Barron's owner's manual for Labs, which I've recruited as representative of the residual strict-father-family frame of understanding dogs, captures both frames in its description of Labs as service dogs: "Such a human-dog bond reaffirms the valued place canines have assumed in our modern world. Guide Dog and owner are a special pairing—a dog that lives to serve and an owner who is able to live life to its fullest aided by the service of a life-long companion and friend."[36] The service dog is both at the service of humans and one half of a special pairing.

The use of Labs and other dogs has expanded over the last few decades. By the 1990s, they were aiding people with other kinds of disabilities. The Americans with Disabilities Act of 1990, recognizing the importance of service animals, legalized their presence in public spaces otherwise off-limits for dogs. Once again, the Labrador offered the ideal breed for this work. In fact, Canine Companions for Independence, a major nonprofit organization for breeding and training assistance dogs since 1975, uses only Labrador Retrievers, Golden Retrievers, and Lab-Golden crosses. Likewise, NEADS World Class Service Dogs, which raises and trains service dogs, employs primarily Labrador Retrievers.[37]

Law enforcement has also relied on Labs for help. Labs' superb senses of smell aid military and police to sniff out bombs and land mines, as well as detect the presence of drugs and other contraband items. You'll also find Labs working in public spaces such as in airports or on street patrol. As the Barron's manual says in 1995, "Labradors are becoming more popular in this job and have been touted for their ability to work among civilians without creating anxiety (which is often known to occur when the more traditional police dogs—German Shepherds and Dobermans—are used)."[38] Perhaps their floppy ears, rounded faces, big eyes, and overgrown-puppy-like builds help with this perception.

Labradors have also proven an excellent breed for search-and-rescue work, such as in the aftermath of an earthquake. Their excellent scenting skills allow them to find people through smoke-choked disaster zones, while their calmness allows them to work amid clamor and sirens, and their athleticism allows them to climb ladders or army-crawl through small windows.

Other types of service work performed by Labs and other dogs include assisting people with impaired mobility, acting as "hearing ear" dogs, mitigating the effects of PTSD, predicting epileptic seizures and other medical emergencies, and providing emotional support.

I've never lived with a retriever, but some of my best friends have been retrievers, both Labs and Goldens, their close cousins. One was a retriever named Sadie, a therapy dog for a student with PTSD after serving in Iraq. The student was a creative writer, and by the time she was attending my classes, she was doing a lot better both physically and psychologically, so she gave Sadie a little more free rein when appropriate. In creative nonfiction workshops, Sadie was free to wander the room. Incredibly, she inevitably went and sat at the feet of the person whose work was being critiqued. Since I used the "muzzle rule" in that class—where the writer doesn't speak until the very end—the silent writer should have been the one least likely to receive Sadie's attentions. And yet Sadie somehow sussed out the person under the most stress—perhaps by observing subtle body language, perhaps by smell—and there she was for them, offering up her support.

In an era when we began to care en masse about the emotions of dogs—and even their emotional well-being—dogs also supported our emotions. At its best, we became mutual emotional support animals for each other. Perhaps this was already true, but in the 1990s this trans-species love dared to speak its name. And the face of this love was most commonly that of a Lab, often looking uncannily like a yellow Lab puppy with plaintive eyes and a head tilted innocently in response to his questioning, possibly scolding human.

Chapter Five. A Dog for All Seasons

A Golden Retriever Search-and-Rescue Dog being transported out of the debris of the World Trade Center September 15, 2001, days after the September 11, 2001, terrorist attack (U.S. Navy photograph by Jim Watson/Getty Images).

Athlete and "big lug," servant and partner, hunter and heart-warmer—the Lab was one of those rare creatures able temporarily to reconcile Americans' irreconcilable differences.

Coda: September 11, 2001

The 1990s could arguably be said to end on September 11, 2001. For many people, that was a "before-and-after" moment in their life—a time that divided their lives into a pre- and a post-. In that horrible tragedy, Labs represented hope, helping to bring us back from the brink.

Amidst the devastation of Ground Zero, dogs offered rare images of hope. Two Labrador Retrievers, Salty and Roselle, guided their sight-impaired owners down more than seventy flights of stairs to safety amidst smoke, screams, rumbles, crackling, and crashing. A heartwarming *New York Times* article soon afterward featured a large photo of Omar Rivera and his dog Salty, tongue out and dog-smiling. Mr. Rivera says that Salty was very nervous, "[b]ut he didn't run away."[39] Roselle, too, stayed by her human's side, and calmly led Michael Hingson down 1,463 stairs amidst flying debris. Hingson later commemorated Roselle in his book *Thunder Dog: The True Story of a Blind Man, His Guide Dog, and the Triumph of Trust at Ground Zero*.[40]

In the wake of that disaster, Search and Rescue (SAR) dogs were deployed—most famously Labs and Goldens (among other breeds). Alongside firemen and other first responders, these dogs descended into the rubble. I remember latching on to the image of Riley, a Golden Retriever, being pulleyed in a basket onto Ground Zero. That retriever became my personal image of hope. Even after the search for survivors shifted into a search for cadavers, these SAR dogs comforted many of the humans amidst the wreckage.

These Ground Zero dogs were honored at the next Westminster Kennel Club Dog Show, which donated $275,000 to the National Association for Search and Rescue.[41] Perhaps these rescue dogs received as much media celebration as they did because we were desperate for any positive story of heroism. But it was also, I believe, because they gave us an image of a particular kind of heroism—and of resilience—that was hard to find in the human realm. While too many humans would soon use 9/11 as a launch-pad for fear-mongering, tribalism, and vengeance (not to mention opportunism), the service dogs focused on recovery. Indeed, in this civic space, the image of these gentle Labrador and Golden Retrievers could replace those of dogs in earlier eras, such as the image of snarling German Shepherds used against African Americans in

1950s and 1960s Civil Rights protests. Soft muzzles could replace sharp teeth.

In the ensuing months—for many of us appalled by the Bush administration's military response to the terrorist attacks and the country's resurgence of racism, tribalism, and religious intolerance—search-and-rescue retrievers offered a symbol of an America we wanted to believe in. And in a divided country, the images of these Labrador heroes offered the nation a point of unity. These dogs served as emotional support animals for the country at this time of trauma. In this key event defining our nation, these search and rescue dogs became the nation's therapy dogs.

Chapter Six

Mutty Waters
Mixed Breeds in the 2000s

> We are, then, not only preoccupied with race, as we know we are, but with good and bad breeds as well.
> —Nancy Isenberg, *White Trash*

On November 7, 2008, in his first press conference as president-elect, Barack Obama said that the first presidential campaign promise he would keep was the one he made to his daughters: to get a dog. When asked by an interviewer what breed of puppy the Obama family would get, the president-elect deadpanned, "With respect to the dog, this is a major issue.... We have two criteria that have to be reconciled. One is that Malia is allergic, so it has to be hypoallergenic. There are a number of breeds that are hypoallergenic. On the other hand, our preference would be to get a shelter dog. But, obviously, a lot of shelter dogs are mutts, like me." On the word "me," Obama gently touched his fingers to his chest. His audience laughed a bit uncertainly, as if not quite sure it was okay that Obama called himself a mutt.[1]

The status of the mutt, a non-pedigreed mixed-breed dog, had clearly risen if it was being considered for the First Dog. In the past, muttiness was a deficit to be overcome. One might say that mutts had to be twice as good as purebred dogs to earn half as much respect. It's true that, back in the 1950s, the mutt Tramp might have earned protagonist status in *Lady and the Tramp*, but in that film he was promoted to the clearly more desirable level/class of the purebred. By the end of the film, as a reward for his service to the "leash and collar" class, and particularly to the highly cultured Cocker Spaniel Lady, he was given honorary purebred status. By the 2000s, however, the muttiness of the mutt was becoming classy. Or, put another way, the mutt had gone middle class.

Many elements likely contributed to mutt's elevation in class. One may well have been that purebreds too often presented congenital breed-related problems, which resulted from the more limited gene pool of most purebreds. Even if a defect is linked to a recessive gene, the more limited the gene pool the greater the odds that both parents will have that recessive gene. Unfortunately, as John Bradshaw dramatically states in his book *Dog Sense*, in "some dog breeds today it is difficult to find two parents who are not closely related."[2] In fact, in some breeds, "the amount of variation within *the whole breed* amounts to little more than is typical of first cousins in our own species."[3] Common gene mutations among the gene pool of a breed can produce a high incidence of specific defects. Among Labrador Retrievers, for

Mutts unmake breeds. This mutt named Pretzel possibly mixes Border Collie with Cocker Spaniel lines, 2008 (photograph by the author).

example, widespread hip dysplasia conditions, as well as epilepsy, were increasingly recognized. Bradshaw notes, "In the 1950s, most breeds still had a healthy range of genetic variation; by 2000, only some twenty to twenty-five generations later, many had been inbred to the point where hundreds of genetically based deformities, diseases, and disadvantages had emerged, potentially compromising the welfare of every purebred dog."[4] In the U.K. in 2008, the BBC aired the documentary *Pedigree Dogs Exposed*, which showed heartbreaking images exposing problems with breeding to an artificial standard for looks without regard to health.[5] In the fall-out from this documentary, the BBC decided not to air the Crufts show beginning in 2009.[6] Although this documentary only aired on a very few stations in the United States,[7] and although many responsible dog breeders do prioritize the genetic health of their breeds, the message of *Pedigree Dogs Exposed* left its mark on American cultural consciousness.

Another factor elevating the status of the mutt is that the 2000s saw a backlash against the puppy mills that produced so many purebreds. (My own Cocker Spaniel, Houdini, whom I got in 2001, was one such puppy mill dog. When I sent off for his papers, I learned that he, too, was inbred, though not quite as badly as I'd feared.) While these purebred puppy mill puppies were being raised, consciousness was also being raised. In fact, while writing this book, when I told friends and colleagues its subject, several admonished me for dignifying the notion of breed altogether, since it's done so much harm. It would be better not to call attention to breed at all, they contended. This "breed-blindness" reminds me of well-meaning (usually white) people who counter racism by adopting a "color-blind," "I don't see race" approach. (Famously, Stephen Colbert regularly parodied this approach on his television show *The Colbert Report*, which ran from 2005 to 2014. His clueless character made it clear that the problems of systemic racism are not going to be solved by ignoring individual race.) I've also noticed, while writing this book, that when I ask people what kind of dog they have, owners of pure-breeds will admit as much only apologetically, even confessionally, often adding an exonerating detail—as I did in Chapter One. I'll admit that most of my friends and colleagues lean left, and that it's cliché (backed up by some preliminary research) that progressives tend to favor rescue mutts while conservatives tend to prefer pedigreed purebreds. Still, by the 2000s, purebred status had lost its cache. Shelter dogs and mutts became cool.

Endearing as the scene is of the president-elect—not yet polished enough to avoid a line like "mutts, like me"—such a line evokes a whole history of troubles. First, any metaphor comparing people of color with animals comes with heavy baggage. Even when it's a person of color referring to himself, as in this case with Barack Obama, that history lingers, and a whole narrative and metaphoric structure (or "mythology") gets activated, whether consciously or not. Obama himself, in his campaign speech about race in America, quoted William Faulkner's famous statement, "The past isn't dead. It isn't even past." The rhetoric of racial animus doesn't disappear with the election of an African American president.

A second set of troubles with Obama's "mutts" line is its suggestion that races are comparable to breeds. Comparing *all* humans to breeds of dog may seem a progressive step forward from making the analogy (discussed in Chapter Four) that nonwhites are to whites what dogs are to humans, but perhaps it's more like "two steps forward, one step back." The uncomfortable suggestion that races are like breeds is both right and wrong. It's right in that it names a generally unspoken and highly operative metaphor in American culture, but it's wrong in that the comparison obscures, more than it clarifies, the true nature of both race and breed. Indeed, the 2000s challenged both the "truth" and the "nature" of race and of breed. This decade popularized the "deconstructive" notion (already advanced in academia for at least two decades) that both races and breeds are cultural constructs that hide their constructedness. They then become "truths" around which we structure our identities.

For these reasons, at the risk of perseverating, Border Collie–like, over what must surely have been an ad-libbed comment, I want to spend the bulk of this chapter "unpacking" Obama's metaphor. In the process, I'll make the case for mutts as the "breed" of the 2000s—or rather, as the non-breed that functions in the place of a breed. Muttiness represents the spirit of the time when we were trying to figure out not only what race we "really" are (both individually and culturally) but also, more importantly, what race really is.

Uncertain Origins

Chapter Four already ventured into these muddy race-as-breed waters. The discourse of breed has dogged the discourse of race—and vice versa—since their inceptions. Both *race* and *breed* are tricky concepts. They can sometimes feel self-evident even when the evidence belies them. Because race has proven so difficult to understand, and can feel so dangerous to formulate, the mind may latch on to concepts of breed and breeding to understand race. In the most literal versions of this trope, race is the human version of breed; race is to humans what breed is to dogs. In more metaphorical versions, dog breeds become merely a way to help us conceptualize and understand race. Such rhetoric, of course, can lead to dangerous ideas about racial purity as a parallel to canine purebreds.

The alignment of breeds with classes or types of men long pre-exists the United States as a country. It's no mere coincidence that people of the privileged classes were said to be of "good breeding." Teaching a freshman class on Shakespeare recently, I was surprised to come across these lines I had forgotten in *Macbeth*, which compare different types of men to differently bred classes of dogs. Speaking to potential assassins, whom Macbeth enlists to kill his rival, he says:

> Ay, in the catalogue you go for men,
> As hounds and greyhounds, mongrels, spaniels, curs,
> Choughs, Water-rugs, and demi-wolves are clept
> All by the name of dogs. The valued file

> Distinguishes the swift, the slow, the subtle,
> The housekeeper, the hunter, every one
> According to the gift which bounteous nature
> Hath in him closed; whereby he does receive
> Particular addition, from the bill
> That writes them all alike. And so of men
> [act. 3, scene 1, lines 103–113].[8]

Men are like dogs, Macbeth says; they come in a range of types and classes with distinct pedigrees (or "valued files"). While they may all be called (or "clept") "by the name of dogs," they are not all equal. Their different values come, in this speech, from "bounteous nature," or, more specifically, from what we today might call genes ("the gift which bounteous nature/ Hath in him closed"). Inequality (says the murderous king) is natural.

It's worth noting how much Macbeth's listing of dog types differs from our contemporary notion of breeds, and that Shakespeare separates dog types more by the work they do (housekeeper, hunter) and the way they function (fast, slow) than by phenotypic characteristics. (If not by function, a few dog types were identified by the region from which they arose, such as "spaniel" for a type of dog originating in Spain.) Breeding for appearance or body-type rather than function would, for the most part, come much later.

It's worth noting as well that Shakespeare uses the terms "cur" and "mongrel," which, like their synonym "mutt," are of uncertain origin. The *cur* dog perhaps comes from the onomatopoeic word for growl ("currrrr") or perhaps a Middle English word for house: is it a growling dog, a housedog, both, or neither? *Mongrel* comes from an Old English word for mixture (as preserved in *among* and *mingle*), a word that comes to English by way of a Proto-Germanic word for kneading. *Mutt* has even more uncertain origins. It may come from the word mutton. Sheep were seen as stupid animals, so a "muttonhead" signaled a stupid person, and a muttonhead dog a stupid dog. But this etymology remains speculative, and the true source of the word unknown, just like the creature it describes. The term probably wandered hither and thither for centuries before taking on its current form. The term is itself a mutt—as, ultimately, almost all terms are, with a few odd and unnatural exceptions. Words are wanderers, unfixed, inextricably mixed, and irrevocably mutty. They've defied our attempt to fix them.

Such is the case for the terms "race" as well as "breed." An emerging term for these groupings of specialty dogs, in Shakespeare's time, was "race," from Old Italian *razza*. Before a clear Linnean taxonomy, the terms "race" and "species" were used loosely, and somewhat interchangeably.[9] That's the sense in which Voltaire wrote, in the eighteenth century, "The Negro race is a species of men different from ours as the breed of spaniels is from that of Greyhounds."[10]

Voltaire's eighteenth century, delving into the "origins of man," gave birth to the field of anthropology. In fact, the study of the origin of humans in the eighteenth century is reflected in many ways in the study of the origin of dogs today. Current debates concern whether dogs as a species are monogenic or polygenic—whether they emerged from their wolf precursors at one time and one place only, or whether the emergence happened more than once in different parts of the world. Similar monogenism vs. polygenism debates with regard to humans played out in the eighteenth century, with some scientists explaining the variety of races by a "multiple origins" theory. Like its dog version, the "multiple origins theory" of human evolution posits that different races originated differently, and not from a common ancestor, as we now (mostly) believe. The multiple origins theory often bolstered a scientific racism in which different races were fundamentally different— and, usually, some were inherently superior to others. (I'll bet you can guess which was which.) Though polygenism usually supported scientific racism, monogenism could also take very racist forms, positing that though all humans emerged from a common progenitor, the differences had become as distinct and undeniable as Chihuahuas and Great Danes. Today, the homo sapiens version of the debate is pretty much settled (in favor of monogenism), but the dog version goes on.

Well into the eighteenth century, the terms "species," "race," and "breed" seem, as far as I can tell, to have been used interchangeably, and only during the Enlightenment, with its zeal for taxonomy—or systems of classification—did the terms come to be defined and differentiated. By the nineteenth century, the term "race" came to denote a generally similar set of animals or plants within a species. These "races" could be further subdivided into "breeds." That's how Darwin uses the term "race" in his *Origin of Species*. For example, what the American Kennel Club currently calls "groups" (Sporting, Working, etc.) would, in earlier eras, have been called "races." By the twentieth century, though, the term "race" narrowed to humans[11] and "breed" to nonhuman animals. Their interwoven histories and connotations, however, continue to intermix in each other's bloodlines.

Constructing Breed

In the late twentieth century, the idea that "race is a construct"— that race is a made-up classification system—took hold in academia and beyond, as I'll discuss below. Race as a social construction can be a difficult concept to wrap your head around. Seeing "breed" as a construct, though, is a bit easier. Breeds of dogs were clearly a human creation from the start, though what's sometimes forgotten is that the very concept of "breed" itself is a human creation, not something already "out there" in nature that humans merely came along and named.

Humans have lived with dogs since before recorded history. While natural variations in genetic traits among dogs have always popped up, the forces of natural selection kept some genetic codings in play and others not. (If you look at today's communities of street dogs who've interbred among themselves for generations, you see this limited range. There are variations among individual dogs, but as a group they're more homogenous than the array of dogs you see in dog shows—or even in today's dog park. There's a generic "street dog look" that they tend to hover around.) Even when people began to breed dogs selectively, they did so for function rather than for specific physical traits. Dogs got categorized by the work they did. Remember Macbeth's list of the different types of dogs according to function, such as guarding, hunting, herding, baiting, and fighting. Dogs as pets were the domain of the privileged; only the aristocracy could comfortably afford pets, who didn't earn their keep. The majority of dogs were working dogs. However, by the eighteenth century in Europe, and eventually in North America, more people from a range of classes, not just the upper classes, were able to keep dogs as pets. Alongside this phenomenon of dogs as non-working pets, "dog fancy" emerged, and the concept of "breed" crystallized.

"Dog fancy" encompasses the breeding, showing, and appreciating of purebred dogs. The term draws on the meaning of the (very British) verb "fancy" as something like "having a special interest in." As a noun, a fancy was a hobby. This was the meaning when the term arose, but other, more contemporary (to us) connotations of fancy serve as well. Dog fancy created "fancy" breeds, in the sense of elaborate and imaginative. "Fancy"'s origins run through the word "fantasy," and, ironically, some of the breeds created by dog fancy seem to spring from someone's highly generative imagination.

Not only did dog fanciers of the nineteenth century develop most the breeds we know today, but they also developed the *concept* of breed as we know it today—the state in which distinctive traits can reliably appear over generations when dogs with these traits are only bred with each other. When they reach this state, dogs are said to "breed true" or "breed pure," and can then be called a distinct breed.

In her book *The Animal Estate*, historian Harriet Ritvo discusses how the creation of breeds played out in Victorian England. The dog fancy, she writes, developed a "series of finely graded differentiations, which functioned both to establish the unique character of each breed and to assess the relative excellence of dogs of the same breed."[12] The repetition of these valued traits in show after show and in breeding manual after breeding manual solidified them into established standards. Breeders bred dogs selectively for those traits that the show ring most often rewarded. Competition led to exaggerating those traits. Those enhanced traits then became the renewed standard for the breed.

Ritvo describes a similar phenomenon already happening with cattle; gentlemen farmers entered in livestock shows as a leisure "sport." Over time they created distinct breeds with exaggerated traits, often selected to display a look of grandeur and amplitude that actually impeded the animals' ability to function as cows and bulls. These grand cattle would, by association, reinforce the grandeur of their aristocratic owners. Unlike the aristocratic gentlemen who owned the cattle of stock shows, though, the owners of dogs mostly "belonged to the urban business and professional classes."[13] The dog shows, as a microcosm of society, "offered a vision of a stable, hierarchical society, where rank was secure and individual merit, rather than just inherited position, appreciated."[14] Dog fancy both reinforced the class structure and shifted the means of achieving its ranks. The greatness of dogs (and, by association, their humans) wasn't just a gift passively received from nature; it could be achieved by actively manipulating nature.

Love for dogs was most definitely a factor in the proliferation of dog fancy in this so-called "sentimental" era, but dog fancy also served as a form of conspicuous consumption. Owning dogs as "luxury items" rather than as laborers signaled an elevated class status. And so,

> [d]espite its genuinely sentimental roots, much middle-class pet-keeping was shadowed by [status-seeking]. After all, the maintenance of idle animals was a custom borrowed from the upper echelons of society and constituted a metonymic attempt at assimilation; the elaborate certification and registration of pedigreed animals was hardly designed to guarantee their emotional qualities.[15]

Elite pets worked to characterize their middle-class owners as elite by association; through the transitive property, fancy dogs conferred status on their people.

In its zeal for proliferating categories, dog fancy offered a microcosm of the larger society. The nineteenth century ushered in great activity in all kinds of registering, tracking of pedigree, and drawing up genealogies—and not just for dogs. The creation of breed coincided with an era that set about classifying, categorizing, and distinguishing everything from insects and plant species to types of mental illness in humans to sexual identities. (This zeal to taxonomize human conditions and identities is the subject of much of Michel Foucault's historical theorizing.) The creation of specific types of dogs fit well with the zeitgeist.

As breeds were normalized, their constructedness got forgotten. "Although this system appeared secure and stable, grounded in biological imperatives and validating centuries of English dog breeding, in fact it resulted from an impressive collective act of will and imagination."[16] Victorians created the concept of breed and of breed standard, and then acted as if it were some kind of natural or Platonic ideal. For example, the Beagle, seen as an ancient breed, was once loosely understood as a type of hound dog, but then narrowed to mean a small dog of 13–15" height at the shoulder, with a square-cut muzzle, short and muscular back, sturdy bearing, and ears and tail neither too long nor too short. Fanciers may have disputed exactly what defined an ideal Beagle, but—even though this shaping of the Beagle could be clearly traced— "all the disputants assumed that a standard or ideal Beagle existed, even though there was no historical evidence for a single, true, ancient Beagle type."[17]

By then, the mongrels, not the pure breeds, were perceived as the abnormal ones, and definitely as inferior. Ritvo writes that, "[f]rom their initial appearance in 1859, public dog shows had been dedicated to the achievement of three related goals: to improve the various breeds of dogs, to display model specimens, and to discourage the breeding of mongrels."[18] Discouraging the breeding of mongrels was as important as the creation of pure breeds. Purity was at a premium. In an era when the discourse of racial purity became rampant, and "miscegenation" an affront to the social order, mongrel (or mixed-breed) dogs nicely served as a culture-wide metaphor for mixed-race humans.

Mongrels symbolized both racial and class instability. Most Victorians of the dog fancy world "felt that ownership of mongrels revealed latent commonness."[19] The natural state of dogs (mutts) was seen as inferior to the designed versions (purebreds)—but then the construct was itself naturalized. Breeds came to be seen as natural and ideal, and mutts as inferior aberrations.

Constructing Race

In the context of American (and European) history, this "scientific" language of races and breeds developed for people too. The activity in classification of types of people resulted in the field of anthropology, which arose in parallel with "natural history." In a sense, anthropology—the study of humankind—did for the concept of race what dog fancy did for the concept of breed: it naturalized the concept. That is, nineteenth-century anthropology helped make race (along with class) seem to be a natural phenomenon, rather than a human-invented set of standards, an imaginary ideal against which to measure individual bodies.

The discourse of race was long in the making, and rose in tandem with the discourse of breed. Since before the inception of the United States as a nation, some people were even commodified as breeding stock. In 1600s Virginia colony, notes Nancy Isenberg in her book *White Trash: The 400-Year Untold History of Class in America*, "[s]lave children were actually listed in the wills of planters as 'breedings,' and a slave woman's potential to breed was denoted as 'future increase,' a term that applied to livestock as well."[20] Women of all races, naturally, were seen as breeders, and a "woman's breeding capacity was a calculable natural resource meant to be exploited and a commodity exchanged in marriage."[21]

Since some "breeds" of humans gained more power than others, it was important to keep the "breeds" of humans distinct. So, as Africans and Europeans proliferated in the Americas (alongside Native Americans), selective breeding was instituted. This took the form of an array of laws barring miscegenation, or the genetic mixing of races. The emerging economic system depended on racial distinctions, and on the belief that those distinctions were natural (and therefore God-given). So an unnatural selection was imposed to maintain the illusion of the naturalness of race. In this sense, humans in America selectively bred for race.

Even within whiteness different "breeds" vied for top caste. Many ethnicities other than what we might now call the "WASP" ethnicity (white, Anglo-Saxon, Protestant)—such as Irish, Jewish, and Italian—were seen as not-quite-white. Here, the rhetoric of race also intermingled with and justified class. White "trash"—dispossessed and disposable whites—were also seen as not-quite-white, a sort of sub-race within the white race, and these class divisions among whites, too, were supported with the language of breeding. It was common among the United States' founding fathers to speak of "breeding" when referring to classes of people. People could be "well bred" and come from "good stock." "Breeding" naturalized class, just as it had race, making class seem to be a result of nature rather than of enculturated power structures.

The rhetoric of good and bad breeding, then, offered a way to disguise the existence of class in America. It became a way to avoid the language of class while at the same time registering class. Nancy Isenberg notes that "[t]he poor were not only described as waste, but as inferior animal stocks too."[22] She observes that Thomas Jefferson, in his *Notes of the State of Virginia* (1787), argued that American stock could be "cultivated" and "bred up": "The circumstance of superior beauty is thought worthy of attention in the propagation of our horses, dogs, and other domestic animals; why not in that of man?"[23]

Thinking of races (and sub-races) as breeds culminated in the deplorable eugenics movement of the 1920s. The eugenics movement generally embraced the idea of selectively breeding humans; the practice served as a necessary corrective for the "unnatural" state of a society that allowed unfit individuals to reproduce. That is, eugenicists argued that human society already violated the natural order of "survival of the fittest" by allowing the "unfit" to survive and thrive. Eugenics was therefore necessary to mimic natural selection by eliminating bad genes from the gene pool. "Almost all eugenicists analogized human and animal breeding," notes Isenberg.[24] Charles Darwin himself equated the two, using language similar to Jefferson's from a century earlier: "Man scans with scrupulous care the pedigree of his horses, cattle and dogs before he mates them; but when it comes to his marriage, he rarely, or never, takes such care."[25] (This is of course very ironic given that the laws and social pressures against miscegenation did just that; they "took care" to manipulate the distribution of gene pools.)

Such racial mythologies cast some types of humans as so genetically inferior, so "degenerate" (or badly gene-ed), that their genes must be bred out (or de-gene-ed), just as responsible dog breeders would not allow genetically inferior purebred dogs to reproduce. These so-called degenerates, imbeciles, and morons, carrying faulty genes, were subject to sterilization, not always voluntary. In 1927, Chief Justice Oliver Wendell Holmes famously ruled, in *Buck v. Bell*, "It is better for all the world if, instead of waiting to execute degenerate offspring for crime or to let them starve for their imbecility, society can prevent those who are manifestly unfit from continuing their kind.... Three generations of imbeciles are enough."[26] Privileged whites saw the less privileged of their race ("white trash") as products of unnatural breeding, not natural selection. Not only did they see such people, along with their genetic make-up, as expendable ("trash"), but they felt it was their moral duty to intervene in this unnatural sub-race and to impose what they saw as a simulation of natural selection where natural selection itself seemed to have been thwarted.

In the drive to breed for untainted whiteness, "better baby" and "fitter family" contests were held at state fairs: "The contests were held in the stock grounds, and families were judged in the manner of cattle."[27] The winning baby best fit the ideal of the healthy, wholesome, and beautiful (white) infant. The resemblance of "better baby" contests to dog shows is uncanny. In their attempts to refine the gene pool, dog fancy and eugenics shared parallel goals and parallel logic.

In the ensuing decades, and particularly after the Nazi death camps operated in the name of racial purity, eugenics on humans itself became tainted. Miscegenation laws were slowly challenged and overturned, and "mulattoes" were no longer see as "tragic." The gucky residue of this discourse of racial purity still sticks to American culture, of course, as when right-wing Rocker and gun rights advocate Ted Nugent called Barack Obama a "subhuman mongrel."[28] Though Nugent later apologized for the metaphor, his mind's pulling up that particular figure of speech in the first place speaks volumes about how present it still is in some segments of the U.S. population.

Still, although racism was alive and well in the U.S. of the 2000s, its biological and moral bases were somewhat discredited. Anti-racist Americans strove toward "color-blindness"—to minimize the importance of race, and to judge people, in Martin Luther King, Jr.'s words, "not by the color of their skin but by the content of their character." (A similar move has recently occurred in the dog world; an anti-breedist movement encourages us to see each dog as a unique individual and to ignore breed-based stereotypes.) The "color-blind" approach to countering racism was flawed in many ways, not least of which was that it ignored decades and centuries of inequality already baked into American social, economic, and justice systems. It also overlooked the ways that our standards and ideals for humans ("the content of [one's] character"), like the standards for breed against which dogs are judged in dog fancy competitions, favored their creators. By the late twentieth century, race was so endemic to the history, identity, and structure of the United States that ignoring it only had the effect of denying the reality of racism. That is, not seeing race was a way of not seeing racism. At the same time, even as this "color-blind" approach minimized the importance of race, it didn't challenge the status of race itself as a scientific, objective, biological fact. It still operated on the model that race pre-existed racism.

Deconstructing Race

And then a funny thing happened to this in-bred American discourse on the way to the twenty-first century. Or rather, a series of funny things happened all at once. Advances in genetics, demographic changes, cultural movements, and shifts in human-dog relations all aided and abetted a rather thorough deconstruction of the concepts of both race and breed. Simultaneously, they revealed the mixedness, the hybridity, of the seemingly pure. At a time when some of our biggest celebrities—golfer Tiger Woods, CNN anchor Soledad O'Brien, wrestler and actor Dwayne Johnson (The Rock), singers Mariah Carey, Norah Jones, and Bruno Mars, and President Barack Obama himself—identified (or could be characterized) as biracial if not multiracial, muttiness went from being the result of an accident and the exception to the rule to being the paradigm. The 2000s generated significant shifts in our understanding both of race and of breed, in practical as well as in conceptual realms. Our values also shifted—from racial purity as the standard of beauty to hybridity as a valued trait. Hybridity was the new authenticity.

By the 2000s, advances in genetics allowed scientists to affirm what cultural critics had long been arguing: that race is a "construct." Such thinking seemed to flout common sense. In everyday life, race seems factual, biological. It seems real in the way that pigmentation is real rather than in the way that the word "pigmentation" is real; the reality seemed to pre-exist its formulation. However, cultural critics of the 2000s were arguing the opposite and challenging the "realness" of race. The deconstructive model of race—the model that sees race as a construct rather than a biological fact pre-existing language—might say that the word "pigmentation" is real because, through repeated speech acts, we've brought it into being. Actual pigmentation exists, at the cellular level anyway, whether or not we repeatedly refer to it, but it only exists as an "it"—it only becomes "a thing," as we'd say in contemporary parlance—through the word. To say that race is a construct is to say that the classification system is real in the way that words are real, rather than in the way that molecular structures are real. Race is real because we constantly invoke it and treat it as real, and so, over time, it comes to feel real. It becomes "a thing."

By the late twentieth century in academia, and by the 2000s in the wider realm beyond academia, race came to be understood less as an essence than as a "construct," even a "fiction." But a "lived fiction"— which is to say, a "mythology." Race wasn't biological, it was cultural (though no less real for being "merely" cultural). Indeed, some cultural critics may put quotes around the term "race" or its alleged constituents ("black," "white," etc.)—or, like journalist Ta-Nehisi Coates, they talk about "people who identify as white" rather than using (and therefore implicitly validating) the phrase "white people."[29] For the most part, I don't do that in my writing because race can be so real in the way it's lived. But when I use racial terms here, they should be understood as

Chapter Six. Mutty Waters

lived metaphors, and race as a culturally imposed concept with very real material effects.

Scientists of the 2000s, too, argued that although we certainly live race as real in everyday life, the science doesn't support the inevitability of our racial categories. For one thing, there's no good scientific reason to prioritize skin pigmentation over any other heritable trait as the basis of identification. We're all a mass of thousands of heritable traits coded by thousands of genes, some falling on the same chromosome, others not. These gene sets get all mixed up in endless varieties, as new DNA-testing technology makes increasingly clear. The bulk of genetic varieties in human beings emerged over one hundred thousand years ago, and already existed before humans migrated beyond the African continent. We all consist primarily of genes of the earliest *homo sapiens* in Africa. For this reason, as Daniel J. Fairbanks bluntly titles his book on the subject, *Everyone Is African*.

What's more, there's at least as much genetic variation among African people today as there is between Africans and people who don't trace their ancestry to Africa. As Lynn Jorde and Stephen Wooding put it in a 2004 study, "Approximately 85–90% of genetic variation is found within" the population groups of Africa, Asia, and Europe, "and only an additional 10–15% of the variation is found between them." In other words, "humans vary only slightly at the DNA level and [...] only a small proportion of this variation separates continental populations."[30] Any given "black" person may be more genetically different from another given "black" person than they are from a "white" person.

Further, throughout human history, genes followed migration patterns at least as complex as the humans they rode in on. Current advances in genetics allow us to trace genetic varieties previously unavailable to us. It turns out that many of the genetic markers associated with race may pop up in unpredictable places. Here's just one example: In his book *The Wandering Gene and the Indian Princess: Race, Religion, and DNA*, Jeff Wheelwright writes about the BRCA variation as a "wandering gene," which, like the "wandering Jews" of my own ancestry, moved around, thereby transforming both themselves and the cultures they entered with each move.[31] BRCA is a variation on a gene that helps cells protect against breast cancer—indeed, its acronym is an abbreviation of BReast CAncer—and is unusually common among people of Ashkenazi Jewish descent. The mutated gene doesn't function as it's supposed to, increasing a person's chances of developing breast cancer in her (or his) lifetime.

This gene probably mutated in ancient Jerusalem prior to the Judean exile to Babylon in the sixth century BCE and stayed mostly among Jewish communities, fanning out with the Jewish diaspora.[32] Because Jews, as an ethnic group (which was historically also referred to as a race), tended to concentrate in tight communities and to intermarry, rather than mix with non–Jews (akin to selective breeding in dog fancy), genetic traits, including genetic defects, tended to concentrate too.

However, at times of persecution of Jews, such as during the Spanish Inquisition of the fifteenth century, some Jews "passed" as *goy*, and passed on some of their genetic make-up to the community into which they assimilated. Hence, BRCA, a mutation associated with Eastern European Jews, can pop up in unlikely places, as it did in an "Hispano" woman in southern Colorado in the twenty-first century. The gene may well have wandered from the Middle East through eastern Europe to Spain to Mexico and up into the United States, appearing in a woman who self-identified racially as the descendant of Pueblo Native Americans and Spanish conquistadors.

I use this example of a "wandering gene" to illustrate how intermixed genetic ancestries can be. The example may seem an exception to the typical trends of genetic inheritance, but contemporary genetics suggests that it's more the norm than the exception. The species *homo sapiens* is much less diverse from continent to continent than many species in part because we have been much less inhibited by geography to intermix. Our genes wander all over the place. Scientists, who were never really comfortable speaking of race as a biological fact, can now speak more definitively of race as biologically ungrounded.

Tracing our wandering genes became a fad and an industry in the 2000s—most visibly so in 2007, when 23andMe began offering DNA testing from saliva samples. We began to discover just how mixed we were, how much hybridity was the norm. Some of us delighted in seeing articles about white supremacists whose gene testing revealed black or Jewish heritage. It may feel like a bit of a paradox that at a time when scientists are debunking "race" as biologically ungrounded, scientific testing could give us our exact racial composition. But that's not quite accurate. What genetic testing traces is the presence (or absence) of gene mutations traceable to specific, usually fairly closed communities. We give the shorthand name "race" or "ethnicity" to such relatively self-enclosed gene pools. Gene testing shows us just how much these genes have wandered around the world. Most Americans carry genes originating in more than one continent. Ultimately, of course, we all carry fundamental genes originating in Africa.

That this activity of "Finding Your Roots" became popular can be seen in Henry Louis Gates, Jr.'s creation of a PBS show by the same name

Chapter Six. Mutty Waters

in 2012. I'd known Henry Louis Gates for decades as a literary critic; his 1988 book *The Signifying Monkey: A Theory of Afro-American Literary Criticism* was what really made the political implications of deconstruction click for me, and his body of work on African American literature taught me to understand the notion of race as a lived construct or mythology. "Blackness exists," he wrote, "but 'only' as a function of its signifiers." That is, race is real because we constantly rename it and reconstruct it; it's "a thing" because we make is so.

Gates' goal for his TV show is to "get into the DNA of American culture." Each episode follows the genealogy and genetic ancestry of several famous or significant Americans. Almost every episode confirms the mythological nature of our racial categories. Almost all of us are far more mixed, complex, multi-familied, and mysterious than the neat label of the racial category we identify with would suggest. Gates himself, the famous African American literary critic, reveals that his great-great-grandfather was most likely a white man who hailed from Irish or Scottish ancestors. Our gumbo of DNA does not respect our crude racial categories.

But not so fast. Race may be a myth and a construct, but it's a *lived* myth. That is, we live it as if it were real (and thereby make it real). Gates' race as a black man must have felt all too real to him when, in 2009, he'd struggled with a jammed front door to his house, and a neighbor, seeing a black man trying to break into a home in a wealthy neighborhood, instinctively called the cops, who subsequently arrested an angry Gates. The incident became a national event when Barack Obama, upon hearing of the event, and still new to his office, rather stupidly said, instinctively, that the (white) police officer had behaved "stupidly." This led to the famous "beer summit," in which Obama invited Gates and the police officer to sit down and talk it out over a beer. This incident was not read by all Americans as three mixed-race men talking through the muddy waters of race in America; many Americans read it as two black men and one white man unable to understand the "opposite" race. Ironically, the incident had the effect of reconstructing race rather than de-mythologizing it.

Soaking in the zeitgeist of DNA revelations, I recently had my own tested. I always considered myself something of a mutt, at least as far as white people go, with my Eastern-European-Jewish mother and my WASPy, working-class American South father. I figured my roots probably extended every which way across Europe, and if I'm honest I was hoping for some splashes of something further afield. However, 23andMe begged to differ. According to them, 50 percent of my ancestry comes from a shtetl in Eastern Europe, and nearly all of the other 50 percent comes from London. That is, I'm more of a designer dog (which I discuss in the next chapter) than I am a mutt.

Deconstructing Breed

Tiger, however, is a different story. After having my own DNA tested, I decided to have my "wire-haired Husky" mix tested. I knew he was half Husky mixed with some sort of Terrier, but I was dying to know which one. Airedale? Fox Terrier? Something scruffy, for sure. But the Wisdom panel reported that Tiger is 25 percent Siberian Husky, 25 percent Malamute, 25 percent Shiba Inu (!!!), and 25 percent could-be-anything. My first reaction was to assume the test must be wrong (and to be fair, it does warn of its error margins). I've thought of

Some mutts present mysteries. Tiger's genetic test suggests Siberian Husky, Malamute, and Shiba Inu, but he's got to have some sort of scruffy Terrier smuggled in under the DNA radar, 2020 (photograph by the author).

Tiger as a Husky-Terrier mix for too many years to adapt. But in the end, I find myself proud that, unlike me, he is about as mutty as dogs get in North America. John Bradshaw has noted that most mutts in America are one or two generations away from purebreds.[33] They are not the mongrel street dogs that you might find in, say, the streets of Kolkata.[34] Like that of their human counterparts, the DNA of American mixed breeds still carries a history of enforced segregation. They are bi-breedal or multi-breedal, rather than beyond breed, just as most mixed-race Americans are bi-racial or multi-racial, rather than beyond race.

The valuing of the "pure breed" (among dogs) has outlasted the concept of racial purity (among humans). (As I write this, however, the drive toward racial purity among white supremacists seems to be making a significant comeback. On the other hand, the Urban Dictionary, that keeper of slang terms, defines a "purebred" as "the child of an incestual relationship."[35]) Still, by the 2000s, the superior status that purebreds conventionally held over non-pedigreed dogs and mutts lost some of its luster, in part because of increasing genetic problems with purebreds. "Puppy mill" dogs were already known to show problems resulting from inbreeding, or breeding from within a closed genetic pool. Unbeknownst to breeders, often the desired traits were genetically linked with less desirable traits, such as tendencies to develop hip dysplasia, heart defects, and certain cancers.

Even among carefully bred lines by responsible owners, however, congenital defects reared up—in ways similar to the incidence of the BRCA mutation gene in Ashkenazi Jews. Such congenital defects are inherent to the process of pure-breeding itself. A purebred dog is one that will "breed true"—that is, it will reliably produce the desired breed traits in its offspring. This happens when the genetic line has been carefully controlled to weed out genetic variations. But genetic variation is itself a key adaptation that nature evolved to ensure maximum health. In *Dog Eat Dog*, their book on the world of dog shows, Jane and Michael Stern explain,

> genetic deficiency is an issue all breeders of purebred dogs must deal with. Because they rely on selective breeding, they all inbreed to a certain degree in hopes of maintaining and magnifying the best qualities of their best dogs. The result is that not only beauty, but also flaws, are perpetuated and amplified.[36]

Citing *Time* magazine's cover story of December 1994, the Sterns note that as many as one in four purebred dogs may be "afflicted with some serious genetic malady." Some common ones include hip dysplasia in German Shepherds and Golden Retrievers, deafness in Dalmatians, high incidence of heart attacks in Great Danes and Newfoundlands, and breathing problems in Bulldogs. Even the gene pool of the Sterns' beloved Bullmastiffs "swirls with weaknesses and hazards: cruciate ligaments that tend to tear, arthritic hips, thyroid deficiency, dermatological disorders. And now, maybe, something new: uncontrollable tremors."[37] Even with the most careful breeders, who won't breed dogs with genetic maladies, dog breeding depends on restricting the gene pool.

As the practical reasons for concerns over purebreds mounted, so did ethical and philosophical reasons. Ethically, as shelters filled with unwanted dogs, it became less viable to support a practice that produced many undesirable dogs in order to create one top show dog.

Philosophically, too, the notion of "purity" was losing its credibility as well as its value. Increasingly, purity was seen as a construct with ideological implications. Purity of breed, which had signified high status, increasingly just meant a narrowed gene pool. The disastrous experiments in eugenics in the twentieth century cast suspicion on the manipulation of gene pools to weed out variation among humans. Breeds were merely the results of dog eugenics, or unnatural selection—and were the product of selecting for traits that would not have survived natural selection. Nature would not have selected for brachycephalic (smushed) faces, which give dogs the look of human babies but hamper their ability to smell and even (sometimes) breathe. Nature would certainly not have made Pugs who can't mate on their own and require artificial insemination[38] or Bulldogs unable to deliver without C-sections. I loved my inbred, puppy-mill-produced Cocker Spaniel, but nature would not have made a dog dumber than a hamster, unable to find the open door to a gate much less find his way home, and susceptible to eating intestinal-blocking, non-biodegradable substances in such massive quantities they required surgical intervention. At this point, for some dog lovers, the values have almost flipped, with hybrids now seen as healthier, more authentic, and more special than racially "pure" dogs.

What's more, the notion of "breed," like "race," is ultimately a fiction and a construct. There are no natural borderlines between breeds as there are, say, between species (though even there the boundaries can be fuzzy). Many breeds were themselves, in fact, the result of mixing other already established purebreds together, and then re-breeding until they bred true again. At the origin of every purebred is a mix. Breed-mixing is not the aberration but the norm, the source of health and revitalization.

But not so fast. Breed still matters. It may be a myth, but it's a myth we live, with very real and material effects. Pit Bulls, for example, are still disproportionately euthanized in shelters because the prejudice against them keeps them from being adopted. (It matters little that Pit Bull-type dogs don't even qualify as a "breed" when they are treated as such.) Indeed, that breed matters is the very basis for this book. I've been arguing that our cultural mythologies of breeds matter, that they have material effects, and that they reflect and serve American culture. Saying that even breed itself is a mythology does not in any way lessen the power of breed mythologies. Mythologies, like the ideologies they encapsulate, are strong and resilient. They're very good at reconstructing themselves.

Even so, the status of impure-breeds had shifted by the 2000s, and mutts were newly cool. As dogs shifted from status symbol to companion, and as health became valued over arbitrary standards of conformation, the mutt shifted from being the underdog to the top dog—and, indeed, almost the First Dog.

In the end, the Obamas didn't get a mutt, they got a purebred. Because of Malia's allergies, they adopted a (hypoallergenic) Portuguese Water Dog from their ailing friend Ted Kennedy, who was not only a senator but also a dog breeder. I respect this choice, of course, but I would have loved to see a First Mutt getting the celebrity status that Bo, the Portuguese Water Dog, went on to garner. Had the Obamas adopted a rescue mutt, they might, by example, have changed the face of the iconic American dog, as they have the race of the iconic American family.

Chapter Seven

Made to Order
Designer Dogs in the 2010s

Doodling

In their search for a hypoallergenic dog, the Obamas briefly considered a Labradoodle. This "breed," a cross of Labrador Retriever and Poodle, had become the dog of choice for allergy sufferers (and others) in the 2000s, joined by Goldendoodles (Golden Retrievers crossed with Poodles) and other Poodle hybrids. Had the ailing Ted Kennedy not gifted the First Family a Portuguese Water Dog, his beloved breed, not long before his death, a designer dog may have marked the White House.

By the 2010s, the phenomenon of "designer dogs," of which the Labradoodle is a prominent example, was in full swing. The variety of designer dog toys and canine couture offered in pet stores was matched by the variety of designer dog "breeds" emerging. A *Newsweek* article from 2009 says that, at that time, "about 20 percent of the dogs raised in puppy mills are designer breeds, with Puggles, Labradoodles and Yorkiepoos (Yorkshire Terrier-Poodle mixes) among the most popular," and that designer dogs are more lucrative for breeders than purebreds.[1] As this decade ends, you can now find Cavapoos (Cavalier King Charles Spaniel and Poodle), Schnoodles (Schnauzer and Poodle), Puggles (Pug and Beagle), Maltipoos (Maltese and Poodle), Morkies (Maltese and Yorkshire Terrier), and Dorkies (Dachshund and Yorkie), among many other concoctions. People now joke about a new designer dog called the Bull-Shit (Bulldog-Shi Tzu), a pairing as unfortunate to imagine as to utter.

Although the term "Doodle" suggests the haphazard, serendipitous creation of a mindless pencil on paper, Labradoodles are, to the contrary, far from unplanned. They debuted in 1988 when an Australian man, Wally Conron, sought to create guide dogs for people with dog allergies. Labradoodles combined the hypoallergenic qualities of

Chapter Seven. Made to Order

A Labradoodle, designed to combine the temperament of the Labrador Retriever with the hypoallergenic fur of the Poodle (photograph by Bruce Williamson via Unsplash).

Poodles with the Labrador Retriever temperament (good-natured, mellow, resilient, and eager to please). They also happen to be adorable, both soft and scraggly, looking somehow both droopy and perky. After an initial reluctance among purebred loyalists to accept the purity of this new cross-breed, Conron created the term "Labradoodle" to give it legitimacy. Demand for Labradoodles quickly spread beyond the disabled community and into the entitled community, and they've been a hot item ever since they made their debut in the United States in 1998.[2]

I get it. I almost bought a Goldendoodle from a pet store. I was already well into the research for this book, and had determined for myself that any future additions to my family would come from rescue shelters. I'd also decided that I wasn't going to do puppies again. I'd enjoyed raising Chappy and Houdini from puppyhood, but I was getting too old for potty runs in the middle of the night. Then I saw the puppy in the window and had to hold him, which stirred up that old, almost hormonal, ache of desire that normal women (so I'm told) have for human babies. The soft, golden-white coat, more fluff than fur; that goofy beauty. It took almost more willpower than I could muster for me to return the soft, cake-batter-breathed creature to the store clerk. True, I fall for any and every puppy I encounter, and fall hard, but it didn't help that the puppy was a Doodle. I hurt as I walked away from the pet store, and throughout the rest of the day, and all through the night. So I get that Doodle desire.

Doodles are recent arrivals in a long line of designer dogs (sometimes called hybrid breeds). These dogs are bred by deliberately mixing two purebred lines. Cockapoos (sometimes called Cockadoodles)—Cocker Spaniels crossed with Poodles—have long occupied the designer dog pantheon, first sold as novelty dogs in the 1950s and quickly mass-produced by "puppy mills." However, the designer dog fad greatly expanded only recently to include the incredible array of -doodles and -poos and -orkies and -weenies that we see today. These are the dogs-of-the-decade for an era in which individuality—both of humans and of dogs—is completely integrated into the economy.

These dogs are not mutts, even if they are mixes. Nor are they new breeds. To make a Labradoodle requires a purebred Labrador Retriever to be mated with a purebred Poodle. That's the only way to ensure a reliable mix of Lab and Poodle traits. Even then, not all puppies from the litter will show the appropriate combination of traits. Labradoodles mixed with each other could produce a whole range of offspring, from pure Lab to pure Poodle and everything in-between. Producing a true Labradoodle takes all the inefficiencies of pure-breeding and multiplies them. Pure-breeding limits a gene pool, which means that along with favorable traits, genetic problems, even recessive ones, get passed down from both parents far more often than they would in a general gene pool. Mutts, with their open gene pool, have greater variation in their DNA and are less likely to carry two recessive genes for undesirable health predilections (hip dysplasia, congenital heart disease, epilepsy) as are purebreds. Designer dogs, however, as the offspring of two purebreds, introduce the artificially preserved genetic lines of one purebred breed with a new set from another purebred breed. (On the other hand, an acquaintance recently told me that she'd purchased a puppy marketed as a "Double Doodle"—the offspring of a Goldendoodle and a Labradoodle. I'm interested to see if this improvised pseudo-breed catches on.)

The Doodle fad, which encouraged less than scrupulous breeding practices, has amplified this phenomenon so much that Wally Conron, the inventor of the Labradoodle, now regrets it, saying he's "opened a Pandora's box" and "released a Frankenstein."[3] In fact, when President Obama announced that he was considering a Labradoodle, Conron "wrote him a letter saying what the pitfalls were…. A lot of them are untrainable, and a lot of them are no good for people with allergies." Conron's term "Frankenstein" for his hybrid suggests a kind of mad scientist overstepping, as if such a creation goes against nature.

Chapter Seven. Made to Order 161

But if designer dogs are unnatural, then, by the same logic, purebreds are unnatural, too. All purebreds are the temporary triumph of selected genetic order over nature's radical randomness. What's more, most purebreds were once designer dogs, the result of crossing prior purebreds to create specific desired traits. Then again, any attempt to override Darwinian natural selection with deliberate selective breeding might be seen as unnatural. Jon Mooallem, in an article pitting Pug purists against a Puggle inventor and breeder, notes that "designer dogs may only promise what dog breeding always has: the chance to create a custom-designed ideal, a more convenient, useful animal suited to our needs, whatever they happen to be."[4] Designer dogs may be less "a remedy for what's wrong with our old dogs" and more "a symptom of what's wrong with us" and with what we expect of our dogs.[5]

Some people prefer to call designer dogs "hybrid breeds," objecting that the term "designer dogs" suggests that such dogs are "made to order," customized to the personal needs of customers. In a sense, though, the idea of a customized, personalized dog is a driving mythology behind the designer dog phenomenon. Designer dogs emerge in a consumer culture in which we express ourselves—or, really, design ourselves—through our consumer choices. Our economy has been moving from macro-consumerism to micro-consumerism. In the micro-economy, we expect the marketplace to offer us seemingly infinite options for self-expression and personalization. It makes sense that in such a culture we would approach shopping for dogs as we approach shopping for clothes or cars (or dog toys), with the ability to specify size and color from a mix-and-match menu. The hybrid "breed"—or *hybreed*?—operates as a kind of personal brand, in this era when having a brand is becoming synonymous with having an identity. We acquire our dogs the way we acquire our selves—by which I mean our *images*—selecting our own hair color, body size, and facial features, using technology when nature's options seem insufficient.

It's not true, of course, that we can make dogs to order, genetically. Not yet, anyway. The designer dogs we get as a result of interbreeding purebred lines might turn out very different than the blend of breeds might seem to predict. But that's not my point here. What I want to point to is that in the 2010s, we've seen dogs, and so much else, including ourselves, as things we can design. Even genetic traits are commodities, things that can be selected and purchased. It's as if we're so trained by consumer culture that we see the world of possibilities as a mail-order catalogue.

The phenomenon of designer dogs runs on the ultimate customer fantasy of customizability. Designer dogs are one way to personalize

The Puggle is a designer dog combining Pug with Beagle (photograph by Tom Hills via Unsplash).

dogs—to make them to order for the people who "own" them, and to treat nature as a starting point rather than a limiting factor. There are other ways that go even farther beyond nature than selective breeding.

From Snoopy to Snuppy

On February 28, 2018, I awoke to the news on NPR that Barbra Streisand had cloned her dog. Sipping my morning coffee, I learned that before the death of her beloved dog Sammie, a Coton de Tulear, Streisand had cells taken from the canine's mouth and stomach. After Sammie's death, Streisand had the cells cloned, resulting in three little cottonball Coton puppies, of which Streisand kept two.

My response was two-fold: first, a knee-jerk horror at the possibilities unleashed by cloning dogs (along with thoughts of all those dogs languishing in shelters), but second, and quick on its heels, a feeling of longing to clone my own beloved dogs. Why hadn't I saved cells from Pretzel, my first dog? A Cocker Spaniel-Border Collie mix with a crooked jaw, an adorable underbite, and a head that, Dr. Seuss-like, was too small for his body, he was one of a kind, and therefore should have been cloned.

Chapter Seven. Made to Order

The news of Streisand's clones had emerged as a result of a seemingly off-hand comment Streisand had made in an interview with *Variety* magazine. "During the photo shoot, Streisand joked that a portrait with her three Coton de Tulear dogs should be captioned 'Send in the Clones.'"[6] The pun is especially apt for *Cotons*, which the AKC website describes as "a bright, happy-go-lucky companion dog whose favorite activities include clowning, cavorting, and following their special human around the house."[7]

Unfortunately, the clownish pun seems to make light of, even trivialize, a very serious issue. Streisand received such a backlash from some Animal Rights defenders for her seemingly glib comment and cavalier attitude to dog cloning that she published an opinion piece in the *New York Times* defending her choice. "I was so devastated by the loss of my dear Samantha, after 14 years together, that I just wanted to keep her with me in some way. It was easier to let Sammie go if I knew I could keep some part of her alive, something that came from her DNA." She concluded, "You can clone the look of a dog, but you can't clone the soul. Still, every time I look at their faces, I think of my Samantha ... and smile."[8]

Streisand's self-justification, though, prompted further backlash, this time from the angle of psychological health. Stuart Heritage of *The Guardian*, for example, wrote that "a big part of owning a pet is to learn about death." When your pet dies, "you're bereft, and then, slowly, you learn how to move on. Little by little, pets equip you with the tools to deal with grief." The "saddest part of this Barbra Streisand news," he says, is "that she refused to let go. She failed to grasp the most fundamental point of life: it ends. And once it's over, you can never get it back."[9]

I can certainly empathize with the pain of losing a loved one and the refusal to let go. Still, Streisand's "Send in the Clones" incident came as a shock to me. I'd thought the cloning of pets was still a futuristic scenario, only to learn that the clones have already been sent in. They're here, and they're adorable. Over the coming days and months I would learn that the animal cloning is well under way, not only in the realms of research but also in the realms of commerce and industry. Like most people, I'd heard of the first successfully cloned mammal, the sheep Dolly, in 1996. Since Dolly, scientists successfully cloned at least eighteen species of mammal, including rats, rabbits, cats, cattle, horses, deer, and, in 2005, the first dog.

Snuppy—the nickname for the Seoul National University puppy—was born in a South Korean Laboratory. It took a lot of dogs to create one clone. The team, led by the "King of Cloning," Woo Suk Hwang, removed 1095 eggs from dog wombs, extracted their nuclear DNA, replaced it with the DNA of a three-year-old Afghan Hound, zapped the cells with an electric current to stimulate cell division, and then implanted those newly formed embryos into 123 surrogate mothers. Each removal and each implantation of eggs requires surgery. Only three pregnancies resulted: one miscarried, one puppy died at twenty-two days old, and one was Snuppy.[10]

That inefficiency of oocytes alone makes the ethics of cloning dogs questionable, as do the multiple, unnecessary surgeries performed on donor and surrogate dogs. As John Woestendiek details in his 2010 book *Dog, Inc.: The Uncanny Inside Story of Cloning Man's Best Friend*, dogs pose particular difficulties for cloning compared to many other mammals. Unlike the sheep, pigs, cats, and some dozen other mammals that preceded them in cloning, dogs go into estrus only once or twice a year and produce only about eight eggs per cycle. When extracted, these eggs are opaque, making them harder to work with. Woestendiek's book details the many years, multiple laboratories, and hundreds of dogs it took to develop the technique to make the first dog clone. Even by 2010, Woestendiek estimates, it still took about twelve dogs to make one clone. That's twelve dogs subjected to unnecessary surgeries (and their concomitant incarcerations).

What's more, South Korea, where these cloning procedures are performed, imposes far less rigorous animal welfare laws than does the United States for animals used in research and industry, so the fate of these egg-donor and surrogate-mother dogs is unknown. (Woestendiek reports rumors that some of the dogs used in cloning were euthanized or sold to the dog meat industry. Even Snuppy himself spent the bulk of his life kenneled in the laboratory.) While the cloning process will become more efficient with time and experience, there are still thousands of uncloned dogs euthanized every year, dogs who could make just as good pets.

Cloning pets was not the original goal of all this research. In 2005, a member of Snuppy's research team insisted, "We are not in the business of cloning pets." Gerald Schatten, of the University of Pittsburgh School of Medicine, further stated, "We perform nuclear transfer for medical research."[11] They intended to clone dogs only for research, and only then when clone studies could tell us things that we couldn't learn any other way. Although commercial applications had been discussed from the start, and although pet-tissue banks were already storing pet cells in the United States and elsewhere, at the time of Snuppy's creation in 2005, the feasibility of pet-cloning as a profitable business must have seemed unthinkable. Even if ethical issues were of no concern, dog cloning was too difficult and wasteful and expensive a process to seem viable. But just a few years later, commercial pet cloning was under way. By the time Streisand had Sammie cloned, the cost was down to a mere $50,000.

Underlying the decision to clone a pet is the sense of one's dog as unique and individual. Cloning is the fantasy of replacing the irreplaceable. People clone their dogs because they see the dogs as individuals, who can't simply be replaced by another dog. So although the impulse to clone a dog may at first seem like an erasure of individuality, I think it's actually—or also—just the opposite. The impulse to clone a dog comes from recognizing the absolute individuality of the dog.

Ironically, of course, individuality can't be replicated. That's the tragic paradox of cloning for people seeking to recreate their dog's personhood and personality. In reality, the clone is not a return of the same dog, but another dog, a genetic twin of the original dog, not a resurrection. Although clones share physical characteristics of their cell donor, they often have very different personalities. As Streisand wrote, "you can't clone the soul." Not yet, anyway.

Designer Genes

The difficult science problems raised by cloning resolved much more quickly than the difficult ethical issues, for which we're still developing tools. Meanwhile, additional genetic technologies are arising and raising corresponding philosophical questions.

The phenomenon of humans manipulating the genetic make-up of dogs is not new, of course, and may even be as old as dogs themselves. The vast range of dog sizes, shapes, proportions, and colors testifies to humans' ability to override nature. We've manufactured greater variation in this species—from the two-pound teacup Yorkie to the two hundred-pound Great Dane—than exist in any other species. Indeed, dogs have been our greatest success in genetic engineering. However, genetic manipulation formerly took many generations. In the twenty-first century, radical genetic change can be made in a single generation.

Once upon a time, "genetic" used to mean "natural," at least when it came to the nature/nurture or nature/culture divides. To say something was "genetic" was to pronounce it natural, inevitable, and beyond question. That's no longer the case. Now we can not only "fix" genes we find "faulty," but design new genetic combinations never designed by "nature." We now live in an era when genes are seen as raw materials for bioengineering and when, for that matter, the field of epigenetics—which looks at the role of the environment in activating or deactivating gene expression—is teaching us that genetics were never the bottom line anyway. The nature/nurture opposition is being thoroughly deconstructed, disrupting other foundational oppositions—non-human/human, object/subject, non-person/person—in its wake.

One example of designing genes emerged on August 30, 2018, when *Science* magazine ran an article reporting that Beagle puppies with the canine equivalent of Duchenne muscular dystrophy (DMD), a muscle-wasting disease, were successfully treated using CRISPR/Cas9.[12]

CRISPR, or *Clustered regularly interspaced short palindromic repeats*, is a "gene-editing" tool, which can be used to patch in corrections to faulty genes. DMD is caused by mutations to the gene that makes dystrophin, a protein needed to support muscle structure and function. Repairing those mutations could restore muscle production. In the Beagles, the repaired genetic material was carried on a benign virus injected into one-month-old puppies. Later measurements revealed increased dystrophin function throughout their bodies. While this technology is still years away from human application, with a number of things that could go wrong still to be worked out, a cure for DMD in humans is at least theoretically feasible.

Such research is not without costs for dogs, of course. For starters, it requires the breeding of a large number of Beagles with the dog version of Duchenne's muscular dystrophy. Some of the Beagles would then be injected with the CRISPR-edited gene (carried on benign viruses) and monitored in laboratory confinement. That makes for a life of much suffering and early death for many dogs. Still, Duchenne's is a devastating disease for humans; children with it rarely live past their twenties, and suffer significantly during their short lives from their body's inability to produce muscle adequately. I don't think I would be able to tell (human) families with Duchenne's babies that a cure wasn't worth the cost to dogs.

On the other hand, CRISPR brings up a slew of ethical issues involving genetic manipulation, issues that our philosophical tools struggle to keep up with. As always, animals, and particularly dogs, occupy the realm where we dry run not only our technical tools but also our ethical tools before we apply them to humans. Remember that the selective breeding of animals formed the template for human eugenics. CRISPR represents a renewed potential for "fixing" all kinds of genetic variations currently understood as "defects." Is it ethical and/or desirable to eliminate human "defects"? In the case of Duchenne's, a painful and life-shortening disease, I think I'm comfortable answering "yes." But what about diseases and conditions that don't lead to suffering, reduced lifespan, or severe limitation that can't be accommodated?

Chapter Seven. Made to Order 167

Many disability rights advocates would prioritize progress in terms of access and accommodation over "prevention." As Tom Shakespeare has noted in his "Manifesto for Genetic Justice," "the real problems for many disabled people are not medical or physical, but social, environmental and attitudinal."[13] However, as Ruha Benjamin argues, "[t]he rhetoric of gene salvation has lead to the promotion of individual, medical solutions to problems which are social and structural. We blame the victim, rather than challenging the oppression." Such rhetoric enforces an "ableist" ideology; that is, it assumes "that disability is an abnormality instead of a feature of human diversity."[14] This can lead to what some disability rights activists call "genetic cleansing." And since medical innovation tends to get inequitably distributed, we must, Benjamin argues, "either decide to prioritize issues of equity and justice early and often, or we ensure a world in which the health and longevity of some are predicated on the disposability of others."[15]

I would add that the longevity of some, predicated on the disposability of others, is already the case with dogs, as cloning has so dramatically illustrated. In order to extend the genetic life of one dog, many other dogs must be "sacrificed." In the marketplace of health, a wide gap lies between the haves and the have-nots.

Additional ethical problems come into play when we go from "correcting" perceived "abnormalities" to "improving" the norm itself. Such ethical problems loom on the horizon with humans, as we venture into CRISPR-enabled human gene editing. They're already unleashed when it comes to dogs. For example, the technique for Duchenne Beagles could be used to produce hyper-muscular dogs. Indeed, it already has, as part of the preliminary work for treating DMD puppies. Mimicking a genetic mutation that occurs in some Whippets, scientists at the South China Institute for Stem Cell Biology and Regenerative Medicine in Guangzhou created two puppies with CRISPR-edited myostatin genes. As summarized in *Science News*, "Gene edit creates buff Beagles." Tina Hesman Saey provocatively writes, "Bully Whippets may have competition in doggy body-building contests."[16] Would it be okay to give puppies genetic material resulting in abnormally high muscle mass? Will we, in the future, use CRISPR to create hypoallergenic dogs? Or non-shedding dogs? Will we make coats silkier? Where will we put the limits on making dogs to order?

And further: what else might be possible, whether or not we find it ethical? Will we design entirely new breeds through gene editing? One of the researchers creating the first dog clone has been able to combine cloning with gene splicing techniques to make a dog that fluoresces green. The technology already exists to create novelty pets. How far will we take it? Although the cost for more frivolous uses of CRISPR is currently prohibitive, remember how quickly that changed with dog cloning.

And then, how much of the technology tested out on dogs will we transfer to human applications? How much are our designs with dogs preparing humans to design ourselves?

One Medicine

In the laboratory, as elsewhere, dogs often serve as surrogates or proxies for humans. One of the long-recognized paradoxes of animal research is that we understand dogs to be different enough from humans that we can justify trial-running both our technology and our ethics on them (rather than directly on humans), but they're similar enough to us that those trial runs are meaningful. Their status as persons, if not as people, is liminal or ambivalent. We see them both as radically distinct from humans and as honorary humans. And this ambivalence can result in seeming contradictions, such as sacrificing multiple nameless laboratory dogs in order to clone one individual dog, or subjecting laboratory dogs to amplified versions of the kind of suffering we're seeking to prevent in other dogs (and in humans). Another term for this ambivalence might be *inequality*; there's a huge class divide among dogs. Indeed, the class divide among dogs in America is probably greater now than it's ever been, as is arguably the case among humans in the United States as well.

A recent trip to the dentist brought this inequality, as well as the invisibility of laboratory dogs, home to me. My dentist regularly asks about my dogs, and while I believe he's being genuinely friendly, it's also a good technique to get me to relax. (I know my students also use this technique on me, priming me by asking how my dogs are before, say, requesting an extension on a paper.) On this visit for my dentist to check on my recent tooth implant (I'd gotten hit by a half-blind Great Dane and cracked my teeth—long story), he also asked me about my writing, and I told him about this book. As we got to talking about the ethical issues emerging with CRISPR, he mentioned in passing that when he was in dental school, students practiced their implant techniques on dogs. He remembered that some dogs would get multiple teeth pulled, to be replaced with implants. At various stages of healing, dogs would be "sacrificed" and autopsied, so that the dental students could learn from within how well the bone grafts were taking. As my dentist spoke, I put my tongue to my new implant, which now echoed with the pain of countless unseen dogs. It had never even occurred to me when I got the implant that it had been practiced on non-humans before being transferred across species. Do I dare investigate further how many non-human animals were sacrificed to make all of my mundane medical and dental procedures possible?

Increasingly, however, as dogs (or at least some dogs) move toward semi-personhood status, some medical experiments intended for human applications reflect this move. As I wrote in Chapter Two, by the 1960s Beagles were regularly bred as laboratory dogs, and the industry of breeding laboratory animals has only grown over the ensuing decades despite increasing public pressure against abusive treatment of lab animals. In the past, those experiments often involved making normal dogs unhealthy and then experimentally treating the malady, or breeding for a diseased condition and then treating the disease. A newer movement, common in research at veterinary schools, now takes pet dogs who developed the disease "naturally"—or at least not by laboratory induction—and then drawing data from treatment the dogs need anyway.

I have been the recipient of such an approach—or, more accurately, two of my dogs have been. Houdini, my Cocker Spaniel, whom I mentioned in Chapter One, turned out to have a congenital heart condition. My vet sent us to a cardiologist at the Colorado State University's Veterinary Teaching Hospital, where they prescribed $100-a-month medications. After a year of pills ($1200), poor Houdini was, at age twelve, declared "end stage," meaning that he had thirty days or fewer of expected life left. That's when the cardiologist told us about an experimental study carried out by her colleague. Dr. Chris Orton was developing an artificial heart valve that might eventually be used on humans.

At that point, Houdini kept gasping for breath. I'd go to sleep to the sound of half-coughs and wake up every morning holding my own breath until I heard his; I only exhaled after I knew he was still alive. His every breath was such a labor that his diaphragm heaved under his protruding ribs, and his heart had so expanded in his emaciated body that you could practically cup your palm over it at the side of his chest. So the proposition seemed to me a win-win. The study would pay for Houdini's medical expenses, his demise would yield useful data, and he might just buy several more years of his own special brand of fussy, sometimes hissy, always Cockery happiness.

In the waiting room during the surgery, where I petted one-eyed and three-legged dogs waiting for chemo, a liaison checked in on me regularly, brought me coffee, and printed out more word scramble puzzles from the internet when she saw that I'd completed all the ones I'd brought. No one ever did this for me when my husband had any of his procedures or surgeries or radiation or chemo treatments. Oddly, people treated me more "humanely" at the veterinary hospital than at any of the hospitals for humans.

The wait, though, was agonizing. Finally, Dr. Orton came out in his scrubs and said that the valve placement was successful. Immediately after the surgery, he said, Houdini's heart "sighed," and his breathing and blood flow improved.

But then a few days later Houdini developed a clot. The team tried to treat it with clot-busting medication, but then Houdi developed internal bleeding. It went back and forth. After a week, the team decided not to make Houdini suffer any more.

When I went back to the ICU to say goodbye to my little buff Cocker, I noticed a red blotch on the top of his head. I was a little teary and not seeing straight. "Is that blood?" I asked, but when I turned to the team of cardiologists and vet techs for the answer, I saw that several of them were weeping as effusively as me, and realized in the instant that the red splotch was lipstick from somebody's farewell kiss. Clearly, Houdini was not some anonymous laboratory animal.

Although Houdini did not survive, the team told me that he still yielded them useful data. They might have told me that just to make me feel better, but I doubt it. One of the cardiologists showed me expensive scans and graphs with calculations beside them. In the end, I was very glad I allowed Houdini to be used in the artificial valve trial. He might ultimately contribute to the development of a valve that may help humans—and, I hope, a few other dogs, too.

For some people, of course, doing heart surgery on aging pet dogs to extend their lives by another year or two is absurd. For other people, it's as much a no-brainer as extending the lives of humans by any medical means necessary.

Currently, Tiger, my Husky mix, is on a clinical trial for a cancer vaccine. The Vaccine Against Canine Cancer Study (VACCS) is being conducted by Dr. Doug Thamm at Colorado State University's Flint Animal Cancer Center along with researchers at the veterinary schools of Arizona State University and University of California–Davis. Tiger has had four shots of either the cancer vaccine or a placebo (which gave me the idea to name my next dog Placebo). Over the next five years, researchers will track his health, along with the other 799 dogs in the study. Eventually the vaccine, if effective, may have human applications. Indeed, the original aim was for the vaccine to work on humans. Dogs make a good intermediary step both because their tumors resemble those in human bodies and because they live in (nearly) the same environments as their human companions. Personally, I'll be thrilled if the vaccine just lowers the cancer rate in dogs.

The experiments that both Houdini and Tiger took part in represent the new "One Health" movement, which sees humans as one unique species of animals among other unique species of animals. Because humans are animals, the interests of humans and of other animals align. Rather than choosing between animal welfare and progress in human health, the One Health movement emphasizes the commonality of (human) medical and veterinary care in order to advance both. Testing on dogs for human applications doesn't have to take the form of humans benefiting at the expense of dogs. Likewise, spending money to treat a dog doesn't have to mean wasting funds that could have been used to save *actual human beings* (as I've been accused of doing). Ideally, we can help each other.

Tiger seems not to mind his medicalized life too badly, in part because I've given him long walks around the duck pond (now really a goose pond) before and after each shot, and the vet techs bribe him with a bonanza of treats. In the waiting room, though (at least in the pre-pandemic days before the parking lot became the waiting room), I continued to be struck by how medicalized pet life has become. As we wait outside the oncology wing, I see how much this waiting room resembles the human counterparts I've sat in when my life-partner, Rajiv, was treated for cancer. I'm also struck by the way the veterinary hospital is, indeed, a hospital, and the veterinarians are doctors, with the range of specialties—oncology, cardiology, anesthesiology, orthopedic surgery, etc.—of medical doctors for humans.

In fact, based on the small sample sizes of veterinary and human medical care afforded to my dogs and my husband, I'd prefer to be treated in a veterinary hospital. There were times when I sat in the CSU vet school waiting room, my heart pounding as I waited for Houdini's results, when I wondered if I would have a heart attack myself. If I did, I decided, I wanted them to wheel me back to the OR and operate on me alongside Houdini rather than transport me to the people hospital across town.

The Medicalized Dog

This brings us to the other side of the "One Health" movement: If dogs are all that similar to humans, shouldn't medical conditions that we wouldn't hesitate to treat in humans be treated similarly in dogs? As canine medical care nears human medical care, so do its costs.

Currently, Olive, my Border Collie, is aging, and has entered that expensive period of a dog's life. She needs her decayed back tooth pulled, but because of her heart murmur, she'll need to be monitored by a cardiologist while under anesthesia. Some of my friends say that spending thousands of dollars to pull a nearly fourteen-year-old dog's tooth is a poor use of resources, but most of my friends just shrug their shoulders and bemoan the cost of health care these days for both human and dog. Like human medicine, today's veterinary medicine, too, can bankrupt us.

Olive's geriatric medical costs offer just one small example of how medicalized a pet dog's life has become. Scholars influenced by Michel Foucault have noted that the late twentieth and early twenty-first centuries have seen a dramatic increase in the medicalization of personhood. Many Americans today believe "heath care is a human right," which suggests how much we now see being subject to medical care as fundamental to our status as individual human subjects. We take it as a given that our medical condition belongs in a network of charts and records. Our being "in the system" of records gives us proof of personhood.

What's more, we have "medicalized" personality. Traits that once were understood as aspects of one's personality are now treated as medical conditions. People (like me) who were once seen as (and understood themselves to be) grumpy or morose or melancholy are now treated as suffering from depression. Formerly shy people (again, like me) now have social anxiety disorder. Once-scattered people currently have ADHD. The "weird kids" in school whom the other kids once so cruelly made fun of are now diagnosed with autism, treated, and accommodated. I'm not saying that these conditions are "really" just personality traits mis-diagnosed as medical conditions. Quite the opposite, actually. We now *experience* depression, shyness, anxiety, autism, etc., both in ourselves and in others, *as illnesses* that can (and should) be treated. Nor am I saying this is a bad thing. I do very much like my enabling anti-depressant pills. What I am saying is that personality—the essence of personhood—has become medicalized and that medicine has become personalized. And medicalization, of course, is a particularly effective way to induce spending, even among people who might still snub the watermelon-scented dog shampoos and diamond-head-polished nails they can get at today's pet stores and doggy spas.

This medicalization of personality (and the concomitant personalization of medicine) that we see among humans is increasingly true of dogs. Through chemistry, we can design dogs to serve as better pets for us. Dogs who hate to be left alone all day suffer from—and can be treated for—"separation anxiety." There's a pill for that, as there is for aggression, OCD, and, yes, depression. In the 2010s in the United States, many of us already treat depression and anxiety in humans pharmaceutically, just as we do arthritis or high blood pressure. The same is becoming true for such conditions in pet dogs. (I want to be clear that I'm talking about *pet* dogs here. At the end of the decade, what we see in the 2010s in humans we also see in dogs: the divide between rich and poor seems to be getting wider. And nowhere is this divide more clear than in the difference in health care between the haves and the have-nots, the pedigreed and the undocumented, the over-sheltered and the homeless.) Personality drugs don't always live up to their hype, as a recent headline in the parodic newspaper *The Onion* recently captures: "Study Finds Giving CBD to Pet Fails to Address Root Issue of Letting Crazed Monster Live in Your Home." The article implies that it's foolish, if not immoral, to try medicating away nature; CBD proves barely more effective than the placebo "at reversing millions of years of evolution that led to savage creature fundamentally at odds with domestic existence."[17] Still, if we do keep dogs in our house despite their thousands of years of genetic development for outdoor living, isn't it more, well, *humane* to at least ease the anxiety their confinement causes?

What I'm suggesting is that both humans and, increasingly, dogs have become designed: both medicalized and personalized. That is, they are seen as medical subjects, and all the routine aspects of living in a body are now understood as medical conditions. Even personality, for both human and dog, is a medical condition. What's more, we have the option—and perhaps even the obligation—to treat personality disorders. In buying medication, we select and upgrade our personalities. This cultural logic of buying our personalities fits with the logic of designer dogs, even though they may seem opposite phenomena. One phenomenon fixes unwanted personality traits, alongside physical traits, with genetic interaction. The other does so with drugs or surgery. In either case, American culture now sees the genes that nature gave us no longer as destiny but as raw material to engineer—often at great cost. The personality of dogs, like that of people, is now a matter of consumer choice.

From Rex to Rx

Just look at the "health and wellness" aisle of the pet store. There you can buy many of the same over-the-counter medications and dietary supplements you might buy for yourself: glucosamine chondroitin with MSM for arthritis, probiotics to "support" a healthy gut, fish oil and CBD cream for joint pain, and supplements for healthy skin and shiny hair. You can also purchase calming spray for the anxious dog, or buy an infuser so the substance can permeate the house. Indeed, many of the pharmaceutical companies, such as Pfizer and Eli Lilly, which make human medications, have branched into the canine and feline markets. So too have some of the companies of the alternative and complementary medical industry, such as GNC, which makes GNC pets, and Arm & Hammer, which sells enzymatic, baking soda-infused toothpaste for dogs.

Even dog food has been medicalized. In Chapter Three I discussed the "wilderness" trend in dog food, which reflects a model of dog origins as descending directly and naturally from wolves. I see in this phenomenon the residual (or perhaps reviving) mythology of the rewilding era. There's also a well-established hearth-and-home trend in dog food, reflecting the model of dogs as family members and the origins of dogs as a result of human rearing of wolf cubs. Increasingly, though, I'm also seeing a branch of medical-themed dog food in the pet store. The palette of the package is no longer the browns and greens of the "blue" wilderness but sterile whiteness. Sometimes the letters Rx appear against this backdrop. Here, dogs are neither wild others or four-legged people, but human inventions, and feeding them requires scientific and medical intervention, which is at least as pricey as the wilderness.

This food isn't depicted as being made in a kitchen or as running in the wild but as concocted in a laboratory. The package labels I read tend to refer to their contents less often as "recipes" or "entrées" and more often as "formulas." Authority brand dog food, made by GNC Pets, offers "Fish and Potato formula with Omega Fatty Acids, Natural Fiber, and No Preservatives" for "Skin, Coat & Digestive Health Support." Science Diet offers "Clinically Proven Antioxidant benefits." Blue's Life Protection Formula with LifeSource Bits provides "Active Nutrients and Antioxidants for Your Dog's Health & Well-Being"; this line of Blue also offers "Health Bars." Hills Prescription Diet dog food, in sterile white packages, offers Joint Care, Kidney Care, Dental Care, and Urinary Care versions. Fat dogs can be treated with "Metabolic (weight management)" food. Sensitive dogs (about which I know a little something) can seek comfort in "Skin and Food Sensitivities" options and "Derm Defense (for Environmental Sensitivities)" options. Food can no longer be taken for granted; eating naturally requires expert intervention. We see the medicalization of dogs reflected in their kibble; dog food, too, is a medical matter.

We see this trend of medicalizing food in human models as well. We may crave nature and seek out what's "natural" and "organic," but we're also suspicious of nature; it's dirty and messy and has bugs in it, not to mention foreign microbes. We're also suspicious of our own bodies in this dangerous modern world. Our immune systems are under constant threat, and we need supplements that "support a healthy immune system." There's more than a bit of magical thinking mixed into the vitamins-and-supplements marketing, in spite of the "scientific" and "clinical" packaging; a trip to the health food store presents ample examples of our cultural schizophrenia about nature and science. We believe in the healing power of nature but think it needs to be supplemented; we want our vitamins organic but also hermetically sealed in medicine bottles. We supplement the natural with the artificial. Once again, dogs are a place where we play out our conflicting ideas about nature.

I can't deny, at this point in history, that dogs as we know them today are not "natural," if by natural we mean created without human interference. Dogs may or may not have originally been the product of natural selection, but at this point all dogs for whom we're buying dog food have centuries of selective breeding twisting in their DNA strands. The origin story of this dog mythology emphasizes the human intervention in dog creation. Today's dogs are clearly man-made, which makes it easier to believe the model of dog origins that says dogs were man-made from the start. As I've said in earlier chapters, different decades and eras seem to favor different origin stories of dogs. Some of the shift in dog origin mythologies over the decades stems from new scientific evidence revealed by new technology. However, an era's mythology of choice can't be explained entirely by the availability of scientific evidence. The dominant origin story of this era of prescription dog food, dogs as health care consumers, and dog cloning, seems to be that the very species itself only exists through human intervention (or invention). Underlying the scientific approach to dog food, I see a narrative that treats dogs as human creations. Dogs are neither our children, nor wild Others, but our own inventions. In this sense, all dogs are designer dogs from the start. Like the packaged dog food they eat, dogs, in all their array of breeds, are artificial human creations. They're products that we designed and own.

Personal Shoppers

It's not just in the medical and nutrition arenas that dogs became consumers and marketing demographics. By the 2010s, dogs had not just entered our houses, our kitchens, and our bedrooms, but—perhaps even more personal to Americans—our wallets. They now occupy a significant place in our economic infrastructure, and are thoroughly integrated into the neoliberal marketplace, both as consumers (or surrogate consumers) and as objects of consumption.

It's proportionally more expensive to own a dog than ever. In part this is because of the medicalization of dogs; more veterinary services are not only offered to but also expected of the dog owner than ever. Goods and services for dogs that were once considered luxuries—toothpaste, joint pain supplements, geriatric blood panels—are now just part of dog ownership. As we increasingly grant pet dogs personhood, with the rights and privileges of other (human) members of the family, they are increasingly treated to our medicalized life and its expenses.

Dogs now also require other services that they didn't in the past. Dogs whose humans work outside the home all day need daycare, in the form of day camp or dog walkers. Dogs stuck in the home all day need a plethora of strong, enticing toys to keep them from eating the sofa. Because they live as humans, dogs need to be taught manners, such as how to greet visitors at the door, which requires classes or home visits by personal trainers. Because dogs lie in our beds, they need to be kept clean and free of bugs, allergens, and foul odors—so, shampoo and regular grooming. As they increasingly occupy human domestic spaces, their goods increasingly occupy human retail spaces. Dogs have their own aisles in our grocery stores and their own section in IKEA (not to mention their own retail boutiques). Dogs in the 2010s in the United States could be called *canis lupus economicus.*

It's no surprise to anyone who's visited a pet store in the past few decades that dogs are now as thoroughly integrated into the marketplace as anyone. I experience this reality regularly when I pick up my dogs from day camp at PetSmart PetsHotel (which its customers no longer call a kennel). On our way out, we like to weave our way through the aisles and go shopping together before making our way out the door. Olive and Tiger especially like the aisle with the bones and chew treats and bully sticks, where the most expensive goodies are lined up not at eye level for me but at nose level for them. Truly, the dogs are the ones doing the shopping. Or, perhaps, it's the dog-human hybrid, operating as a single unit, that's the individual consumer, with the dog end leading the way. Olive stops at each bin and sniffs its contents thoroughly before moving on, while Tiger is a bit more random in his investigations. Both, though, are clearly doing the olfactory version of window shopping, and the merchandise is lined up to accommodate their shopping styles. PetSmart's lay-out recognizes dogs (not just their human guardians) as consumers.

The aisle of bones, pig's ears, antlers, and bully sticks, all laid out at dog's-nose level, is flanked by an endcap displaying individually wrapped dog treats in open glass (well, actually, acrylic) jars. Their open mouths offer individually wrapped Vera brand treats: chicken meatballs, beef patties, nature bars, pork sausage links, mini fillets, and superfood beef mini burgers. I feel like a kid in an old-timey candy shop, and am tempted to take one of each.

Around the corner are dog toys, with practically as much choice as in a toy store for children. Indeed, the recently bankrupt Toys R Us still offers Toys R Us Pets, a line of pet toys sold at PetSmart. People who like to dismiss pet dogs as substitutes for children would find plenty of material here to support that argument; these highly personalized toys suggest that pets are joining or even displacing children in the hearts and homes of at least some adults in the United States. These tennis balls, ring toys, squeaker sticks, footballs, and Frisbee-style flyers come in the bright reds, yellows, greens, blues, and oranges of a children's playroom. As dogs move from the margins into the center of human households, they often get put in roles already carved out for them, such as the role of child.

A whole array of puppy toys come in baby pastels: pinks, powder blues, and soft yellows, with basinet-sized fleece blankets and teething toys shaped like keys, indistinguishable from the human version. Others come in in bright, nursery-room reds, pinks, oranges, and greens outside the dog's visual range. Even Kong makes a pacifier-shaped toy. Some toys come in shapes dogs don't recognize (cupcakes, Jack-o-lanterns, dreidels, wrapped presents with bows on top). They're seasonal for holidays, so you can include your dogs in the gift-giving celebrations. (My dogs always get toys off-season from the clearance bin; they play with candy cane shapes in January, hearts in March, and bunnies in May.) Owners like me take great pleasure in shopping for their dogs, and in including their dogs in the shopping experience. We're buying (for) our selves as much as we are for the dogs.

Individuality has long been a dominant American ideology, and a primary medium for the expression of individuality has been the marketplace. We construct and curate our sense of self through consumer choices. Indeed, part of being an individual in the 2010s is having a personal "brand." The maintenance of individuality through specialized purchases in turn keeps the economy flowing. You could say that, in the United States, life begins at consumption—or at least life as a personalized individual. Part of being a person in the United States is being a shopper; indeed, shopping is one of our few forms of agency. The irony is that, in the neoliberal economy of the present, while individuality poses as the ideal to strive for, actual individuality is more impossible than ever. To bolster our sense of individuality, or at least of agency, we shop for our selves (with those selves as both the consumers and the objects being purchased). And now we shop for our dogs.

Why else would Nylabone offer not just the standard doggy flavors of chicken, bacon, beef, and peanut butter, but also Meatloaf and Gravy; Bacon Cheeseburger; Chili Cheese dog; Cherry Slushy; and Buttered Popcorn (among others)? Why would Top Paw offer dog spritzes in scents like Cucumber Melon and Peaches & Cream? Of course these are for the owners—or at least the owner end of the human-dog unit. Dogs don't like imposed, synthetic scents, and would prefer to roll their own *eau de garbage*. Why else would PetSmart offer all manner of doggie "apparel": raincoats, sweaters, designer jackets, beach hats, football jerseys, cheerleader uniforms, and Halloween costumes? Why else, too, would we find among the dog food aisles such an array of medleys, stews, and casseroles?

The different dog toys and foods are not as different from each other as is their packaging. What all this variety and specificity suggest is that, as dogs acquire the role of consumer, they have become personalized and individualized. On the one hand this means recognizing the individuality of dogs, as we see in specialized toys for different levels of play and for chewing styles ranging from "Gentle Chewing Style" to "Extreme Chewing Style." We recognize that some dogs (like my Tiger) adore squeakers and crumply sounds. Others, like Olive, prefer the interactive puzzles. On another hand, the personalization of dogs means that dogs become personalized as an extension of their human guardians—dressed up to reflect the style and politics of the owner, and sometimes even made to order. In our economy of mass-production—and, increasingly, of micro-consumption—dog toys reflect a fundamental contradiction of consumerist personhood. We live in a period of mass-produced individualism. Our signifiers of selfhood are produced by anonymous workers across the global economy.

Even as we grant dogs increasing personhood, some of us dream of personalizing dogs to our own wants and needs. It makes sense to me that people trained in marketplace desire would shop for the dogs themselves in the same way they shop for the toys for those dogs. The logic of shopping for individuality—the logic of self as brand—finds its soul mate in designer dogs and in personal clones.

What the dogs themselves think of these designer dog foods and toys and outfits is another matter. Shopping with my dogs, as I look mesmerized at the aisles of packaging, Olive and Tiger sniff out the contents of the shelves, then dive deep underneath to dig out stray kibble. Their butts stick out from under the shelves as they scavenge, before emerging with dusty muzzles over their happily chomping jaws.

Passing the cash registers on our way out of PetSmart, my dogs both sit, knowing that they'll be rewarded with a canine cookie. The cashiers, who know my dogs by name, remember that I like my pups to earn their treats, so Olive and Tiger immediately flip out, rolling and spinning in circles and trying to "high five" the cashier. The dogs have learned that if they do a trick for her they'll get a treat, so they offer up everything in their repertoire. The cashier, though, can't be enticed that easily. She knows that my dogs have been through Beki's "Click-a-Trick" class (offered in October in time for Halloween), and that I like my dogs to wait for the command. So she sits out their shenanigans and waits for them to watch her.

I recognize that PetSmart has trained me, along with Olive and Tiger, that the cash register is our happy place. Here, where the cashier knows the dogs by name, they become individuals. Indeed, the more they're treated as individuals, the more I want to buy things for them. The cashier doesn't know my name, only those of my dogs. So here, at the cash register, they're more individualized than I am, and I wouldn't have it any other way. It's as if they're displacing me, the human, in the role of individual. Or, perhaps they *are* my individuality, at the core of my identity.

Just as drops of saliva are ready to slide off their tongues, the cashier "shoots" Olive, who dies a drama-queen death, and makes Tiger army-crawl for his biscuit. What these strange behaviors mean to my dogs I can't fathom. For that matter, what our relationship "means" to them is beyond my knowing. It's as opaque to me as the bone-shaped "cookies" are to them—or *were*, because they've already snatched the treats from the cashier's fingers and swallowed down in one gulp before begging for more. The dogs always leave satisfied, their tricks exclaimed over and rewarded, which makes me happy. In spite of my conscious efforts not to get swept into consumerist ideology, I unconsciously express my love through buying stuff for my dogs, from chew toys to drugs to surgery. PetSmart's old motto "Where Pets Are Family" could be updated to "Where Pets Are Individuals." What doesn't even need stating is "Where Pets Are Shoppers." It's where we all—humans and dogs alike—confirm our personhood through acts of individual consumption.

Coda: Miss Olive

As I was completing this chapter, Olive's health seemed to worsen. Though her heart condition was stable and her kidney disease was only mild, she just didn't seem herself. I took her to the dog park to cheer her up. Big mistake. Now quite hard of hearing, Olive hated to be startled by dogs coming up on her from behind. And now with her arthritis, she had a hard time standing her ground—she who used to burn grooves beside the fence from running back and forth. When a Corgie-Sheltie mix tried to instigate play, she whipped around and snapped at the hapless dog, which turned into an instant fight. I can't say Olive's behavior was entirely out of character, but its extent disturbed me. We left the dog park in shame.

A couple of days later, I came home from my morning workout to find Olive immobile in the living room amid feces and vomit. Tiger, all distressed, kept sniffing her up and down. I took her to the urgent care center at CSU's veterinary hospital, where they did an ultrasound and found internal bleeding due, almost certainly, to a burst hemangiosarcoma tumor. (It's the most common form of cancer in dogs, and it can sneak up from nowhere. It's what took out Pretzel and Chappy both.) Just like that, we were talking about euthanasia. Already, Olive's once-red tongue had drained to a pale pink.

It seemed impossible. She was a force of nature. Having adopted her at two years old, I used to joke that Olive was never a puppy; such a dog could only have emerged goddess-like into the world, fully formed and full of fury. I found it equally incredible that such a dog could die.

Although friends and family all sympathized, it was, ironically, Olive's two main places of business—her veterinarian's office and her training/daycare center—that sent sympathy cards with hand-written notes from all the employees who'd interacted with her. While a smart business move, the notes also seemed genuine. Amidst the commonplaces about leaving "pawprints in our hearts," assurances that "she will be missed," and white lies that "she was always so sweet and polite," the day camp crew also called her the "best trick Border Collie ever" and mentioned her specialties: *say your prayers* (paws raised and head bowed below them), *bang bang* (resulting in a very dramatic slow-motion "play dead"), and *back up like a truck* (when someone beep-beep-beeped in falsetto). They eulogized her as an individual.

This is what I mean by saying that in the 2010s, dogs, like people, are so thoroughly integrated into the marketplace as both the consumers and as the consumed that it has become our place of personhood. It is as a consumer of care and medicine that Olive's personhood was most recognized, and it was her medical care and daycare providers who most marked her death, as they did her life. I don't think that Olive's (and my) marketplace relations were fake, but rather that, for better or worse, they're the new real. And it is as a consumer that she seems to be most missed.

Chapter Seven. Made to Order

Post-Coda: Send in the Penguin

Tiger, always prone to separation anxiety, missed Olive's company so desperately that I had to adopt another dog. Or so I told myself, knowing full well that I'd premised the book I was finally completing on the idea that (human) individuals, like their cultures, project themselves onto dogs.

My next dog would be the anti–Olive, I decided. Much as I missed her. Olive, my Bully of a Border Collie, who made puppies cry if they licked her face, had been resource-protective, leash-aggressive, and ever-shrieking in her war on squirrels. This time I'd go for sweet, shy, and submissive. So when I saw the little stick-figure dog huddled in her crate on adoption day at PetSmart, her tail tucked between her legs so tight she gave herself a wedgie, I thought I'd found my ideal for my sixth and final dog. She was some sort of Rat Terrier/Blue Heeler mix, with maybe some sight hound stirred in. Her long beak-snout, black masked face, and white body inspired the name Penguin.

Just after I got her, the pandemic lockdown happened, and much of the work I was doing with Penguin to help her get over her fear of the world went on hiatus, and the day camp I tried seem to traumatize her worse. Little Penguin is sweet, in her way, and plays well with Tiger, but there are issues. She turns out to have a bad case of coprophagia (shit-eating), and gets so anxious she shakes as if reliving old traumas. She was rescued from a puppy mill, so who can blame her? When all the toys and training failed to calm her, I turned to drugs. (For her.)

So now I'm one of those people who give their dogs Prozac as well as expensive supplements to make their poop less appetizing. Serves me right. Re-reading this chapter, I detect a hint of smugness when I discuss treating canine personality disorders pharmaceutically—as if I somehow stood apart from the society I was diagnosing. As it turns out, both Penguin and I are very much creatures of the tail end of the 2010s.

Afterword
How Will We Look with Dogs?

I wrote this book during the Trump presidency. When Donald Trump took office in 2017, his White House did not include a dog (setting aside pundits' jokes about all the lapdogs in his cabinet or Jimmy Kimmel's calling Mike Pence the "Vice Poodle"). For the first time in my living memory, the United States did not have a First Dog. Ironically, at a time when dogs have become more central than ever to the American home, its most iconic House lacked a DOTUS.

Even though I know, at least intellectually, that your don't have to like dogs to be a good person, I can't help it: I'm tempted to read Trump's lack of a dog as a symptom of a much larger character flaw. I could easily draw a line from the dogless White House to the way the Trump Administration gutted protections on endangered animals, unlocked wildlife habitats for drilling and mining, lifted new treatment standards for farm animals, and impeded public access to the Department of Agriculture's information on violations to the Animal Welfare Act—violations committed, for example, by circuses, zoos, scientific laboratories, and puppy mills. I'm tempted to draw equations between the dogless White House and its dangerously animal-blind policies, even though I know that having dogs as pets doesn't necessarily make you any more responsible toward other creatures, and that keeping pets itself, no matter how responsibly, demands ethical compromises. I know that loving a dog doesn't necessarily make you more compassionate or more aware of the non-human animals of this world. While I'd like to think that dogs inevitably teach us about other ways of seeing and smelling and understanding the world beyond the human one, I know that many a dog lover has missed this lesson. And yes, I know, too, that Adolf Hitler, purportedly, was a dog lover.

I imagine that if Trump had gotten a dog, he would have selected a designer dog—most likely (given his penchant for gold) a Goldendoodle.

But that's merely speculation. Trump, for his part, speculated in his own way about entering into the human-dog bond. At a rally, after praising the bomb-sniffing capabilities of German Shepherds, he riffed, "How would I look walking a dog on the White House lawn?" He seems to have meant it as a rhetorical question, as if, obviously, it would appear undignified for a president to walk a dog. But when the crowd seemed supportive of his getting a dog, Trump added, "I don't know, I don't feel good.... Feels a little phony to me."

Again, I'm tempted to read his negative comment about dogs negatively, as a character flaw: For Trump, a person only has a dog for show, as an accessory. Dogs are a question of looks; they're signifiers, or even symbols, in the service of their masters. Trump's scenario of dog as accessory (rather than, say, as a buddy, a family member, or even a hunting partner) mirrors the dog's current role as commodity and shopper, the consumer of consumers, prominent in the 2010s. In part, perhaps, Trump's reduction of dog-owning to how he would look represents in microcosm the way we're all embedded in a "society of the spectacle" in which, in Guy Debord's famous formulation, the history of social life is characterized by "the decline of *being* into *having*, and *having* into merely *appearing*."

The more intellectually generous route, though, would be to read "How would I look walking a dog?" as not just a rhetorical question, but also a real one, whether Trump intended it that way or not. How would Trump look walking a dog? To the extent that Trump is representative of at least some Americans, his comment testifies to dogs' role as accessory, as image, and as statement. Dogs *mean*, and are there to be read. Dogs act as signifiers whether we mean them to or not (and, indeed, whether the dogs themselves are actually there or not).

"How would I look walking a dog?" (or, more generally, "How do we look with dogs?") is in fact, the question I've been trying to answer in these many pages. How we "read" a human being and their chosen dog draws on whole sets of cultural assumptions and mythologies about nature, humanity, race, class, gender, genetics, and the role of human intervention. As our understanding of these concepts change, the mythologies supporting our understanding changes, and consequently the meaning of dogs changes, as do the breeds we see as most exemplary. Once again, dogs serve as the more visible example of what humans are also experiencing. Dogs are our premier cultural accessory.

This book has been considering some of our cultural mythologies, as they're tested out on and reflected in dogs from the 1950s to the present. As I said in the introduction, mythologies come and go (or, more often, metamorphose), but do so unevenly. At any given time, the dominant ideology is nipped on all sides by residual, emergent, and sub- or co-cultural ideologies. Correspondingly, at any given moment in culture, dogs (and dog breeds) mean different things to different people, and contradictions abound.

Dogs in America today show our current cultural moment a-swirl with competing ideological strands. From the era of the Cocker Spaniel's heyday, we still have puppy mills, or mass-produced puppies, and the concomitant ideology of dogs as commodities. But we also, increasingly, see dogs as members of the family, and even as persons. A major component of personhood in the United States is being a consumer of merchandise, and a trip to any pet store will show how thoroughly dogs are integrated into the marketplace. We humanize our dogs by including them in our consumer economy as both the consumer and the consumed.

We still use dogs, especially Beagles, as surrogates for humans in laboratory testing, which implies dogs' subordinate value in relationship to humans. At the same time, we're also beginning to challenge human supremacy and to grant to (some) dogs some of the rights previously reserved for humans.

We continue to seek in dogs, especially wolfy-looking ones like huskies, a wildness that feels all but lost to many of us otherwise, even as we continue to devastate the habitats of our dogs' closest kin, and to kill wolves and coyotes on massive scales.

We still discriminate against some breeds, such as Pit Bulls, and use them to enact racism by other means, even as we fight such discrimination both against dogs and against people. We still include dogs as key players in our class and racial dramas at a time of both prevalent racial mixing and a resurgent white supremacy.

We increasingly attribute subjectivity to dogs at the same time as we control and restrain them more intensely than ever. We're increasingly recognizing the dogness of the dog—their radical differences from humans in how they experience and understand the world—at the same time as we humanize dogs, forcing them to live ever more of their lives in human spaces and according to human dimensions.

We see dogs as the last bastion of Nature in human lives even as we use genetic-level technology to change dogs' nature. Indeed, dogs' bodies stage the deconstruction of the nature/nurture opposition. Dogs even stage the breakdown of the natural-vs.-artificial, subject-vs.-object, consumer-vs.-consumed, and even person-vs.-property binaries. We treat our dogs—and ourselves—as both objects and subjects simultaneously.

All of these ideological strands coexist in the present moment of the United States. Which ones will triumph, and which fall away? Is the dog becoming a person? A human, even? Will humanization be good for dogs, or will it force them into ever more un-dog-nified lives? Will dogs become full family members as our culture redefines its definition of family? And if so, will this be a good or a bad thing for dogs? Will we increase our understanding of dogness, and honor it, perhaps even allowing dogs to canine-ize us (as we humanize them)? As we devastate our planet, will dogs lead us toward sympathy for other living creatures beyond our doorstep, and help us get past speciesism and human exceptionalism? Will dogs be the gateway drugs to harder zoology? Will we continue bringing dogs further into the human realm, or will we allow them to help us out of it? How will the United States define itself in the future, and what will its mascot be?

Whatever direction(s) we take, dogs will continue to be part of our everyday myths. We will continue to both project ourselves onto them and to pose them as our foils. To both identify with them and to put ourselves in opposition to them. They will be our surrogates and our alternatives, our second selves and our others. They'll unwittingly serve as our objects of fantasy and as our "guinea pigs," or test subjects, not just in the scientific laboratory but also in the cultural laboratory. However we breed dogs in the future we will continue to breed stories about dogs, and we will look to dogs to help us understand ourselves.

As we move forward in a new Joe Biden presidency, like many Americans, I'm still recovering from a bitter election season and its ongoing aftermath. Amidst some very serious (and often disturbing) campaign ads, however, one tongue-in-cheek ad, sponsored by "Dog Lovers for Joe," asks us to put a dog back in the White House.[1] The ad goes through a series of photos showing presidents bonding with their dogs, from Ronald Reagan and his Bouvier, Lucky; to George H.W. Bush and his Springer Spaniel, Millie; to Bill Clinton and Buddy; to George W. Bush and Barney the Scottish Terrier; to Barack Obama and Bo. Then there's that clip of Donald Trump asking, "How would I look walking a dog on the White House lawn?" and then shrugging and shivering at the thought while making a "That's ridiculous!" face. Finally, there's a picture of Joe Biden down on the ground and burying his face in the scruff of Champ, his German Shepherd. The ad ends by exhorting us, presumably from the dog's-eye view, to "choose your humans wisely."

Biden's two German Shepherds, twelve-year-old Champ and two-year-old Major, are now the new First Dogs. Whether or not this means an imminent rise in German Shepherd popularity remains to be seen. Perhaps more noteworthy, Major will be the first rescue dog from a shelter to serve as DOTUS, having been acquired by the Bidens as a foster fail. Amidst the current surge of quarantine pet adoptions, perhaps we will enter a new era of mutual rescue between humans and dogs. I hope so.

Beyond the Biden presidency, though, who will the future First Dogs be, and what will they mean to the human citizens of their country? Who will be our next canine celebrities and icons? What breed will stand as the next mascot of the next cultural moment? And how will we look with our dogs in the future?

How will we look walking our dogs? Well, if I know anything about walking a dog from the many hours I've clocked in over three decades with my five—now six—dogs, it's that the dog decides much about how we are to look, and that despite the best efforts of people to discipline and control the dog, the dog has a mind of their own, which is still, largely, a wonderful mystery to us, begging for further exploration. Like the cultural meaning of the dog we're trying to walk, the dog itself sometimes defies our control. Just when you think you've tied down the meaning of the dog, it sniffs an invisible squirrel and goes off in another direction.

Chapter Notes

Introduction

1. "The Unkindest Cut of All," *Frasier*, dir. Rick Beren, writ. David Angell, Peter Casey, and David Lee, exec. prod. David Angell, 24 February 1994.
2. Jon Mooallem, *Wild Ones: A Sometimes Dismaying, Weirdly Reassuring Story About Looking at People Looking at Animals in America* (New York: Penguin, 2013) 6.
3. Mooallem 6.
4. Meisha Rosenberg, "Golden Retrievers Are White, Pit Bulls Are Black, and Chihuahuas Are Hispanic: Representations of Breeds of Dog and Issues of Race in Popular Culture," *Making Animal Meaning*, ed. Linda Kalof and Georgina M. Montgomery (Michigan State UP, 2012) 117.
5. Raymond Williams, *Marxism and Literature* (Oxford UP, 1977).
6. iditarod.com/about.
7. CNN, "Barack Obama, First Press Conference," 7 November 2008, YouTube video, youtube.com/watch?v=4uHn6ydl6TM.

Chapter One

1. Kim Kavin, *The Dog Merchants: Inside the Big Business of Breeders, Pet Stores, and Rescuers* (New York: Pegasus Books, 2016) 11.
2. Roland Kilbon, "Born Hunters, the Bird Dogs," *The National Geographic Book of Dogs* (Washington, D.C.: The National Geographic Society, 1958) 101.
3. Kilbon 101.
4. Sharon Damkaer, "Albert Staehle," 2003, American Art Archives, 16 June 2020 http://www.americanartarchives.com/staehle.htm.
5. Damkaer http://www.americanartarchives.com/staehle.htm.
6. Damkaer http://www.americanartarchives.com/staehle.htm.
7. Andrea Degener, "Celebrate National Dog Day with Butch the Cocker Spaniel," 26 August 2014, Washington University Libraries, 6 June 2020 https://library.wustl.edu/celebrate-national-dog-day-with-butch-the-cocker-spaniel/.
8. Damkaer.
9. Katherine C. Grier, *Pets in America: A History* (Orlando: Harcourt, 2006) 160–233.
10. Andreas Platthaus, "Creating Enchantment: The Making of *Lady and the Tramp*," *The Walt Disney Film Archives: The Animated Movies 1921–1968*, ed. Daniel Kothenschulte (Taschen, 2016) 473.
11. Platthaus 485.
12. "American Rhetoric: Richard M. Nixon—'Checkers' Speech," 8 July 2019 http://www.americanrhetoric.com/speeches/richardnixoncheckers.html.
13. Alice George, "The Sad, Sad Story of Laika, the Space Dog, and Her One-Way Trip into Orbit," 2018, Smithsonian.com, 6 December 2019, http://www.smithsonianmag.com/smithsonian-institution/sad-story-laika-space-dog-and-her-one-way-trip-orbit-1-180968728/.
14. Kurt Caswell, *Laika's Window: The Legacy of a Soviet Space Dog* (San Antonio: Trinity UP, 2018) 25.
15. Grier 303.
16. This history is nicely summarized in Chad Lavin, "Factory Farms in

a Consumer Society" *American Studies* 50.1/2 (2009): 71–92.
17. Kavin 11.
18. Kavin 11.
19. "mill, n.1," *OED Online*, Oxford University Press, June 2020, www.oed.com/view/Entry/118469. Accessed 27 June 2020.
20. Arthur Frederick Jones, "How to Choose, Care for, and Train Your Dog," *The National Geographic Book of Dogs* (Washington, D.C.: The National Geographic Society, 1958) 398.

Chapter Two

1. "President's Two Beagle Pups Sound Off for Guests; Johnson Lifts Dogs to Hear Them Yip; Action is Criticized," *New York Times*, 27 April 1964.
2. Associated Press, "Johnson Lifts Dogs by the Ears Again to Prove They Enjoy It," *New York Times*, 5 May 1964: 1.
3. Richard Benedetto, "LBJ Had a Bone to Pick," *USA Today*, 17 February 1997, 1A.
4. AKC Staff, "Top Ten Breeds of the 1960s," *The American Kennel Club*, 13 February 2015, 12 June 2020 http://www.akc.org/news/top-ten-breeds-of-the-1960s/.
5. David Michaelis, *Schulz and Peanuts: A Biography* (New York: Harper Perennial, 2008).
6. Lee Mendelson, *Charlie Brown & Charlie Schulz* (United Feature Syndicate, Inc., 1970), 33.
7. Charles Schulz, *Peanuts Treasury* (New York: Fall Rivers Press, 1968) unpaginated.
8. Mendelson 45.
9. "Snoop Dogg Tells Money Honey He Was Named After Snoopy," 16 November 2009, 12 June 2020 https://www.nbcchicago.com/news/national-international/snoop_dogg_tells_money_honey_he_was_named_after_snoopy/1883645/.
10. Mendelson 40.
11. All strips discussed in this paragraph are from Schulz, *Peanuts Treasury*, which is unpaginated.
12. Mendelson 126.
13. Jeremy Beckham, "Why Are Beagles Used for Lab Experiments? A Look Back at the Nuclear History of This Dog Breed," *One Green Planet*, 2017, 12 June 2020 www.onegreenplanet.org/animalsandnature/nuclear-history-of-lab-beagles/.
14. Cited in Beckham.
15. Stephen Withrow, personal interview, 15 September 2015.
16. C.W. Miller, personal interview, 16 March 2016.
17. C.W. Miller, personal interview, 16 March 2016.
18. C.W. Miller, personal interview, 16 March 2016.
19. Bernard Rollin, personal interview, 15 October 2016.
20. Bernard Rollin, personal interview, 15 October 2016.
21. Coles Phinizy, "The Lost Pets That Stray to the Labs," *Sports Illustrated*, 29 November 1965.
22. Stan Wyman, "Pets for Sale Cheap—No Questions Asked: Concentration Camps for Dogs," *Life Magazine*, 4 February 1966, 60 (5): 22.
23. https://awic.nal.usda.gov/public-law-89-544-act-august-24-1966.
24. Glenn Greenwald and Leighton Akio Woodhouse, "Bred to Suffer: Inside the Barbaric U.S. Industry of Dog Experimentation," *The Intercept*, 17 May 2018, 12 June 2020 https://theintercept.om/2018/05/17/inside-the-barbaric-u-s-industry-of-dog-experimentation/.

Chapter Three

1. Barry Holstun Lopez, *Of Wolves and Men* (New York: Charles Scribner's Sons, 1978) 12.
2. U.S. Fish & Wildlife Services, "Gray Wolf (Canis Lupus) Biologue," *Gray Wolf Fact Sheet*, January 2007, 12 June 2020, https://www.fws.gov/midwest/Wolf/aboutwolves/biologue.htm.
3. USF&WS Fact Sheet.
4. USF&WS Fact Sheet.
5. Aldo Leopold, *A Sand County Almanac* (Oxford UP, 1949) 138–9.
6. Leopold 140, 141.
7. Lopez 63.
8. Farley Mowat, *Never Cry Wolf* (Toronto: Bantam Books, 1973) 40.
9. Mowat v.
10. Mowat 27.

11. Mowat 28.
12. Mowat 29.
13. Mowat 29.
14. Mowat 35.
15. Mowat 36.
16. Mowat 136.
17. Mowat 45.
18. Mowat 51.
19. Mowat 162.
20. Mowat 163.
21. Jean Craighead George, *Julie of the Wolves* (New York: HarperCollins, 1972) 14–15.
22. George 120.
23. George 7.
24. George 78.
25. George 133–4.
26. George 133.
27. George 170.
28. Mark Derr, *A Dog's History of America: How Our Best Friend Explored, Conquered, and Settled a Continent* (New York: North Point Press, 2004) 61.
29. Derr 67.
30. Jason Mark, *Satellites in the High Country: Searching for the Wild in the Age of Man* (Washington, D.C.: Island Press, 2015).
31. www.fws.gove/home/wolf recovery/
32. Konrad Z. Lorenz, *Man Meets Dog* (Cambridge, MA: The Riverside Press, 1954) 1–15.
33. Evan Ratliff, "Taming the Wild," *National Geographic* 219.3 (March 2011), 46.
34. Mordecai Siegal and Matthew Margolis, *Good Dog, Bad Dog, New and Revised: Dog Training Made Easy* (New York: Henry Holt and Company, 1991) 75.
35. Siegal and Margolis 76.
36. Siegal and Margolis 84.
37. The Monks of New Skete, *How to Be Your Dog's Best Friend* (New York: Little, Brown, 2002) 16.
38. Lopez 32.
39. John Bradshaw, *Dog Sense: How the New Science of Dog Behavior Can Make You a Better Friend to Your Pet* (New York: Basic Books, 2011) 260. See also his article "Paedomorphosis affects agonistic visual signals of domestic dogs," *Animal Behaviour* 53 (1997): 297–304.
40. Quoted from the official Iditarod website iditarod.com/about.
41. iditarod.com/about.

Chapter Four

1. E. M. Swift, "The Pit Bull: Friend and Killer," *Sports Illustrated*, 27 July 1987.
2. "'Time Bombs on Legs': Violence-Prone Owners Are Turning Pit Bulls into Killers," *Time*, 27 August 1987.
3. Mark Uehling and Sue Hutchison, "'The Macho Dog to Have': Pit Bull Terriers May Prove to Be a Dangerous Fad," *Newsweek*, 14 July 1986, 40.
4. Michelle Green and Dirk Mathison, "An Instinct for the Kill," *People*, 6 July 1987 (28.1) 28.
5. Michael Satchall with Tracy Shryer, "The Most Dangerous Dog in America," *U.S. News & World Report*, 20 April 1987, 24.
6. Kurt Lapham, quoted in Swift.
7. Satchall 24.
8. David Brand, Scott Brown, and D. Blake Hallanan, "'Time Bombs on Legs': Violence-Prone Owners Are Turning Pit Bulls Into Killers," *Time*, 27 July 1987 (130.4) 60.
9. Laurence Battett, "Shifting Mist: Pit-Bull Politics and Weak Voter Conviction Make the Polls Bounce," *Time* 132.11, 12 September 1988.
10. Nancy Traver, "The Republicans' Pit Bull," *Time* 133.24, 12 June 1989, 22.
11. Peter Applebome, "Pit Bull Politician," *New York Times Magazine*, 28 October 1990.
12. Bronwen Dickey, *Pit Bull: The Battle Over an American Icon* (New York: Vintage Books, 2017) 32–43.
13. Dickey 14–16.
14. Laura Schenone, *The Dogs of Avalon: The Race to Save Animals in Peril* (New York: W.W. Norton & Company, 2017) 96.
15. Jeffery J. Sacks et al., "Breeds of Dogs Involved in Fatal Human Attacks in the United States between 1979 and 1998," *JAVMA* 217.6 (2000): 836–840.
16. Dickey 16–17.
17. Rosenberg 113–125.
18. Kelly M. Hoffman, Sophie Trawalter, Jordan R. Axt, and M. Norman Oliver, "Racial Bias in Pain Assessment and Treatment Recommendations, and False Beliefs About Biological Differences Between Blacks and Whites," *Proceedings of the National Academy of Sciences U.S.A.*, 19 April 2016, 113(16): 4296.

19. "Killer Genes Ate My Dog," *The Economist*, 1 June 1991: 83.
20. "'Time Bombs on Legs': Violence-Prone Owners Are Turning Pit Bulls into Killers," *Time*, 27 August 1987.
21. Mark D. Uehling, "'The Macho Dog to Have': Pit Bull Terriers May Prove to Be a Dangerous Fad," *Newsweek*, 14 July 1986: 40.
22. Green and Mathison, "An Instinct for the Kill."
23. Jane Alvaro of the Anti-Cruelty Society, cited in David Brand, "'Time Bombs on Legs': Violence-Prone Owners are Turning Pit Bulls Into Killers," *Time*, 27 July 1987 (130.4) 60.
24. Dickey 56.
25. Marjorie Spiegel, *The Dreaded Comparison: Human and Animal Slavery* (New York: Mirror Books, 1988) 27.
26. Spiegel 29.
27. Spiegel 41.
28. Spiegel 26.
29. Spiegel 27.
30. Tricia Rose, *Black Noise: Rap Music and Black Culture in Contemporary America* (Wesleyan University Press, 1994) 3.
31. Teresa Wiltz, "Hustling to the Beat: Pitbull Perez Has Worked His Way Into the Hip-Hop Mix.," *The Washington Post*, 25 July 2004, N01.
32. Dickey 220.
33. Jim Gorant, *The Lost Dogs: Michael Vick's Dogs and Their Tale of Rescue and Redemption* (New York: Gotham Books, 2011) 30.
34. Dickey 221.
35. Angela Davis, "Rape, Racism and the Myth of the Black Rapist," *Women, Race and Class* (New York: Random House, 1981).
36. Valerie Smith, "Split Affinities: The Case of Interracial Rape," *Conflicts in Feminism*, eds. Marianne Hirsch and Evelyn Fox Keller (New York: Routledge, 1990) 272–275.
37. Uehling 40.
38. Uehling 40.
39. Michelle Green and Dirk Mathison, "An Instinct for the Kill," *People*, 6 July 1987 (28.1) 28.
40. City and County of Denver, Colorado, "Sec. 8–55.—Pit Bulls Prohibited," 26 July 2017, *Code of Ordinances, Supplement 130*, 9 September 2017 https://library.municode.com/co/denver/codes/code_of_ordinances?nodeId=TITIIREMUCO_CH8AN_ARTIIDOCA_DIV3PRAGAN_S8-55PIBUPR .
41. Carl Semencic, *The World of Fighting Dogs* (Neptune City, NJ: T.F.H. Publications, 1982) 53–4.
42. Kevin Strooband, "The P Word: Breed Bans and Other Issues Facing Ontario's Shelters," *Bark* (June-August 2011) 14.
43. Malcolm Gladwell, "Troublemakers: What Pit Bulls Can Teach Us about Profiling," *New Yorker*, 6 February 2006.
44. Villalobos Rescue Center, *Villalobos Rescue Center Home*, 29 September 2017 vrcpitbull.com.
45. Animal Legal Defense Fund, 2012.
46. Steve Almond, *Against Football: One Fan's Reluctant Manifesto* (Brooklyn: Melville House, 2014) 110–111.
47. Almond 110.
48. Almond 111.
49. Almond 111.
50. Almond 112–13.
51. Almond 111–12.
52. Peter B. Kraska, "Militarization and Policing—Its Relevance to 21st Century Police," *Policing* (13 December 2017) 6.
53. Kraska 3.
54. Kraska 6
55. Kraska 7.
56. West 10.

Chapter Five

1. Audrey Pavis, *The Labrador Retriever Handbook* (Barron's Educational Series, 2001) 1.
2. Rosenberg 119.
3. Rosenberg 119.
4. Pat Buchanan, "1992 Republican National Convention keynote" http:/buchanan.org/blog/1992-republican-national-convention-speech-148.
5. Pat Buchanan, "The Cultural War for the Soul of America" http://buchanan.org/blog/the-cultural-war-for-the-soul-of-america-149.
6. George Lakoff, *Don't Think of an Elephant*, 6.
7. Lakoff 7.
8. Lakoff 11.
9. Lakoff 12.
10. Lakoff 13.

11. Lakoff 17.
12. The American Kennel Club, *The Complete Dog Book*, 19th Edition, Revised (New York: Wiley Publishing, 1998) 64.
13. The American Kennel Club, *The Complete Dog Book*, 65.
14. Kerry V. Kern, *Labrador Retrievers*, 2nd Edition (Hauppage: Barron's Educational Series, 1995) 50.
15. Kern 60.
16. Kern 74.
17. Kern 52.
18. Kern 53.
19. https://www.akc.org/dog-breeds/labrador-retriever/.
20. https://www.akc.org/?s=husky.
21. Michael Schaffer, *One Nation Under Dog: Adventures in the New World of Prozac-Popping Puppies, Dog-Park Politics, and Organic Pet Food* (New York: Henry Holt & Company, 2009) 154.
22. www.akc.org/products-services/training-programs/canine-good-citizen/.
23. Definitions from Glossary, Karen Pryor, *Reaching the Animal Mind: Clicker Training and What It Teaches Us About All Animals* (2009) 238 and 240.
24. Pryor 2.
25. Pryor 153.
26. Pryor 18.
27. Pryor 35.
28. Pryor 35.
29. Pryor 180.
30. The Monks of New Skete 16.
31. Jean Donaldson, *The Culture Clash* (Berkeley: James & Kenneth Publishers, 1996) 97.
32. Donaldson 97.
33. Donaldson 99.
34. The Seeing Eye
35. Seeing Eye fact Sheet "By the Numbers" from website.
36. Kern 54.
37. AKC Service Dogs 101
38. Kern 57.
39. Winnie Hu, "Violent Sounds of an Escape From the 71st Floor," *New York Times* 7 October 2001: 58.
40. Michael Hingson, *Thunder Dog: The True Story of a Blind Man, His Guide Dog, and the Triumph of Trust at Ground Zero* (2011).
41. Ellen J. Horrow, "Dogs Honored for Ground Zero Duty," USA Today, 11 February 2002.

Chapter Six

1. https://www.youtube.com/watch?v=4uHn6ydl6TM (viewed May 23, 2020).
2. John Bradshaw, *Dog Sense: How the New Science of Dog Behavior Can Make You a Better Friend to Your Pet* (New York: Basic Books, 2011) 255.
3. Bradshaw 255.
4. Bradshaw xix.
5. Kavin 128.
6. Kavin 131.
7. Kavin 123–4.
8. Folger 87.
9. This discussion of race and related terminology comes from Daniel J. Fairbanks, *Everyone Is African: How Science Explodes the Myth of Race* (New York: Prometheus Books, 2015) 14–15.
10. Quoted in Fairbanks.
11. Fairbanks 15.
12. Harriet Ritvo, *The Animal Estate: The English and Other Creatures in the Victorian Age* (Cambridge: Harvard University Press, 1987) 84.
13. Ritvo 84.
14. Ritvo 84.
15. Ritvo 87.
16. Ritvo 93.
17. Ritvo 106.
18. Ritvo 101.
19. Ritvo 91.
20. Nancy Isenberg, *White Trash: The 400-Year Untold History of Class in America* (New York: Viking, 2016) 41.
21. Isenberg 41.
22. Quoted in Isenberg xvi.
23. Quoted in Isenberg, 85.
24. Isenberg 194.
25. Quoted in Isenberg 175.
26. Quoted in Isenberg 174.
27. Isenberg 196.
28. Grow, Rolling Stone.
29. See, for example, Coates' *Between the World and Me*.
30. Cited in Fairbanks 24.
31. Jeff Wheelwright, *The Wandering Gene and the Indian Princess: Race, Religion, and DNA* (New York: W.W. Norton & Company, 2012).
32. Wheelwright 42.
33. Bradshaw 254.
34. I wrote about them in my essay "The Street Dogs of Kolkata," which appears in *Pretzel, Houdini, and Olive:*

Essays on the Dogs of My Life (Pasadena: Red Hen Press, 2020).

35. *Urban Dictionary*, Purebred, https://www.urbandictionary.com/define.php?term=Purebreed, accessed December 29, 2020.

36. Michael Stern and Jane Stern, *Dog Eat Dog: A Very Human Book About Dogs and Dog Shows* (New York: Scribner, 1997) 141.

37. Stern and Stern 141.

38. See Jon Mooallem, "The Modern Kennel Conundrum," *New York Times Magazine*, 4 February 2007, for a graphic scene depicting this procedure.

Chapter Seven

1. Suzanne Smalley, "A (Designer) Dog's Life," *Newsweek*, 13 April 2009: 52–55.

2. Smalley 52–55.

3. Stanley Coren, "A Designer Dog-Maker Regrets His Creation," *Psychology Today*, 28 July 2019 https://www.psychologytoday.com/blog/canine-corner/201404/designer-dog-maker-regrets-his-creation.

4. "The Modern Kennel Conundrum."

5. "The Modern Kennel Conundrum."

6. Scott Neuman, "Send in the Clones: Barbra Streisand Reveals Fluffy Canine Copies," NPR, 28 February 2018. Transcript on https://www.npr.org/sections/thetwo-way/2018/02/28/589404560/send-in-the-clones-barbra-streisand-reveals-fluffy-canine-copies, accessed 30 June 2020.

7. https://www.akc.org/dog-breeds/coton-de-tulear/.

8. www.nytimes.com/2018/03/02/style/barbra-streisand-cloned-her-dog.html.

9. http://www.theguardian.om/commentisfree/2018/mar/02/barbra-streisand-dog-cloning-pets.

10. John Woestendiek, *Dog, Inc.: The Uncanny Inside Story of loning Man's Best Friend* (New York: Avery, 2010) 176.

11. Woestendiek 177.

12. Amoasii et al., *Science* 363 (2018)|, 86–91.

13. Tom Shakespeare, "Manifesto for Genetic Justice," *Social Alternatives* 18.1 (1999): 31.

14. Ruha Benjamin, "Interrogating Equity: A Disability Justice Approach to Genetic Engineering," *Issues in Science and Technology* XXXII.3 (2016).

15. Benjamin.

16. Tina Hesman Saey, "Gene Edit Creates Buff Beagles," *Science News* 188.11 (2015): 16.

17. "Study Finds Giving CBD to Pet Fails to Address Root Issue of Letting Crazed Monster Live in Your Home," *The Onion*, 16 October 2020, theonion.com/study-finds-giving-cbd-to-pet-fails-to-address-root-iss1845384712?utm_source+TheOnion_Daily_RSS&utm_medium=email, accessed 30 December 2020.

Afterword

1. dogloversforjoe.com, accessed 30 December 2020.

Bibliography

Access Entertainment News. "Snoop Dogg Tells Money Honey He Was Named After Snoopy." 16 November 2009. Access Online. 12 June 2020. accessonline.com/articles/snoop-dogg-tells-money-honey-he-was-named-after-snoopy-78807.

AKC Service Dogs 101—Everything You Need to Know. https://www.akc.org/expert-advice/training/service-dog-training-101/. Accessed May 13, 2020.

AKC Staff. "Top Ten Breeds of the 1960s." 13 February 2015. The American Kennel Club. 12 June 2020. http://www.akc.org/news/top-ten-breeds-of-the-1960s/.

Almond, Steve. *Against Football: One Fan's Reluctant Manifesto*. Brooklyn: Melville House, 2014.

The American Kennel Club. *The Complete Dog Book*, 19th Edition, Revised. New York: Wiley Publishing, 1998.

Andersen, Allen C., and Loraine S. Good., eds. *The Beagle as an Experimental Dog*. Iowa State UP, 1970.

"Animal Shelter Euthanasia." American Humane. August 25, 2016. http://www.americanhumane.org/animals/stop-animal-abuse/fact-sheets/animal-shelter-euthanasia.html

Animal Testing & Cosmetics. U.S. Food & Drug Administration. 22 November 2017. https://www.fda.gov/cosmetics/product-testing-cosmetics/animal-testing-cosmetics

"Animal Welfare Act." Animal Welfare Information Center, USDA. https://awic.nal.usda.gov/public-law-99-198-food-security-act-1985-subtitle-f-animal-welfare

Applebome, Peter. "Pit Bull Politician." *New York Times Magazine*, 28 October 1990.

Arrington, John, and Walt Zeintek. *Labrador Tales: A Celebration of America's Favorite Dog*. Azul Editions, 1998.

ASPCA. "Pet Statistics." ASPCA. 2 July 2020. http://www.aspca.org/animal-homelessness/shelter-intake-and-surrender/pet-statistics.

Associated Press. "Johnson Lifts Dogs by the Ears Again to Prove They Enjoy It." *New York Times*, 5 May 1964: 1.

Barthes, Roland, trans. Annette Lavers. *Mythologies*. London: Paladin, 1972.

Bass, Rick. *The Ninemile Wolves*. New York: Ballantine Books, 1992.

"Battling Over Pit Bulls." *Time*, 11 August 1986: 17.

Beckham, Jeremy. "Why Are Beagles Used for Lab Experiments? A Look Back at the Nuclear History of This Dog Breed." *One Green Planet*, 2017. www.onegreenplanet.org/animalsandnature/nuclear-history-of-lab-beagles/. Accessed June 12, 2020.

Benedetto, Richard. "LBJ had a bone to pick." *USA Today*, 17 February 1997, 1A.

Benjamin, Ruha. "Interrogating Equity: A Disability Justice Approach to Genetic Engineering." *Issues in Science and Technology* Vol. XXXII, No. 3, Spring 2016.

Berns, Gregory. *What It's Like to Be a Dog: And Other Adventures in Animal Neuroscience*. New York: Basic Books, 2017.

Best Friends Animal Society. *Best Friends Animal Society*. 12 March 2013. 4 October 2017. https://www.youtube.com/watch?v=6goNpMIsiyU.

Bradshaw, John. *Dog Sense: How the New Science of Dog Behavior Can Make You a Better Friend to Your Pet.* New York: Basic Books, 2011.

_____. "Paedomorphosis affects agonistic visual signals of domestic dogs." *Animal Behaviour* 53 (1997): 297–304.

Brand, David. "'Time Bombs on Legs': Violence-Prone Owners Are Turning Pit Bulls into Killers." *Time*, 27 August 1987.

Brody, Howard. *Hooked: Ethics, the Medical Profession, and the Pharmaceutical Industry.* Lanham, MD: Rowman & Littlefield, 2007.

Buchanan, Pat. The Cultural War for the Soul of America, http:/buchanan.org/blog/the-cultural-war-for-the-soul-of-america-149, speech dated September 14, 1992.

_____. 1992 Republican National Convention keynote, http:/buchanan.org/blog/1992-republican-national-convention-speech-148, speech dated August 17, 1992.

Canine Companions for Independence website. https://www.cci.org/assistance-dogs/assistance-dog-faqs.html#question5. Accessed May 13, 2020.

Caswell, Kurt. *Laika's Window: The Legacy of a Soviet Space Dog.* Trinity UP, 2018.

Chadwick, Douglas H. "Wolf Wars." *National Geographic,* 217.3 (March 2010), pp. 34–55.

City and County of Denver, Colorado. "Sec. 8–55.—Pit Bulls Prohibited." 26 July 2017. Code of Ordinances, Supplement 130. 9 September 2017, https://library.municode.com/co/denver/codes/code_of_ordinances?nodeId=TITIIREMUCO_CH8AN_ARTIIDOCA_DIV3PRAGAN_S8-55PIBUPR.

CNN. "Barack Obama, First Press Conference." 7 November 2008. 26 June 2020 youtube.com/watch?v=4uHn6ydl6TM.

Coppinger, Raymond, and Lorna Coppinger. *Dogs: A New Understanding of Canine Origin, Behavior, and Evolution.* New York: Scribner's, 2001.

Coren, Stanley. "A Designer Dog-Maker Regrets His Creation." *Psychology Today* https://www.psychologytoday.com/blog/canine-corner/201404/designner-dog-maker-regrets-his-creation. Retrieved July 28, 2019.

Damkaer, Sharon. "Albert Staehle." American Art Archives. 2003. http://www.americanartarchives.com/staehle.htm. Accessed June 6, 2020.

Davis, Angela. "Rape, Racism and the Myth of the Black Rapist." *Women, Race and Class.* New York: Random House, 1981.

Debord, Guy. *La Société du Spectacle* (Buchet-Chastel, 1967). Trans. Donald Nicholson-Smith, 1994, as *The Society of the Spectacle* (Zone Books) (Thesis 17).

Degener, Andrea. "Celebrate National Dog Day with Butch the Cocker Spaniel." August 26, 2014. https://library.wustl.edu/celebrate-national-dog-day-with-butch-the-cocker-spaniel/. Accessed June 6, 2020.

Deloria, Philip J. *Playing Indian.* Yale UP, 1998.

Derr, Mark. *A Dog's History of America: How Our Best Friend Explored, Conquered, and Settled a Continent.* New York: North Point Press, 2004.

_____. *How the Dog Became the Dog: From Wolves to Our Best Friends.* New York: Overlook Duckworth, 2011.

Dickey, Bronwen. *Pit Bull: The Battle Over an American Icon.* New York: Vintage Books, 2017.

"Dog Bite-Related Fatalities from 1979 Through 1988," *JAMA,* 15 September 1989.

Dog Lovers for Joe, dogloversforjoe.com, 2020. Accessed 26 November 2020.

Donaldson, Jean. *The Culture Clash.* James & Kenneth Publishers, 1996.

Dowd Modern Graphic History Library Staff. "Celebrate National Dog Day with Butch the Cocker." University Libraries, Washington University in St. Louis. 26 August 2014. http://wulibraries.typepad.com/mghlnews/2014/08/albert-staehle-butch.html.

Fairbanks, Daniel J. *Everyone Is African: How Science Explodes the Myth of Race.* New York: Prometheus Books, 2015.

Gates, Henry Louis, Jr. *The Signifying Monkey: A Theory of African-American Literary Criticism.* Oxford UP, 1988.

George, Alice. "The Sad, Sad Story of Laika, the Space Dog, and Her One-Way Trip into Orbit." *Smithsonian.com.* 2018. 6 December 2019. http://www.smithsonianmag.com/smithsonian-institution/sad-story-laika-space-dog-and-her-one-way-trip-orbit-1-180968728.

George, Jean Craighead. *Julie of the Wolves.* New York: HarperCollins, 1972.

Gladwell, Malcolm. *What the Dog Saw: And Other Adventures.* New York: Little, Brown, 2009.

Gorant, Jim. *The Lost Dogs: Michael Vick's Dogs and Their Tale of Rescue and Redemption.* New York: Gotham Books, 2010.

"Gray Wolf (Canis Lupus) Biologue," Gray Wolf Fact Sheet, USF&WS, January 2007. https://www.fws.gov/midwest/Wolf/aboutwolves/biologue.htm.

Green, Michelle, and Dirk Mathison. "An Instinct for the Kill." *People,* 6 July 1987, Vol. 28 Issue 1, 28.

Greenwald, Glenn, and Leighton Akio Woodhouse. "Bred to Suffer: Inside the Barbaric U.S. Industry of Dog Experimentation." *The Intercept,* 17 May 2018. https://theintercept.com/2018/05/17/inside-the-barbaric-u-s-industry-of-dog-experimentation/. Accessed 12 June 2020.

Grier, Katherine C. *Pets in America: A History.* Orlando: Harcourt, 2006.

Grimm, David. *Citizen Canine: Our Evolving Relationships with Cats and Dogs.* New York: PublicAffairs, 2014.

Grogan, John. *Marley and Me: Life and Love with the World's Worst Dog.* HarperCollins, 2005.

Grow, Cory. "Ted Nugent Apologizes for Calling Obama a 'Subhuman Mongrel.'" 21 February 2014. *Rolling Stone.* 25 June 2020. rollingstone.com/culture/culture-news/ted-nugent-apologizes-for-calling-obama-a-subhuman-mongrel-96782/.

Herzog, Hal. *Some We Love, Some We Hate, Some We Eat: Why It's So Hard to Think Straight About Animals.* New York: HarperCollins, 2010.

Hingson, Michael. *Thunder Dog: The True Story of a Blind Man, His Guide Dog, and the Triumph of Trust at Ground Zero.* 2011.

Hoffman, Kelly M., Sophie Trawalter, Jordan R. Axt, and M. Norman Oliver. "Racial Bias in Pain Assessment and Treatment Recommendations, and False Beliefs About Biological Differences Between Blacks and Whites." *Proceedings of the National Academy of Sciences U.S.A.,* 19 April 2016, 113(16): 4296–4301.

Hooper, Rowan. "First Canine Clone Is a Chip Off the Old Block" *New Scientist,* vol. 187, issue 2511, 2005, p. 15

Horowitz, Alexandra. *Inside of a Dog: What Dogs See, Smell, and Know.* New York: Scribner's, 2009.

Horrow, Ellen J. "Dogs Honored for Ground Zero Duty." *USA Today,* 11 February 2002.

Hu, Winnie. "Violent Sounds of an Escape From the 71st Floor." *New York Times,* 7 October 2001, p. 58.

Ignatiev, Noel. *How the Irish Became White.* Taylor & Francis, 1996.

Isenberg, Nancy. *White Trash: The 400-Year Untold History of Class in America.* New York: Viking, 2016.

"Johnson Lifts Dogs by the Ears Again to Prove They Enjoy It." The Associated Press, *New York Times,* 5 May 1964, p. 1.

Jones, Arthur Frederick. "How to Choose, Care for, and Train Your Dog." *The National Geographic Book of Dogs.* Ed. Arthur Frederick Jones. 1st Edition. Washington, D. C.: The National Geographic Society, 1958. 396–425.

Jorde, L.B., and S. P. Wooding. "Genetic Variation, Classification, and 'Race.'" *Nature Genetics* 36 (2004): S28-S33.

Kaplan, Lawrence. "Inuit or Eskimo: Which name to Use?" Alaska Native Language Center. University of Alaska Fairbanks. www.uaf.edu/anlc/resources/inuit-eskimo.

Karetnick, Jen. *American Kennel Club.* 24 September 2019. 13 May 2020. www.akc.org/expert-advice/training/service-dog-training-101/.

Kavin, Kim. *The Dog Merchants: Inside the Big Business of Breeders, Pet Stores, and Rescuers.* New York: Pegasus Books, 2016.

Kern, Kerry V. *Labrador Retrievers,* Second Edition. Hauppage, NY: Barron's Educational Series, 1995.

Kilbon, Roland. "Born Hunters, the Bird Dogs." *The National Geographic Book of Dogs*. First Edition. Washington, D.C.: National Geographic Society, 1958.

"Killer Genes Ate My Dog." *The Economist*, 1 June 1991, p. 83.

Lavin, Chad. "Factory Farms in a Consumer Society." *American Studies* 50.1/2 (2009): 71–92.

Leopold, Aldo. *A Sand County Almanac*. Oxford UP, 1966, 1949.

Lopez, Barry Holstun. *Of Wolves and Men*. New York, Charles Scribner's Sons, 1978.

Lorenz, Konrad. *Man Meets Dog*. Boston: Houghton Mifflin, 1955.

Mark, Jason. *Satellites in the High Country: Searching for the Wild in the Age of Man*. Island Press, 2015. Excerpted in *Scientific American* as "Can Wolves Bring Back Wilderness?" 9 October 2015. www.scientificamerican.com/article/can-wolves-bring-back-wilderness/.

Masson, Jeffery Moussaieff, and Susan McCarthy. *When Elephants Weep: The Emotional Lives of Animals*. New York: Delacorte Press, 1995.

McConnell, Patricia B. *For the Love of a Dog: Understanding Emotion in You and Your Best Friend*. New York: Ballantine Books, 2005, 2006.

Mendelson, Lee. *Charlie Brown & Charlie Schulz*. United Feature Syndicate, Inc., 1970.

Michaelis, David. *Schulz and Peanuts: A Biography*. New York: Harper Perennial, 2008.

Millan, Cesar, with Melissa Jo Peltier. *Be the Pack Leader*. New York: Three Rivers Press, 2007.

The Monks of New Skete. *How to Be Your Dog's Best Friend*. New York: Little, Brown, 2002.

Mooallem, Jon. *Wild Ones: A Sometimes Dismaying, Weirdly Reassuring Story About Looking at People Looking at Animals in America*. New York: Penguin, 2013.

Mowat, Farley. *Never Cry Wolf*. Toronto: Bantam Books, 1973.

"Murder by Dog." *ABA Journal,* June 1989.

Neuman, Scott. "Send in the Clones: Barbra Streisand Reveals Fluffy Canine Copies." 28 February 2018. *NPR*. 30 June 2020. https://www.npr.org/sections/thetwo-way/2018/02/28/589404560/send-in-the-clones-barbra-streisand-reveals-fluffy-canine-copieshttps://www.npr.org/sections/thetwo-way/2018/02/28/589404560/send-in-the-clones-barbra-streisand-reveals-fluffy-canine-copies.

Nixon, Richard. "American Rhetoric: Richard M. Nixon—'Checkers' Speech." 8 July 2019. *American Rhetoric*. 5 January 2020. http://www.americanrhetoric.com/speeches/richardnixoncheckers.html.

OED Online. "mill, n. 1." *Oxford English Dictionary*. Oxford University Press, 2020.

Orlean, Susan. *Rin Tin Tin: The Life and the Legend*. New York: Simon & Schuster, 2011.

Pavis, Audrey, *The Labrador Retriever Handbook*. Barron's Educational Series, 2001.

PBS. "Wolf Wars: America's Campaign to Eradicate the Wolf." 14 September 2018. *PBS*. 8 June 2019. http://www.pbs.org/wnet/nature/the-wolf-that-changed-america-wolf-wars-americas-campaign-to-eradicate-the-wolf/4312/.

"Pet Statistics." ASPCA. https://www.aspca.org/animal-homelessness/shelter-intake-and-surrender/pet-statistics.

Phinizy, Coles. "The Lost Pets That Stray to the Labs." *Sports Illustrated*, 29 November 1965.

Platthaus, Andreas. "Lady and the Tramp." *The Walt Disney Film Archives: The Animated Movies 1921–1968*. Ed. Daniel Kothenschulte. Disney Enterprises, 2016.

"President's Two Beagle Pups Sound Off for Guests; Johnson Lifts Dogs to Hear Them Yip; Action Is Criticized." *New York Times,* 27 April 1964.

Pryor, Karen. *Reaching the Animal Mind: Clicker Training and What It Teaches Us about All Animals*. 2009.

Ratliff, Evan. "Taming the Wild." *National Geographic* 219.3 (March 2011), pp. 34–59.

Ritvo, Harriet. *The Animal Estate: The English and Other Creatures in the Victorian Age*. Harvard UP, 1987.

Rose, Tricia. *Black Noise: Rap Music and Black Culture in Contemporary*

America. Wesleyan University Press, 1994.
Sacks, Jeffrey J., Leslie Sinclair, Julie Gilchrist, Gail C. Golab, and Randall Lockwood. "Breeds of Dogs Involved in Fatal Human Attacks in the United States Between 1979 and 1998." *JABMA*, vol 217, no. 6 (15 September 2000) pp. 836–840.
Saey, Tina Hesman, "Gene Edit Creates Buff Beagles." *Science News*, 28 November 2015, vol .188, issue 11, p. 16.
Satchell, Michael. "The Most Dangerous Dog in America." *U.S. News and World Report*, 29 April 1987.
Schaffer, Michael. *One Nation Under Dog: Adventures in the New World of Prozac-Popping Puppies, Dog-Park Politics, and Organic Pet Food*. New York: Henry Holt & Company, 2009.
Schenone, Laura. *The Dogs of Avalon: The Race to Save Animals in Peril*. New York: W.W. Norton & Company, 2017.
Schulz, Charles M. *Happiness Is a Warm Puppy*. 1962. Determined Productions, Inc., .
_____. *Peanuts Treasury*. New York: Fall River Press, 1968.
The Seeing Eye. https://www.seeingeye.org/. Accessed May 12, 2020.
Semencic, Carl. *The World of Fighting Dogs*. Neptune City, NJ: T. F. H. Publications, Inc., 1984.
Shakespeare, Tom. "Manifesto for Genetic Justice." *Social Alternatives* Vol. 18 No. 1, January 1999, p. 31.
Shakespeare, William. *The Tragedy of Macbeth*. Eds. Barbara A. Mowat and Paul Werstine. New York: Simon & Schuster, 2013, p. 89.
Siegal, Mordecai, and Matthew Margolis. *Good Dog, Bad Dog, New and Revised: Dog Training Made Easy*. New York: Henry Holt and Company, 1991.
Smalley, Suzanne. "A (Designer) Dog's Life." *Newsweek*, 13 April 2009: 52–55.
Smith, Valerie. "Split Affinities: The Case of Interracial Rape." *Conflicts in Feminism*. Ed. Marianne Hirsch and Evelyn Fox Keller. New York: Routledge, 1990. 271–287.
"Snoop Dogg Tells Money Honey He Was Named After Snoopy." 16 November 2009. https://www.nbcchicago.com/news/national-international/snoop_dogg_tells_money_honey_he_was_named_after_snoopy/1883645/. Accessed 12 June 2020.
Spiegel, Marjorie. *The Dreaded Comparison: Human and Animal Slavery*. New York: Mirror Books, 1988.
Stern, Michael, and Jane Stern. *Dog Eat Dog: A Very Human Book About Dogs and Dog Shows*. New York: Scribner's, 1997.
Strooband, K. "The P Word: Breed bans and other issues facing Ontario's shelters." *Bark* (June–August 2011), p. 14.
Swift, E.M. "The Pit Bull: Friend and Killer." *Sports Illustrated*, 27 July 1987.
"'Time Bombs on Legs': Violence-Prone Owners Are Turning Pit Bulls into Killers." *Time*, 27 August 1987.
"Top Ten Breeds of the 1960s." AKC Staff, The American Kennel Club. 13 February 2015. http://www.akc.org/news/top-ten-breeds-of-the-1960s/.
Uehling, Mark D., and Sue Hutchinson, "The Macho Dog to Have." *Newsweek*, 14 July 1986.
"The Unkindest Cut of All." David Angell, Peter Casey and David Lee. Dir. Rick Beren. Perf. Kelsey Grammar, David Hyde Pierce and Moose. *Frasier*. 24 February 1994.
U. S. District Court Ohio. "*Vanater v. Village of South Point*, 717 F. Supp. 1236 (D. Ohio 1989)." 4 October 2017. *Animal Legal & Historical Center*. Michigan State University. 4 October 2017. https://www.animallaw.info/case/vanater-v-village-south-point.
U.S. Food & Drug Administration. *Animal Testing & Cosmetics*. 22 November 2017. 22 June 2020. www.fda.gov/cosmetics/product-testing-cosmetics/animal-testing-cosmetics.
USDA. "Animal Welfare Act." *Animal Welfare Information Center, USDA*. 22 June 2020. https://www.nal.usda.gov/awic/animal-welfare-act.
USF&WS. "Gray Wolf (Canis Lupus) Biologue." 15 October 2018. *Gray Wolf Fact Sheet*. 2 July 2020. https://www.fws.gov/midwest/Wolf/aboutwolves/biologue.htm.
Villalobos Rescue Center. *Villalobos Rescue Center Home*. 29 September 2017. 29 September 2017. vrcpitbull.com.
Walker, Ben. "Labradoodle Creator Laments Designer Dog Craze." *AP Top News Package*. Associated Press DBA

Press Association, 6 February 2014. https://ezproxy2.library.colostate.edu/login?url=http://search.ebscohost.com/login.aspx?direct=true&AuthType=cookie,ip,url,cpid&custid=s4640792&db=nsm&AN=AP420a5a27f6e34c81923dd09331d3d8c3&site=ehost-live.

Warren, Cat. *What the Dog Knows: Scent, Science, and the Amazing Ways Dogs Perceive the World*. New York: Simon & Schuster. 2013.

Weintraub, Arlene. *Heal: The Vital Role of Dogs in the Search for Cancer Cures*. Toronto: ECW Press, 2015.

West, Cornell. *Race Matters*. Boston: Beacon Press, 1993.

Wheelwright, Jeff. *The Wandering Gene and the Indian Princess: Race, Religion, and DNA*. New York: W.W. Norton & Company, 2012.

Williams, Raymond. *Marxism and Literature*. Oxford University Press, 1977.

Wiltz, Teresa. "Hustling to the Beat: Pit-bull Perez Has Worked His Way Into the Hip-Hop Mix." *The Washington Post*, 25 July 2004, p. N01.

Woestendiek, John. *Dog, Inc.: The Uncanny Inside Story of Cloning Man's Best Friend*. New York: Avery, 2010.

"Wolf Wars: America's Campaign to Eradicate the Wolf." PBS. 14 September 2018. http://www.pbs.org/wnet/nature/the-wolf-that-changed-america-wolf-wars-americas-campaign-to-eradicate-the-wolf/4312/.

Woodhouse, Barbara. *No Bad Dogs: The Woodhouse Way*. New York: Summit Books, 1978.

Wyman, Stan. "Pets for Sale Cheap—No Questions Asked: Concentration Camps for Dogs." *Life Magazine*, 4 February 1966: 22.

Index

Numbers in ***bold italics*** indicate pages with illustrations

Afghan Hound 164
Against Football: One Fan's Reluctant Manifesto 105
air traffic controllers 107
Airedale 154
Akita 79
Alaska 78–81
Alaskan Husky 78
Alaskan Malamute 77
Almond, Steve 105
American Art Archives 20
American Bar Association 85
American Kennel Club (AKC) 8, 13, 35, 39, 45, 77, 98, 114, 118, 121, 123, 163
American Medical Association 85
American Pit Bull Terrier 86, 98
American Society for the Prevention of Cruelty to Animals (ASPCA) 38
American Staffordshire Terrier 86, 98
American Weekly 20
Americans with Disabilities Act (AWD) 133
Amish 33
Amorak Productions, Ltd. 63
animal control 52–3
The Animal Estate 144–6
animal rights 163
Animal Welfare Act (AWA) 10, 35, 50–2, 54, 182
anthropology 143, 146–7
Apollo 10 41
Apollo 11 41
Arizona State University 170
artificial insemination 156
Atomic Energy Commission 46
Audubon, John James 57

Bad Newz Kennels 103–4
BADRAP 102
Balto 11, 78
Barney (dog) 185
Barthes, Roland 3, 4, 79, 117
Bass, Rick 68
Bassett Hound 52–3
Be the Pack Leader 74

Beagle 10, 15, 35, 38–54, 64, 71, 79, 146, 158, 162, 166, 167, 169, 184
Beagle colony 45–8, 50
Beagle Freedom Project 46
The Beagle Project 46
Beckham, Jeremy 46, 48
Beer Summit 153
behaviorism 125
Belyayev, Dmitry 71
Benjamin, Ruha 167
Bentham, Jeremy 45
Berns, Gregory 7
Best Friends Animal Society 104
"better baby" contest 148–9
Bhadra, Rajiv 35–7, 171
Biden, Joe 1856
Big Daddy Kane 96
"Black Lives Matter" 94
Black Panther Party 95
Bloodhound 24, 89, 94, 95
Bloodhound Act 94
Blue Heeler 181
Bo (dog) 157, 158, 185
Border Collie 29, 48, 53, 71, 103, 106, 123, 125, 127, 130, 132, 133, 139, 180
Boston Terrier 86
Bouvier 185
Boxer 86, 87
brachycephaly 156
Bradshaw, John 7, 71, 76, 139, 154
brand 161, 177, 178
BRCA gene variation 151–2, 155
breed specific legislation (BSL) 98–100, 109
breedism 99–103, 109, 111
breedology 3–9, 84, 90, 117, 156
British Society for Happy Dogs 31
Buchanan, Patrick 115–6
Buck v. Bell 148
Buddy (dog) 13, 112–4, 120, 185
Bull Terrier 86
Bulldog 155, 156
Bullmastiff 155
Bullseye (dog) 86

199

Index

Bush, George H.W. 115, 185
Bush, George W. 185
Butch (dog) 9, 19–21, 37

Call of the Wild 2, 69
Canine Companions for Independence 133
Carey, Mariah 150
Carlson, William 47
Caswell, Kurt 31
Cavalier King Charles Spaniel 158
Cavapoo 158
Champ (dog) 185
Chaplin (Chappy) (dog) 8, 36, 123, 159, 180
Charlie Brown 42
Charlie Lab 10
Chiweenie 15
Checkers (dog) 10, 28–9
Chihuahua 107
Chorkie 15
Chow Chow 33–4, 79
Citizen Canine 121
Civil Rights Movement 41, 95, 137
Clean Air Act 55
clicker training 81, 124–7, 131
Clinton, Bill 13, 112–4, 120, 185
cloning 162–8
Coates, Ta-Nehisi 150
Cockadoodle 160
Cockalier 15
Cockapoo 160
Cocker Spaniel 9–10, 17–37, 53–4, 71, 79, 112, 138, 139, 140, 160, 184
Colbert, Stephen 140
The Colbert Report 140
Collaborative Radiological Health Animal Research Laboratory (CRHARL) 46–9
Collie 18, 19
"color-blindness" 149
Colorado State University 46, 48, 169–71, 180
The Complete Dog Book 118
Concentrated Animal Feeding Operation (CAFO) 33
"Concentration Camp for Dogs" 50
conditioning (classical and operant) 125
congenital defect 139, 155
Conron, Wally 158, 160
Coppinger, Lorna 70, 129
Coppinger, Ray 70, 129
coprophagia 181
cordectomy 52–4
"corrective jerk" 73
Coton de Tulear 162–3
CRISPR (clustered regularly interspaced short palindromic repeats) 166–8
Crufts 139
Cujo 2
cultural studies 5
The Culture Clash 131–2

Culture Wars: The Struggle to Define America 115
"cur" (term) 142

Dachshund 158
Daddy (dog) 101
Dalmatian 50, 155
Damkaer, Sharon 20
Darwin, Charles 59, 143, 161
Davis, Angela 97
Debord, Guy 183
deconstruction 141, 150, 184
Deloria, Philip 11
Denver, Colorado 98
Derr, Mark 7, 66
designer dog 15, 154, 158–81, 182
"Dick and Jane" books 21
Dickey, Bronwen 86, 88–9, 90, 92, 96, 97
disability rights 167
Disney 63, 64; see also *Lady and the Tramp*
DMX 96
DNA testing 151–3, 154
Doberman 29, 90, 134
Dr. Dre 96
Dr. Seuss 22
dog bite-related fatality (DBRF) 90, 99
Dog Eat Dog 155
dog fancy 33, 144–6, 149
dog food 75–6, 173–5
Dog, Inc.: The Uncanny Inside Story of Cloning Man's Best Friend 163–5
"Dog Lovers for Joe" 185
Dog Merchants 18
Dog Sense 139
The Dog Whisperer 101
dogfighting 84, 90, 95, 96–7, 99, 103–5, 107–8
"Doggie in the Window" (song) 31
Dogo Argentino 106
A Dog's History of America 66
The Dogs of Avalon 90
Dolly (sheep) 163
Donaldson, Jean 128, 130–2
Don't Shoot the Dog 125
Don't Think of an Elephant 116
Dorkie 15, 158
double doodle 160
Douglas, Ann 4
The Dreaded Comparison 93–4
Duchenne muscular dystrophy (DMD) 166

Earl of Malmesbury 118
Earth Day 55
The Economist 91
Eddie 1, 16
Eisenhower, Dwight 28, 29
Eli Lilly 174
Elixir Sulfanilamide 45
Elkhound 79
emotional support animal 134, 137

Endangered Species Act 11, 67
English Kennel Club 118
English Bulldog 86
Enlightenment 143
Environmental Protection Agency (EPA) 55
epigenetics 165
epilepsy 139
"Eskimo" (term) 63
"Eskimo dog" 78
ethology 74, 125, 129–30
eugenics 14, 148–9, 156, 166
Eustis, Dorothy 133
Everyone Is African 151
evolution of dogs 69–73

factory farm 18, 32, 60, 93
Fairbanks, Daniel J. 151
Fala (dog) 18, 21, 24
"family values" 112, 133
fancy 3, 144–6, 149
Faulkner, William 140
Finding Your Roots 152
First Dog 157, 182–6
"fitter family" contest 148
Flint Animal Cancer Center 170
Food and Drug Administration (FDA) 45, 51
football 103–5
Fort Collins 49, 52
Fortunate Field Kennels 133
Foucault, Michel 102, 146, 172
fox farm experiment 70–1
Fox Terrier 154
framing 116–7, 119, 132
Frasier 1–2
French Bulldog 86
Freud, Sigmund 29
Fritz (dog) 122
Fugitive Slave Act (of 1850) 94
Fun with Our Friends 21

"gameness" 99
Gantt, Harvey 106
Gates, Henry Louis, Jr. 152–3
genetic engineering 165–8, 184
genetically modified organism (GMO) 15
George, Alice 30
George, Jean Craighead 11, 58, 63–7
German Shepherd 17, 18, 19, 29, 39, 90, 95, 122, 133, 134, 136, 155, 183, 185
Gillette, Ed 47
Gingrich, Newt 86, 106
Gladwell, Malcolm 100
Golden Retriever 13, 35, 133–6, 155, 158
Goldendoodle 15, 158–60, 182
Good Citizen Test 123–4
Good Dog, Bad Dog: Dog Training Made Easy 73
Gorant, Jim 96

Great Dane 155, 165, 168
"Great Ear Lift" 10, 38–41, 45, 53
Green, Michelle 98
Greenwald, Glen 51
Greyhound 90, 143
Grier, Katherine 7, 21, 32
Grimm, David 121
Grogan, John 2, 120–1
The Guardian 163
guide dog 132–3, 158
Guide for the Care and Use of Laboratory Animals 51

Happiness Is a Warm Puppy 44
Helms, Jesse 86, 106
hemangiosarcoma 180
Heritage, Stuart 163
Him and Her (dogs) 38–41, 45, 54
Hingson, Michael 136
hip dysplasia 139, 155, 160
hip hop 95–6
Hitler, Adolf 182
Holiday, Billie **88**
Holmes, Chief Justice Oliver Wendell 148
HomeAgain (pet microchips) 45
Horowitz, Alexandra 7
Houdini (dog) 8, 35–7, 123, 140, 159, 169–71
How the Irish Became White 26
How to Be Your Dog's Best Friend 73
Humane Society 85
Hunter, James Davison 115–6
Husky 10, 11, 35, 57, 61, **75**, 76–81, 90, 123, 184
Hwang, Woo Suk 163

Ice-T 96
Iditarod 11, 78–81
IKEA 176
inbreeding 139, 140, 155
Indian Husky 78
Institute of Cytology and Genetics (Siberia) 71
Institutional Animal Care and Use Committee (IACUC) 51
Inuit 63
Ignatiev, Noel 26
Isenberg, Nancy 138, 147–9

Jack Russell Terrier 1
Jaws 83, 85
Jay-Z 96
Jefferson, Thomas 148
Johnson, Dwayne (The Rock) 150
Johnson, Lyndon 10, 38–41
Jones, Norah 150
Jordan, Michael B. 97
Jorde, Lynn 151
Journal of the American Veterinary Medical Association (JAVMA) 90

Julie 67
Julie of the Wolves 11, 55, 63–7

Kavin, Kim 18, 33
Kennedy, Ted 157, 158
Kern, Kerry V. 119
Kimmel, Jimmy 182
King, Martin Luther, Jr. 149
King, Stephen 2
kitsch 17
Kolkata 154
Kong (chew toy) 122–3
Kraska, Peter B. 107

Labradoodle 15, 158–60
Labrador Retriever 35, 86, 87, 109, 112–37, 139, 158
Labrador Retriever Handbook (Barron's) 112
Labrador Retrievers: A Complete Pet Owners Manual 119, 133
Lady and the Tramp 2, 9, 14, 22–8, 29, 37, 121, 138
Laika 29–31, 41, 48
Lakoff, George 4, 116–22, 128, 132
law enforcement, dogs in 133–4
leash laws 22, 121, 123
Lee, Peggy
Leopold, Aldo 58–62, 65, 67–8
Levi-Strauss, Claude 4
Life Magazine **40**, 50
Little House in the Big Woods 88
Little House on the Prairie 55
Little Rascals 88
London, Jack 2, 65, 69
Lopez, Barry 55, 58, 59, 74
Lorenz, Konrad 69, 125
Lucky (dog) 185

Macbeth 141–2, 144
Major (dog) 185
Malamute 76–8, 154
Maltese 158
Maltipoo 15, 158
Man Meets Dog 69
Margolis, Matthew 73
"Manifesto for Genetic Justice" 167
Mark, Jason 67
Markham, Joe 122
Marley and Me 2, 120–1
Mars, Bruno 150
Mastiff 86
Mathison, Dirk 98
Mattingly, Don 83
Mendelson, Lee 42, 44
Michaelis, David 41
Millan, Cesar 74, 128–9, 101, 103
Miller, C.W. 47
Miller, Francis 41
Millie (dog) 185

miscegenation (laws prohibiting) 147, 148, 149
Missy Elliot 96
Mister (dog) **88**
Mitchell, Joni 11
"mongrel" (term) 142
The Monks of New Skete 73, 128
monogenism 143
Mooallem, John 2, 161
Moral Politics 116
Morkie 158
Mowatt, Farley 59–63, 65
mutt 4, 5, 14, 15, 138–57
My Side of the Mountain 63
mystification 3
"Myth of the Black Rapist" 97–8, 102, 104
Mythologies 3, 4, 72, 93, 117

National Aeronautics and Space Administration (NASA) 41
National Association for Search and Rescue 136
National Geographic Book of Dogs 19, 33–4
National Institutes of Health (NIH) 50
natural selection 59, 144, 148, 160, 175
nature/nurture 184
Navy, United States 21
NEADS, Inc. (National Education for Assistance Dog Services) 133
Never Cry Wolf 59–63
New York Times 136, 163
New York Times Magazine 86
New Yorker magazine 100
Newfoundland (breed) 155
Newsweek 92, 98, 158
Newton, Huey 95
"Nihilism in Black America" 89
The Ninemile Wolves 68
Nixon, Richard 10, 28–9, 55, 67–8, 112
No Bad Dogs: The Woodhouse Way 73
Nugent, Ted 149

Obama, Barak 14–5, 138, 140–1, 149, 150, 153, 157, 160, 185
Of Wolves and Men 59
Olive (dog) 8, 124, 125–7, 130, 172, 178–80
One Health 168–71
The Onion 173
Origin of Species 143
origins, dog 11, 69–73, 119, 129, 143, 174–5
Orlean, Susan 37
Orton, Chris 169–70
Our Gang 88
Oxford English Dictionary 33, 78

Page, Pattie 31
Pal the Wonderdog 88
Palin, Sarah 106
Pavlov's dogs 125, 127
Pedigree Dogs Exposed 139

Index 203

Pence, Mike 182
Penguin (dog) 181
People for the Ethical Treatment of Animals (PETA) 46
People magazine 85, 92, 98
Pepper (dog) 50
Perdue, Sonny 51
Perez, Armando 96
personhood 50, 51, 124, 129, 165, 168, 169, 172, 176, 184
pet store 15, 20, 31–5, 75–6, 122–3, 158–60, 172, 173–9, 184
Petey (dog) 88
Pets in America: A History 21, 32
PetSmart 13, 115, 122–3, 125, 177–9, 181
Pfizer 174
Phemister, Robert 47
Pit Bull 12, 83–111, 156, 184
Pit Bulls and Paroleés 101–2
police brutality 95, 107
polygenism 143
Pomeranian 119
Poodle 15, 39, 158–60
Portuguese Water Dog 14, 157, 158
post-traumatic stress disorder (PTSD) 134
Presna Canario 106
Pretzel (dog) 8, 36, 112, 120, 123, *139*, 162, 180
Professional Air Traffic Controllers Organization 107
projection 1–2, 93, 181, 185
Pryor, Karen 125, 127, 128
Pug 156, 158, 160–1
Puggle 15, 158, 160–1, *162*
The Puppy Bowl 105
puppy mill 31–5, 140, 155, 158, 160, 181, 182, 184
"purebred" (term) 155

"race" (term) 142–3
Race Matters 14–5
radiation 46–8
Rat Terrier 181
Reaching the Animal Mind 125
Reagan, Ronald 12, 107, 185
Reaganomics 89, 107
Redman 101
Rex (dog) 88
Riley (dog) 136
Rin Tin Tin 17
Ritvo, Harriet 7, 144–6
Rivera, Omar 136
Rollin, Bernard 47–9
Roosevelt, Franklin Delano (FDR) 18, 21, 24
Rose, Tricia 95
Roselle (dog) 136
Rosenberg, Meisha 91, 114
Rottweiler 90, 98
Royal Society for the Prevention of Cruelty to Animals (RSPCA) 31

Sadie (dog) 134
Saey, Tina Hesman 167
Saint Bernard 90
St. John's Dogs 118
Salt Lake Tribune 46
Salt-N-Pepa 96
Salty (dog) 136
Saluki 119
Sammie (dog) 162–4
Samoyed 79
A Sand County Almanac 58
Satellites in the High Country 67
Saturday Evening Post 20
Schatten, Gerald 164
Schenone, Laura 90
Schnauzer 158
Schnoodle 158
Schulz, Charles 2; see also Snoopy
Schulz and Peanuts: A Biography 41
Science magazine 166
Science News 167
scientific racism 143
Scott-Foresman 21
Scottish Terrier 18, 24, 185
Seale, Bobby 95
search and rescue dog 13–4, 133, 134–7
seeing eye dog 132–3
selective breeding 144–6, 152, 155, 161–2, 166, 175
Semencic, Carl 99
separation anxiety 172
September 11th 13, *135*–7
Serum Run (of 1925) 78
service dog 132–7
Shakespeare, Tom 167
Shakespeare, William 141–2
shelter dog 14
Shiba Inu 79, 154
Shih Tzu 119
Siamese cat 26–7
Siberian Husky 71, *75*–7, 121, 154
Siberian Laika 79
Siegal, Mordecai 73
The Signifying Monkey 153
Simpsons 41
Smith, Martin Cruz 63
Smith, Valerie 97–8
Snoop Dog 43, 96
Snoopy 2, 10, 41–5, 54, 96, 121
Snuppy (Seoul National University puppy) 163–4
Society for the Prevention of Cruelty to Animals (SPCA) 99
"Society of the Spectacle" 183
Socks (cat) 120
Soto, James 98
South China Institute for Stem Cell Biology and Regenerative Medicine 167
speciesism 94, 103, 118, 184–5
Spiegel, Marjorie 93–4, 103

Spitz-type dogs 79
Sports Illustrated 50, 83, 85, 92
Spot (dog) 9, 21–2, 24, 37, 121
Springer Spaniel 185
Sputnik 30–1, 48
Staehle, Albert 20
Staffordshire Bull Terrier 86, 98
street dog 154
Stern, Jane 155–6
Stern, Michael 155–6
Streisand, Barbra 162–3, 165
Summer of Love 41
Swift, E.M. 84

Thalidomide 45
Thamm, Doug 170
therapy dog 134, 137
"Thinking Like a Mountain" 58–9, 61
Thunder Dog 136
Thurber, James 88
Tiger (dog) 8, 79, 80, 124, **154**, 170–1, 178, 181
Time magazine 85, 91, 155
Torres, Tia 101–2
Toys"R"Us Pets 177
training, dog 73–4, 101, 118, 119, 123–32
trophic cascade
Trump, Donald 51, 95, 182–3
23andMe 152, 153

United Kennel Club 98
United States Department of Agriculture (USDA) 51, 182
United States Fish & Wildlife Service 57, 68
University of California–Davis 170
University of Utah 46
Urban Dictionary 155
US News and World Report 85

Vaccine Against Canine Cancer Study (VACCS) 170
Vanater v. Village of South Point 99
Vick, Michael 96, 103–5
Victktory Dogs 104

Vietnam War 41, 55, 80
Villalobos Rescue Center 102
Voltaire 142–3

The Wandering Gene and the Indian Princess 151
"War on Drugs" 107
WASP (White Anglo-Saxon Protestant) ethnicity 147
"We Are Siamese" (song) 26–7
West, Cornel 14–5, 89, 108
Westminster Kennel Club Dog Show 18, 33, 136
Wheelwright, Jeff 151
Whippet 167
White Fang 69
white privilege 102
white supremacy 94, 107, 152, 155, 184
White Trash 138, 147–9
Whole Earth Catalog 55
The Wild Animal Sanctuary (TWAS) 81
Wilder, Laura Ingalls 88
Williams, Raymond 4, 9
Wisdom Panel 154
Withrow, Stephen 47
Woestendick, John 163–5
Wolf 10–12, 55–82, 106, 129–30, 184
Wolf-Dog Hybrid 57, 80
The Wolves Offered Life & Friendship (W.O.L.F.) Sanctuary 81
Woodhouse, Barbara 73
Woodhouse, Leighton Akio 51
Wooding, Stephen 151
Woods, Tiger 150
The World of Fighting Dogs 99
World Trade Center 135

yellowface 26
Yellowstone 68
Yorkiepoo 158
Yorkshire terrier (Yorkie) 158, 165
Yupik 63

www.ingramcontent.com/pod-product-compliance
Ingram Content Group UK Ltd.
Pitfield, Milton Keynes, MK11 3LW, UK
UKHW040610160426
5217IPUK00034B/963